Central America
and the
Western Alliance

CENTRAL AMERICA
AND THE
WESTERN ALLIANCE

edited by
Joseph Cirincione

in cooperation with
The Carnegie Endowment for International Peace
and
The International Institute for Strategic Studies

HOLMES & MEIER
New York   London

First published in the United States of America 1985 by
Holmes & Meier Publishers, Inc.
30 Irving Place
New York, N.Y. 10003

Great Britain:
Holmes & Meier Publishers, Ltd.
Unit 5, Greenwich Industrial Estate
345 Woolwich Road
Charlton, London SE 7

Book design by Rachael Bickhardt

Library of Congress Cataloging in Publication Data
Main entry under title:

Central America and the western alliance.

    1. Central America—Strategic aspects.
I. Cirincione, Joseph.   II. Carnegie Endowment for
International Peace.   III. International Institute
for Strategic Studies.
UA606.C46   1985   355'.0330728   84-19770
ISBN 0-8419-1003-0
ISBN 0-8419-1004-9 (pbk.)

Manufactured in the United States of America

CONTENTS

Soviet Strategy and Central America

Latin American Perspectives

ABOUT THE CONTRIBUTORS

ZBIGNIEW BRZEZINSKI is Herbert Lehman Professor of Government at Columbia University and Senior Adviser at the Georgetown University Center for Strategic and International Studies. From 1966 to 1968 he served as a member of the Policy Planning Council of the U.S. State Department. He was founder and the first director of the Trilateral Commission. In 1977 he joined the administration of President Carter as Assistant to the President for National Security Affairs. Among his numerous publications are *Alternative to Partition: For a Broader Conception of America's Role in Europe; Between Two Ages: America's Role in the Technotronic Era; The Fragile Blossom: Crisis and Change in Japan;* and *Power and Principle*.

JOSEPH CIRINCIONE is the Associate Director of the Central America Project at the Carnegie Endowment for International Peace in Washington, D.C. He is also the Assistant Editor and contributor to the recent Carnegie study *Central America: Anatomy of Conflict* (1983). He has served as Special Assistant to the Associate Director for Programs at the United States Information Agency on issues of international security affairs and Central America. As a research analyst at the Georgetown Center for Strategic and International Studies in 1982 he studied U.S. and Soviet power projection capabilities in the Third World, and is the author of several articles on these subjects.

HORACIO CRESPO specializes in the study of the political history and economics of Latin America, particularly Mexico. He is a member of the Latin American Center for Strategic Studies in Mexico City and a frequent contributor to the journals *Vuelta* and *Revista de la Universidad de México*. He recently authored a chapter in the collective study *América Latina: desventuras de la democracía*, edited by Enrique Krauze (Mexico City: Planeta y Joaquin Mortiz, 1984).

ARTURO J. CRUZ is currently Associate Treasurer of the Inter-American Development Bank. He was a supporter of the Sandinistas as a member of the Group of Twelve during the insurrection period of the revolution and was appointed President of the Central Bank in 1979. He joined the ruling junta in 1980 and later was named Ambassador to the United States. He publicly resigned in Managua in December 1981 and is now a dissident.

WOLF GRABENDORFF is Senior Staff Member of the Stiftung Wissenschaft und Politik, Research Institute for International Affairs, in Ebenhausen, Federal

Republic of Germany. He has been a visiting scholar at the Institute of Latin American Studies, Columbia University; a Visiting Fellow at the Center of Brazilian Studies, School for Advanced International Studies, Johns Hopkins University; and, for three years, the Latin American correspondent for the German Television System (ARD) in Buenos Aires. Among his extensive writings on many facets of Latin American politics and international relations are *Political Change in Central America: Internal and External Dimensions* and *A donde Latinoamérica?*

MICHAEL M. HARRISON is Associate Professor of European Studies at the Johns Hopkins School of Advanced International Studies in Washington, D.C. He is the author of *The Reluctant Ally: France and Atlantic Security* and coauthor of *A Socialist France and Western Security*, and has written many articles on Atlantic affairs.

ROBERT S. LEIKEN is a Senior Associate at the Carnegie Endowment for International Peace and an adjunct Senior Fellow at the Georgetown University Center for Strategic and International Studies. He has been Professor of Economic History at Centro de Investigación y Docencia Económica (CIDE) and at the National Agricultural University in Mexico. He is the author of *Soviet Strategy in Latin America*, and editor of *Central America: Anatomy of Conflict*.

WILLIAM LEOGRANDE is Director of Political Science in the School of Government and Public Administration at the American University in Washington, D.C. He has published widely in the field of Latin American politics and U.S.– Latin American relations; his publications include *Cuba's Policy in Africa, 1949–1980;* "The Revolution in Nicaragua," in *Foreign Affairs;* and "Drawing the Line in El Salvador," in *International Security*.

EDWARD LUTTWAK is a Senior Fellow at the Georgetown University Center for Strategic and International Studies in Washington, D.C., and a professional research consultant to private industry as well as the U.S. government. He is the author of a number of works on strategic issues, including most recently *The Grand Strategy of the Soviet Union*, and the coeditor of the *International Security Yearbook*.

JAMES H. MICHEL currently serves as the Principal Deputy Assistant Secretary of State for Inter-American Affairs, with responsibility for aiding the Assistant Secretary to carry out U.S. foreign policy in Latin America and the Caribbean. He served as an attorney in the Department of State's Office of the Legal Adviser from 1965 and as the department's Principal Deputy Legal Adviser from 1981 until assuming his present assignment.

RICARDO NUDELMAN is a publisher and author in Argentina. He is also an attorney, and taught political science in the Law School of the University of Buenos Aires during 1973–74. He lived in exile in Mexico from 1976 to 1984, teaching political science at the National University of Mexico. He helped found the Latin American Center for Strategic Studies in Mexico City in 1983. He is currently a publisher in Argentina and Mexico and the director of *Folios Ediciones* in both countries. He is the author of numerous articles on international and political affairs and a contributor to the *Diccionario de Ciencias Políticas*.

ROBERT PASTOR is currently on the faculty of the School of Public Affairs, University of Maryland, College Park, where he is teaching and doing research on U.S. policy toward the Caribbean Basin. He was a Guest Scholar at the Brookings Institution in 1981–82, and prior to that, he was the Senior Staff Member responsible for Latin American and Caribbean Affairs on the National Security Council from 1977 to 1981. During 1975–76 Dr. Pastor was the Executive Director of the Linowitz Commission on U.S.–Latin American Relations.

WILLIAM D. ROGERS served as Secretary of State for Inter-American Relations and Under Secretary of State for Economic Affairs for President Ford, and as Senior Counselor to the National Bipartisan Commission on Central America. The President of the American Society of International Law from 1972 to 1974, Mr. Rogers is currently a partner in the Washington law firm of Arnold & Porter. He has undertaken several international efforts at the request of the President, including a good-offices mission to resolve difficulties in connection with the ratification of the Panama Canal Treaties in 1978, and a presidential mission to El Salvador to inquire into the murder of the American churchwomen there in 1980–81. He is the author of *The Twilight Struggle: The Alliance for Progress and U.S.–Latin American Relations,* and numerous articles.

ANIBAL ROMERO is a Professor of Political Science at the Simon Bolivar University in Caracas. A former adviser to the Venezuelan Ministries of Defense and Foreign Affairs, he is the author of several books and articles on Venezuelan national security policy and contemporary strategic problems. At present he is doing research on Venezuelan foreign policy toward Central America and the Caribbean with the support of a Rockefeller Foundation International Relations Fellowship.

STEPHEN S. ROSENFELD is Deputy Editor of the editorial page and a columnist for the *Washington Post*.

FREDERICK F. SHAHEEN is a lieutenant in the U.S. Navy. Formerly naval aide to Vice Admiral A. J. Baciocco, Jr., he is presently pursuing a master's degree in Soviet studies at the Naval Postgraduate School, Monterey, California.

WAYNE SMITH is a Senior Associate of the Carnegie Endowment for International Peace in Washington, D.C. A career Foreign Service Officer until August of 1982, he left the service at that time because of serious disagreements with the Reagan administration's policies in Cuba and Central America. Mr. Smith was the U.S. State Department's top expert on Cuba. For the three years prior to his resignation, he served as Chief of the U.S. Interests Section in Havana (1979–82).

MICHEL TATU is presently an editorial writer for *Le Monde*, after being that newspaper's correspondent in Moscow, correspondent in Washington, and Foreign Editor. He is the author of *Power in the Kremlin*, and *La Bataille des Euromissiles*, and numerous articles on Soviet policy, East-West relations, defense problems, and European problems. He is a member of the International Institute for Strategic Studies and scientific adviser for the Institut Français des Relations Internationales.

VIRON P. VAKY is a retired career Foreign Service Officer who served formerly as the Assistant Secretary of State for Inter-American Affairs and as Ambassador to Costa Rica, Colombia, and Venezuela. He is currently Research Professor in Diplomacy at the School of Foreign Service, Georgetown University, Washington, D.C.

JIRI VALENTA is an Associate Professor in the Department of National Security Affairs at the Naval Postgraduate School, Monterey, California. Dr. Valenta is the author of *Soviet Intervention in Czechoslovakia, 1968: Anatomy of a Decision*, coeditor of *Eurocommunism between East and West*, coauthor of the monograph *The Soviet Invasion of Afghanistan: Three Perspectives*, author of *The Soviet Interventions at Their Periphery* (forthcoming), and coauthor of *Soviet Policies in Latin America* (forthcoming).

CONFERENCE RAPPORTEURS

SUSAN ALBERTS, a former legislative assistant to Representative Tom Harkin, is currently an associate with Foreign Policy Advocates, a Washington-based lobbying group concerned with Central American issues.

MICHAEL CLARK was an associate of the Central American and Caribbean Program at Johns Hopkins School of Advanced International Studies. He completed studies for an M.A. in Latin American Studies at SAIS and is presently working toward a doctorate in American Foreign Policy.

CRAIG VANGRASSTEK is a journalist and consultant specializing in Latin American economic and political affairs. He recently completed a Fulbright Fellowship in Colombia and has worked as the Research Director for Manchester Associates, Ltd., and as Bogota correspondent for the *Journal of Commerce*.

FOREWORD

AMONG THE OTHER gaps in perception that now affect relationships across the Atlantic and inside Western societies on both sides of the ocean—in addition to the nuclear dilemmas, the Middle East, and relations with the Soviet Union—the Central American issue is a growing subject of intergovernmental and domestic debate. President Reagan has succinctly stated his own view: "If Central America were to fall," he has told us, "our alliances such as NATO would crumble. If the United States cannot respond to a threat near our own borders, which ally will trust us elsewhere?" While the administration variously describes Central America as our "backyard," our "frontyard," our "front door," and our "back porch," it clearly considers it very close to home.

Yet any casual American visiting Europe these days quickly learns that popular—and in some capitals, the governmental—unrest over our Central American policies is affecting the Western Alliance. *The Economist* in London has already referred to the Central American imbroglio as "the second Spanish Civil War."

The trans-Atlantic dynamics of the official arguments that are now being put into play are also heavy with potential for further misunderstanding. Pentagon spokesmen and others politely threaten Europe, noting that Central America, unless pacified, will gradually become a greater and greater requirement for Washington, drawing more money, men, psychological attention, and investment all the time, ultimately to the detriment of our commitments elsewhere. Europeans react with renewed bewilderment over American priorities and strategic commitments. American officials complain or explain that "regionally oriented" Europeans lack concern about the global responsibilities and interests of the United States. They engage in perhaps a purposeful myth. The reality is not European lack of interest in United States global pursuits ("outside the treaty area" as the NATO phrase goes) but European skepticism over, and indeed disagreement with, the analysis, prescriptions, and current American policies in the Third World, Central America being a prime example.

The arguments about Central America within Western societies on both sides of the Atlantic illustrate in a dozen contemporary ways the ambiguity of the concept of security. In a sense there is always a latent ideological conflict within Western societies between the security culture and the equity culture. At a time of hyped-up ideological politics these tendencies are bound to be in sharper conflict than otherwise.

Yet in a larger sense security has meaning only for those who have something to preserve. It is a much larger concept than defense expenditures and military deployments. It makes a great deal of difference whether we are talking seriously about the security of a society, a country, a people, or whether we really mean only the security of an interest, an oligarchy, a sector, a class, or an entrenched regime. *Whose* security is an issue that haunts all proceedings on Central America, like Banquo's ghost. As many Europeans remind us, security is one thing when we are talking about just societies full of social stability and thriving economies. It is quite another notion when it is artificially grafted upon a historical compound of repression, poverty, and inherited animosity.

With some awareness of all this, the sponsors of this conference tried to assemble a group drawn from both sides of the Atlantic and both sides of the Rio Grande, and one which at the same time spans both geographical and ideological divisions. Above all we tried to bring together informed people who tend to represent a range of views of security, narrow and broad, thereby assuring us a full perspective on the issues that are now dividing people inside the United States and inside Europe as they look at the Central American predicament. Together we hope to get beyond some of the unexamined premises and automatic stereotypes that so richly encumber this subject.

Finally, in this setting it might be appropriate for me to refer to what one International Institute of Strategic Studies icon, Professor Michael Howard, has written about another strategic icon, Clausewitz. Howard, in his book about Clausewitz, says, "He had the practical man's horror of abstractions that could not be directly related to the facts of the situation, of propositions that could not be illustrated by examples, of material that was not relevant to the problem in hand." It is our hope that after two days of intensive discussion some of the abstractions and propositions that are so freely visited upon the Central American predicament will be more related to the facts and more relevant to the problem.

Thomas L. Hughes
President
Carnegie Endowment for
  International Peace
Washington, D.C.

FOREWORD

THOMAS HUGHES HAS set forth the dimensions of the problems presented to the members of the Western Alliance by the current crises in Central America. They are, in essence, different perceptions of the causes of the trouble, different views on how the crises should be handled, different perceptions on the extent to which the crises are an American problem, confusion as to whether the United States government is willing to accept all the costs of a more militarily oriented policy, and awareness of a need to achieve a stronger Western public consensus on the issue.

On the European side, the Central American question tends to be viewed more in the context of long experience with colonial and former colonial states than it is in the United States. Of course, it is easier for Europeans to take a more philosophical attitude. The problem is not on their doorstep. Nonetheless, it is worth devoting a thought to the Central American problem in the light of European (and especially British and French) experience with developing states in which they have had, and continue to have, political, economic, and security interests. Good relations have often been secured in the longer term by Britain or France, for example, riding out calmly a difficult period in their relations with these states and relying on the eventual reassertion of political and economic interests to restore an effective relationship and to buttress against slippage towards the Soviet Union. Sometimes, but not often, they have resorted to intervention but only as a last resort. Europeans, on the other hand, have to bear in mind the difficulty of remaining relatively cool and detached when regional upheavals coincide with high global tensions and there is a perceived degree of connection between the regional events and the security interests of their major ally.

Not surprisingly, Europeans are generally content to avoid military commitments to Central America, with the exception of the residual British commitment to Belize. Hence, either in justification or rationalization, it is not difficult for them to conclude that military responses are inappropriate. Their own experience in other parts of the world suggests that this deduction is based on a partial reading of the evidence. After all, Britain and France have had their military successes as well as their failures in Asia and Africa. This kind of parallel needs to be drawn to supplement that of Vietnam. It is not only the United States' experience in intervention that is relevant.

One particularly contentious element in trans-Atlantic discussions of the Central American question is the degree to which it is essentially an American problem. For some the Monroe Doctrine is the guiding principle. For others the notion of spheres of influence is seen as an affront or an actual threat to their security. Swedes and Norwegians, sensitive to repeated evidence of Soviet naval infringements of their sovereignty, are bound to reject any validity in the idea that one state can be in another's "backyard"—especially if that other is a superpower—and that having someone in one's "backyard" confers on one certain rights to intervene. The parallel often drawn between Central America and Afghanistan is justified neither by the nature of U.S. involvements in Central America nor by the sovereignty remaining with Central American states. There is, nonetheless, a greater willingness on the part of international public opinion to criticize any military intervention by a superpower in the wake of the Soviet invasion of Afghanistan, to which all Western leaders have to be sensitive. The criticisms of U.S. actions in Grenada seem largely to have been based on questions of sovereignty and the right of an external power to decide the political arrangements of a neighboring state. The different degrees to which this sensitivity is displayed can complicate further the politics of the Western Alliance.

An all-too-frequently encountered element of public (and official) reaction to U.S. involvement in Central America is confusion as to what the United States government's objectives are and how much it is willing to pay to secure them. This confusion is fed internationally both by the United States domestic debate and by the way in which the issues are incorporated into standing ideological disputes in other societies. There is, of course, no complete remedy to this problem that is likely to be acceptable to all democratic states, but the present ambiguity and obscurity of United States aims and policies in Central America are complicating an already difficult situation.

This volume addresses a series of significant problems in trans-Atlantic relations, hoping in time to exert some influence on policies adopted by Western states and on the public debate that will help to shape those policies. There are already more than enough issues on which NATO partners think very differently. The prospects for a continuing high level of tension in East-West relations emphasize the importance of reducing differences of approach to related political and security problems. Such reduction cannot be achieved easily or quickly: the differences in perception are deeply rooted in historical experience, geostrategy, and societal attitudes. It is all the more important to begin the process.

I particularly welcome the opportunity that has been afforded by the Carnegie Endowment and the United States Committee of the International Institute for Strategic Studies to debate and analyse the Central American problem in the light of Alliance concerns and interests. May I also record our warm appreciation of the cooperation given by the authors of the chapters of this volume and by Robert Leiken and Joseph Cirincione, both through the conference on which this book is based and for their contributions to the volume itself.

Robert O'Neill
Director
The International Institute for
    Strategic Studies
London

Europe and the Americas

Chapter 1

AN OVERVIEW AND INTRODUCTION

Joseph Cirincione

ON JUNE 1 President Ronald Reagan began his 1984 tour of Europe with what was planned to be a picturesque journey to his ancestral land. But in Galway, Dublin, and Ballyporeen marching bands gave way to tens of thousands of demonstrators protesting United States actions in Central America and Reagan's nuclear weapons policies. Senior members of the Irish Catholic church hierarchy refused to meet with the president during his visit, and Prime Minister Garret FitzGerald criticized American involvement in Central America at the official banquet.

Tiny Ireland, once a colony of England and beset with its own serious conflicts, would seem the least likely European nation to concern itself with events in Central America, thousands of miles and a cultural leap from its shores. As Prime Minister FitzGerald endorsed the efforts of the Contadora countries (Panama, Colombia, Venezuela, and Mexico) to negotiate a resolution to the Central American crisis, he elaborated on one of the myriad threads that tie Europe to the nations of Central America and therefore to the raucous intercontinental policy debate over the troubled isthmus. "With many of these Latin American countries," he said, "our people have close emotional ties through the work of our priests and nuns and lay helpers there, who seek to relieve the poverty of the people and to give them back their dignity."

If the Catholic nations of Europe share through their missionaries the travails of Central Americans, other Europeans are linked through more material ties such as economic aid, fraternal Christian Democratic, Social Democratic, Socialist and Communist parties, and shared Latin cultural and historical roots.

Overall, the nations of the European Community represent the second-largest market and second-greatest investment source for Central America. While Europe has for years contributed food aid and disaster relief to the region, some aid has more political overtones. The Netherlands, Sweden, and West Germany, for example, have given humanitarian aid to DAZ-PAZ, an agency established by Salvadoran rebel groups to channel aid to guerrilla-run areas. Politically, NATO members West Germany, Spain, and France have supported the efforts of the Democratic Revolutionary Front, the political wing of the Salvadoran guerrillas, to negotiate with the government. These nations have also sent aid to Sandinista Nicaragua and publicly disagreed with the Reagan administration's view that the Central American conflict is essentially an East-West struggle. Endorsing the Contadora Group, the leaders of the European Community have declared that "the problems of Central America cannot be solved by military means, but only by a political solution springing from the region itself." More recently, El Salvador's President José Napoleón Duarte has used his Christian Democratic credentials to win a promise of almost $18 million in aid from the West German government headed by fellow Christian Democrat Helmut Kohl. Duarte's tour of Europe in July 1984 was at least partially successful in improving the image of the Salvadoran government and in neutralizing some of the sympathetic ties the guerrillas had developed over the past few years.

Europeans have demonstrated that they have more than a humanitarian interest in Central America. They are deeply concerned about how the United States has responded to the crisis there and how United States policy in Central America affects the Western Alliance.

For the Europeans, Central America is a test case: United States strategy, tactics, and decision-making processes are scrutinized for their implications for America's ability to lead the Western Alliance. Doubts about the United States' role in Central America erode the political underpinnings of NATO, affecting such vital issues as the deployment of Pershing II and Cruise missiles, basing agreements in Europe, negotiations over economic cooperation and NATO weapons acquisition programs, and European willingness to fund much-needed NATO modernization efforts. Continuing the trend begun during the United States' ill-fated involvement in Indochina, American military measures in Central America have strained Atlantic relations at precisely the time the United States has sought to present a united front against the Soviet Union. British Foreign Secretary Geoffrey Howe, criticizing the United States invasion of Grenada, voiced the concerns of many Europeans when he said, "The events in Grenada have reminded us again that there are times when Europe needs a voice independent of even its closest allies."

Increasing European involvement in Central America and growing concern that the conflicts there could threaten Western Alliance unity moved the Carnegie Endowment for International Peace and the International Institute for Strategic Studies in London to convene a conference, "The Central American Crisis and the Western Alliance," in Washington on May 31 and June 1, 1984. Gathered at the conference was a diverse and exceptionally well informed group of strategists and Central American specialists from Europe, the United States, and Latin America. For two days, the conference rooms, hallways, and banquet tables sizzled with debate on American and Soviet strategy, the political and social aspirations of Central Americans, critiques of European behavior, and how best to prevent further NATO discord.

The papers and discussions from that conference have been collected in this volume after having benefited from comments and criticisms made during and after the conference. Together they offer a strategic overview of the current crisis in Central America and the contribution of that crisis to the existing tensions within the Atlantic Alliance. The conference and this collection constitute an effort to present as fairly and objectively as possible the various and often sharply contrasting views of the participants, leaving the reader to judge which arguments are the most persuasive.

The first and fourth sections are essays based on speeches made at the conference, plus the editor's overview and introduction. All other sections follow the same format: the first chapter in the section is the main paper presented at a conference panel discussion, the second chapter is either a commentary on the main paper or a contrasting view, the third chapter consists of the remarks of the discussant on the conference panel, and finally, the fourth chapter is the rapporteur's report of the conference discussion that followed the formal panel presentations. We have preserved, where appropriate, the informality of some of the speeches and discussants' remarks in order to convey the liveliness of the debate and the often intimate involvement of the speakers with the policy-making process upon which they comment.

This is true, for example, in the illuminating essay by William D. Rogers, which is presented here as chapter 2. Rogers examines some of the reasons why the behavior of the United States in Central America has caused some Europeans to question the consequences of working closely with the United States on other global matters. In so doing, he explains how the Central American debate revolves around two basic, and unresolved, arguments about America's global behavior: Should United States policy strive simply to contain Marxist regimes, or to change them structurally; and is there compatibility between the use of force and the possibility of negotiated solutions? Rogers, from his perspective as a senior counselor to the National Bipartisan Commission on Central America, summarizes that attempt to forge a consensus policy toward Central America and explains why the two central recommendations of the commission are now essentially dead.

Any strategic discussion of Central America must be grounded in the bitter realities of the region. In chapter 3, William LeoGrande of the American University presents a comprehensive overview of the current situation in each of the major Central American countries, detailing the contending factions, the history of the conflicts, and his prognosis for the near future. LeoGrande criticizes the Reagan administration's reliance on military means for dealing with Central America's problems, noting that its efforts have provoked a storm of international criticism, congressional resistance, and wide public opposition in the United States while yielding little improvement in either the living conditions of the majority of Central Americans or prospects for resolving the wars on the isthmus.

In chapter 4, Deputy Assistant Secretary of State James Michel criticizes LeoGrande's paper as "riddled with exaggerations and omissions" and defends the administration's policy as one that is strengthening democratic institutions and laying the basis for equitable economic growth in a more secure environment. Michel believes that because of the successful land-reform programs in El Salvador, that country's military is no longer the guardian of the landed oligarchy but the protector of democratic reforms undertaken by the civilian government despite Nicaraguan-, Cuban-, and Soviet-supported guerrilla attacks. United States policy, he says, is not interventionist, but rather aimed at countering the dramatic Nicaraguan military buildup that now threatens all of Central America.

In chapter 5, former Assistant Secretary of State Viron Vaky, while not endorsing LeoGrande's analysis, notes that the belief that the United States is threatened not merely by Soviet bases in Central America but by the very existence of Marxist regimes leads inexorably to military solutions to the current crisis. He concludes, pessimistically, that the administration's conceptualization of Central America as a zero-sum game points toward increasing confrontation on the isthmus rather than negotiations.

In chapter 6, the conference participants debate the issues, including the actual state of social justice in El Salvador, the nature of Sandinista control of Nicaragua, and conditions that would permit United States coexistence with the Sandinistas.

The third section features a debate between two well-known strategists, Edward Luttwak of the Georgetown Center for Strategic and International Studies, and Robert Pastor, former National Security Council senior staff member for Latin America. Luttwak opens in chapter 7 with his view of the strategic stakes for the United States in Central America: if the United States cannot vanquish the Soviet-backed forces to the south, it will be forced to shift military resources to defend its southern borders, jeopardizing the entire structure of United States global strategy. While he supports the current administration's policies in general, Luttwak warns that there are only two ways to defeat the insurgencies in the region. Either the United States must pull out, leaving the local elites to deal with the problem with their traditional brutal methods, or it must commit the relatively great quantities of modern equipment and training required to implement more sophisticated counterinsurgency strategies. Any compromise between the two will fail.

Robert Pastor totally disagrees. In chapter 8, he rebuts the claim that external powers are responsible for the revolutions in Central America and discounts the probability of an invasion of the United States from the south as "infinitesimal." Pastor urges a redefinition of United States strategic interests in the region. The essence of the national security challenge for the United States in Central America today, he believes, is not how to parry the Soviet Union, but how to influence sociopolitical change in a sensitive Third World environment.

Stephen Rosenfeld of the *Washington Post* turns a pragmatist's eye on this debate in chapter 9 and concludes that there exists a consensus policy toward Central America, but it is neither the hard-line approach of Luttwak nor Pastor's preference for regional negotiations. Rather, he concludes the "congressional muddle" is as close as this country is likely to get to a coherent approach.

The discussion in chapter 10 focuses on the differing appraisals of the insurgent threat and the sharp disagreements among the European and American strategists on the validity of Luttwak's policy prescriptions. It also features an eloquent plea by the former Costa Rican ambassador to the United States, Rodolfo Silva, for a democratic *political* strategy modeled on the successful Venezuelan approach championed by Romulo Betancourt.

Zbigniew Brzezinski's speech to the conference, presented as an essay in chapter 11, examines the long-range consequences of an American defeat in Central America. He warns us that, with the wrong policies, the Central American crisis could escalate into a crisis within the Western Alliance, isolating the United States internationally and fragmenting the Alliance itself. Noting the disparity between United States and Soviet stakes in the region, Brzezinski concludes with policy recommendations essentially in agreement with the approach of the Reagan administration.

In chapter 12, Michel Tatu of *Le Monde* cautions that European opinion on American behavior in Central America is often as divided as opinion in the United States. His essay elaborates the problems of varying perceptions that frequently distort our trans-Atlantic vision, concretely illustrating his analysis with summaries of British opposition to the United States invasion of Grenada and the attitude of French Socialists toward the revolution in Nicaragua. Tatu offers a refreshing critique of the Left's early enthusiasm for Central American revolutionary movements and its present disillusionment.

Wolf Grabendorff, of the Stiftung Wissenschaft und Politik in the Federal Republic of Germany, presents a contrasting view in chapter 13. Grabendorff explains why Western Europe is now more concerned about Central America than any other area of the Third World. The democratic Left, he notes, is concerned that the Reagan administration's policies jeopardize Western relations with the Third World in general by undermining the credibility of the Western industrialized nations' commitment to social change in the developing world. Worse, the Central American crisis could escalate into precisely the sort of great-power conflict Western Europe has striven to prevent. Grabendorff thus argues for a greater European role in mediating the crisis, as part of the more general effort by regional powers on both sides of the Atlantic to negotiate solutions that avoid the unpleasant choice of either United States or Soviet dependency.

Michael Harrison of the Johns Hopkins School of Advanced International Studies analyzes in chapter 14 three dimensions of the Central American crisis for the Europeans. He cautions that, like Poland and Afghanistan for the Soviet Union and like Vietnam for the United States, Central America is a relatively minor issue in its own right, but is of great importance because of its effects on the broader international security order.

In the exchange of views reported in chapter 15, considerable attention is devoted to the nature of Allied obligations with respect to United States policy in Central America. As the participants debate, the discussion provides a useful encapsulation of the Western European political spectrum.

Robert Leiken of the Carnegie Endowment analyzes Soviet strategy in Central America in chapter 16. He notes that Soviet adventurism has decreased in the region—not primarily because of Reagan administration policies, but rather because of a shift in the global correlation of forces, which has strained Soviet capabilities. Leiken bolsters his hypothesis with, first, a comprehensive review of Soviet policy toward the Third World since 1975 and, then, a detailed examination of Soviet support for the Sandinista revolution. He concludes the Soviets have been forced to adopt a policy of "cautious consolidation" in Central America. He warns that United States policies based on a vision of an adventurous, thrusting Soviet military machine may backfire, seriously damaging United States credibility in the Third World and Europe in the long run.

In chapter 17, Jiri Valenta and Frederick Shaheen of the Naval Postgraduate School dispute the idea of a Soviet retrenchment. Soviet commitments in Central America have always been limited, they argue, but their attempts to expand their influence continue and represent a threat that should not be underestimated. Determined United States action in Grenada did give the Soviets pause, they say, but their caution will continue only so long as the willingness of the United States to use its military power remains credible.

Wayne Smith of the Carnegie Endowment believes that American overreaction to Soviet involvement in Central America is a greater danger than Soviet actions themselves. In chapter 18, Smith draws upon his years of experience in the State Department to critique what he considers the failure of American diplomacy in the region.

The discussion presented in chapter 19 features a debate on the Soviet-Cuban threat to the sea-lanes and a discussion between representatives of Salvadoran and Nicaraguan rebel groups on the Soviet role in Central American revolutionary movements.

In chapter 20, Horacio Crespo and Ricardo Nudelman of the Latin American Center for Strategic Studies in Mexico City present the current conflict as a confrontation between possible future paths of regional development. They argue against the prevailing ideologies of both the Left and the Right, which give lip service to democracy but forestall its implementation. The history of

Latin America, they say, demonstrates that the region is ready and able to sustain political pluralism. Analyzing United States and Soviet roles in the region, they urge the United States to abandon its historic support for the status quo and to help eradicate the conditions that invite Soviet destabilization initiatives.

Anibal Romero of King's College in London asks in chapter 21 whether it is realistic to expect change without revolution in Central America. He supports the Nicaraguan revolution as a truly nationalist uprising and points to European aid to Nicaragua as beneficial in moderating the bellicose instincts of the extreme elements in that country.

In chapter 22 Arturo Cruz, a former Sandinista government official, makes a brief but eloquent plea for a third option in Nicaragua. He urges Western Europeans to stop any blank-check support to the Sandinistas in order to help promote a national reconciliation.

Chapter 23 concludes the book with a discussion of the relationship between economic development and political participation, the role of regional militaries, and the possibility of checking both Americanization and Sovietization of Central America in order to allow indigenous solutions to the region's problems.

Many of the authors in this volume have illuminated their arguments with references to United States' intervention in Vietnam, though often drawing different lessons from that traumatic conflict. In many ways, the discussion is reminiscent of the debate over American strategy in Vietnam which raged inside the Johnson administration on the eve of the massive commitment of United States troops to the region. Then, too, officials, experts, and advisors disagreed over the nature of the conflict, the threat presented to the national security of the United States, the role of international communism in the war, and the extent of U.S. assistance to a beleaguered, corrupt regime. Then, too, one of the principal considerations was how the actions of the United States would affect its international relations.

In October 1964, as the strategic debate drew to a close and the decision in favor of escalation appeared inevitable, Undersecretary of State George Ball made a last-ditch plea in a memo to Dean Rusk, Robert McNamara, and McGeorge Bundy. "The view of many of our allies," he said, "is that we are engaged in a fruitless struggle . . . a struggle we are bound to lose." Arguing against those who insisted the credibility of the United States was at stake, he warned, "what we might gain by establishing the steadfastness of our commitments, we could lose by an erosion of confidence in our judgment."

Twenty years later, the debate over United States and Soviet involvement in Third World conflicts continues. This collection captures a moment in the international debate over Central America at a time when the United States seems poised at the edge of either intervention or negotiation. The authors, no matter what their nationality or point of view, agree that the crisis in Central America has dramatic strategic implications for the United States.

Unless this debate forges a policy that Western Europeans and Americans— North and South—can support, the United States will continue to risk losing both the struggle in Central America and the confidence of its allies.

Chapter 2

AMERICAN BEHAVIOR AND EUROPEAN APPREHENSIONS

William D. Rogers

DURING MY TENURE as assistant secretary of state a decade ago, I rather doubt that I spent more than 3 percent of my time thinking about Central America. I remember at one point recommending to Henry Kissinger that we terminate outright what at that time was about a $50 million bilateral aid program for all Central American countries on the theory that our interests were so well protected and things were moving so distinctly in our direction that we could afford to remit the entire responsibility for Central American development to the multinational agencies.

Things have changed. I spent last year in Europe (mostly at Cambridge University). It was fascinating to see Central America as the Europeans see it. There is no question that the Central American vexations of the United States have had and will have an outsized impact on Europe's perception of America's capacity to manage its foreign relations. The Central America crisis, for example, affects Europe's perceptions of what sort of leader Ronald Reagan is. This point was brought home to me vividly one night when I made the mistake of accepting an offer to participate in a general debate in the Cambridge Union. It was my task to defend the proposition that United States foreign policy was not against the best interests of Britain. I lost. The major evidence trotted out by the opposition (and they were extremely effective, I must say) was Central America and Ronald Reagan's capacity to manage what, after all, was obviously a matter of considerable importance to the United States—close to home, simple, small, and yet impossibly muddled.

That issue of America's will and capacity in world affairs has had an impact and will have an impact on Atlantic relations, regardless of which side in the Central American conflict a particular European may favor. There are some in Europe who regard the problem as the incoherence of American foreign policy; others who think that American foreign policy is far too coherent, but also wrongheaded. There are those in Europe, I am sure, who would be mightily in favor of a crushing defeat for the Marxist forces. And there are those, on the other hand, who regard revolution as inevitable, who would like to see them succeed as quickly as possible, and feel that the United States is making a serious mistake in thus opposing the course of history. But for all those Europeans, how we are behaving in Central America is a matter of considerable concern.

Thus far, the United States has succeeded in communicating the impression that we have not figured out how to manage this particular crisis. This extrapolates into larger significances for the nature of the Western Alliance, causing some to question the consequences of working closely with the United States in other global affairs. There are three reasons it should be so, why we are seen to be either incoherent or wrong.

The first reason in my judgment is that this administration has not in fact made up its mind. From a variety of vantage points, there appears to be a debate going on within the administration on the issues of how the United States ought to behave with respect to Central America just now. This is not so obvious on the surface; there the battle seems to be between an administration committed to a certain aid program and a Congress not quite willing to go along. But inside, on the hard issues of how to fit negotiations with a continued military effort, there is division within the administration.

The second reason, and perhaps related to the first, is that the issues in Central America are not much different from the broader questions of how the United States should behave in the wider world. The Central American debate and indeed the broader argument of America's global behavior really are about two questions—and I think the American people have not made up their minds on these questions. The first is whether our policy with respect to Marxist regimes should be containment or structural change. This is an issue that goes to the vitals of how we should act with respect to the Soviet Union. Should we be content if we can work out a system by which the Soviets will agree to play a lawful and sensible role in world systems? Or ought our objectives to be broader and more fundamental—ought we indeed to be seeking the basic alteration of the Soviet Union and its way of life? That issue has echoes in our relationship with Europe. Many in Europe are disturbed in that they sense that the Reagan administration is intent on a larger objective than mere containment. It is this that has induced nervousness in some quarters in Europe. I think that same issue—containment versus structural change—is at the heart of our uncertainty about how in the long term to deal with Nicaragua.

The second fundamental question that is at the heart of the debate over Central America is the relationship between negotiation and force. Is negotiation something separate from force? Are they alternatives? Can a nation pursue only one at a time? Or is there compatibility and a mutual reinforcement between the judicious use of force on the one hand and the possibility of negotiated solutions on the other? Here, too, in my judgment, the issue goes to the heart of the nature of our policy vis-à-vis the Soviet Union and the Soviet system, and also is at the center of the American debate with respect to Central America and Nicaragua at the present time.

These are the philosophical issues of our foreign policy in the late twentieth century. It is perhaps not surprising that we are as unable to resolve them in any final way in the discussion of Central America as we have been unable to resolve them in the case of central East-West relationships.

The third basic reason that the difficulties of the United States in Central America have given pause in Europe rests on an old problem: the incomprehensibility of our system, of the ways in which we manage foreign policy in this country. There is a cacophony that emanates from Washington and around the rest of the United States, and which is even more confusing to Europe (I testify from my experience at Cambridge) than at home.

This brings me to the most recent experience of the nation with the messy process by which we manage our foreign relations, and the recent effort to break away from it, to move on to a somewhat higher ground. I refer to the National Bipartisan Commission on Central America, in which I played a minor role as senior counselor.

I thought the commission was a bad idea when it was first broached. I urged Henry Kissinger not to accept when the rumors began to fly that President Reagan was thinking of asking him to take over as chairman.

He accepted, and I grew even more pessimistic about the possibility of rational results from the commission's efforts when the list of members was announced. I attended the first introductory meeting of the twelve. They were certainly a bipartisan crew, and a distinguished one. But in the group I counted only one who had ever spent a night in any Central American capital other than Panama. Their early discussions reflected that profound ignorance. The first meetings of the commission were filled with a most extraordinary naïveté. The talk was as cliché ridden as that of a group of twelve people selected by chance off the street. I thought that my dire prophesies were indeed going to be fulfilled.

However, I was surprised, gratified, and pleased at the effort that the commission put forward, and at the response that the twelve displayed to what was a very heavy work schedule over a six-month period. We visited all the Central American countries and had intensive meetings with all the great leaders there. We heard more than 250 witnesses, used up an enormous amount of paper, went through intensive debates, and in sum, came out with what was a remarkably better report than anyone had a right to expect at the beginning—a report that, for reasons we will come to in a moment, I think is essentially dead and has not served the extraordinary purpose that it might have.

Why do I think it was such a good report? It contained, I think, what was a real strategy with respect to Central America. Not only did it take a very broad view of the complexity of the causes of the present Central American crisis, not only did it make a relatively elegant analysis of the nature of the economic as well as security issues present in Central America today, but the recommendations themselves broke new ground.

They broke new ground in two respects. First, they represented an effort to move on the entire series of interrelated fronts—the economic, the political, the security, the social fronts—at the same time, and in an integrated way. And in this they mirrored the view that it was impossible to conceive of any single-dimension solution. It was the view of the commission—and I think that in this sense the commission was eminently correct—that a purely military solution will never work, but also that it is a "mug's game" to think that we can stop the violence by a quick dose of economic development. Heavy infusions of medical assistance, for example, are never going to solve the problems of democratization, whereas pleading for democracy without doing something with respect to the security, the economic, and the social issues is to whistle in the wind. The solutions, the commission thought, must be sought on all these fronts, and all at the same time. To that end the commission recommended a major increased commitment by the United States of material resources.

And this brings me to the second element, which I think was basic to the rather new strategy that the commission proposed. That second element was the multilateralization of the effort.

Central America diverged radically from the rest of South America over the last fifteen years. As South America moved toward rapid economic development in the 1970s, accompanied by a major move toward peaceful democratization, Central America deteriorated. One of the major reasons for the different trends is the difference in the historic nature of the relationship between the two regions and the United States. Our historic involvement in Central America was ever so much heavier-handed. It has left a residue of attitudes and self-perceptions in Central America that set it off importantly from the rest of the hemisphere in terms of the nature of its relationship to the United States and what must be done about the future.

It was the view of the commission that one of the great difficulties of United States policy in Central America, therefore, had been the unilateral nature of our behavior there, the unwillingness to take into account the views and the interests of others, and the patronizing character of our attitude and policies. I regret to say that these still exist today among United States ambassadors and United States foreign policy representatives in the region. The commission proposed in essence to delegate to a multilateral mechanism, consisting in the first instance of the nations of Central America themselves, a very large power: the authority to define policy vis-à-vis Central America and to determine how United States resources ought to be provided to Central America.

The ticket of admission for the Central American states to that process would be a development program and an unabashed commitment to democratization.

The commission was guided by considerations similar to those that Rodolfo Silva raised during the Carnegie Endowment–IISS conference discussions—the proposition that democratization, pluralism, and support for the moderate political leadership make up a *sine qua non* to any real hopes for a genuine resolution of the Central American crisis. The commission proposed an offer to put United States money where its mouth was, to turn over responsibility for defining how the carrots were to be handed out to the moderate democrats, to a multilateral organization in which the United States would accommodate its own views as one member of the larger group. In this respect a very large door was opened to the Europeans and the Japanese. They were invited to play a major role in the multilateralization effort.

In these two respects—one, the interrelated nature of the solutions proposed, and, two, the multilateralization of the effort to find those solutions—I think the commission broke new ground.

As I said earlier, I think these two central recommendations are close to dead. This is so for two reasons. First, I think the Reagan administration did not understand them, and it certainly has not communicated the essence of these rather radical proposals to the American people. Secondly, the press muddied the waters. The ten days before the commission's report finally came out on January 11 were marked by much more intense media interest in the commission's report than it ever got after it was issued. This was a reflection of the competitive nature of the contemporary American press. Many of these stories were dead wrong, as was the big piece by Seymour Hersch in *The New York Times* on the Sunday before its release. However, they determined the reaction in Latin America itself. To this day, many Latin Americans entertain the residual impression that what Hersch and others had said about the report was in fact the case. Their misunderstanding, I regret to say, was scarcely forestalled by the inadequate effort of the United States State Department in getting the report around and explaining it in the hemisphere.

Since the commission report was issued in January, the debate in the land has tended to concentrate on the short-term tactical issues. The essence of the strategy that the commission attempted to set before the American people has been lost. It was well enough understood by the twelve commissioners, who ended the process very much more educated than they began. But this newly acquired wisdom was not effectively transmitted to the American people. Thus one effort to attempt to bring coherence, indeed even a bipartisan understanding out of the present cacophonous debate, failed of its ultimate objective.

My own view about Central America's significance for Europe is much like the view I had about Vietnam. The critical aspect of Vietnam was not what happened in Vietnam but what happened in the United States, as far as Europe was concerned. So too as to Central America. It is how the United States behaves—how well it manages the crisis there—which is really of importance to

Europe. Obviously most of Europe would like to see the United States successful—confident, tactically sensible, rational, avoiding excesses. It is when we are not these things, or not all these things, that Europe is disturbed, and when fundamental questions about the Western Alliance are raised.

This conference is an attempt to address some of those very apprehensions, and I congratulate the management for arranging it.

The Central American Crisis

Chapter 3

CENTRAL AMERICA: EXPANDING WARS AND ELUSIVE PEACE

William M. LeoGrande

FROM ALMOST ANY point of view, the situation in Central America has deteriorated greatly since 1981. The war in El Salvador has become much more intense, and the armies on both sides have grown substantially. As the war goes on, the cumulative destruction of the economy, from both war damage and capital flight, is creating a legacy of poverty and misery for the postwar period. There is no sign that the war is any closer to conclusion, either militarily or politically.

A new war has emerged against Nicaragua, fought by an army ten to fifteen thousand strong from bases in Honduras and Costa Rica. It has raised the danger of hostilities between Nicaragua and these two neighbors and has introduced what may well be a permanent element of instability into Central American politics. To Nicaragua, the economic cost has been substantial, and the war has aggravated the already tense relations between the Sandinista government and its internal opposition.

Honduras has seen no progress on the social and economic problems which the civilian government was elected in 1981 to address. Instead, that nation has undergone a tremendous military buildup fueled by the United States—a buildup that has weakened civilian political institutions and involved Honduras directly in the Salvadoran and Nicaraguan wars.

In Guatemala, the armed forces have dealt the guerrillas some serious defeats, albeit at the cost of substantial bloodshed in the countryside. But this success has not produced stability either within the governing coalition of military officers and rightist civilians or in the larger society. Nor have the guerrillas been eliminated; their setback resembles nothing so much as their prior defeats, from which they have always rebounded with even greater strength.

Central America has also experienced a sharp increase in extraregional involvement in its conflicts. The United States has undertaken a massive increase in military aid and advisors in El Salvador and Honduras, has launched the covert war against Nicaragua, and has established a permanent military presence in Honduras under the auspices of major military exercises that are scheduled consecutively through the end of the decade.

The Cuban and Soviet role in the region has increased as well. Their military aid to and advisory presence in Nicaragua escalated rapidly as the covert war expanded. Their aid to the insurgency in El Salvador is a matter of intense debate.[1]

On the positive side, the Contadora nations of Mexico, Venezuela, Colombia, and Panama have intensified their efforts to find a peaceful solution to the regional conflict. Much progress has been made, but much remains to be done before success can be declared.

EL SALVADOR

The Regime

For generations the government of El Salvador has served as the guardian of the landed oligarchy, suppressing by force any challenge to the nation's rigid social order. The army seized power in 1932 to crush a peasant rebellion, which it accomplished at the cost of between ten thousand and thirty thousand lives.[2] The military's monopoly on political power was retained for the next half century through alternating periods of modernization and conservative retrenchment during which two things held constant: the policies of the regime never threatened the socioeconomic privileges of the oligarchy; and the military met all civilian demands for reform and democracy with electoral fraud and repression.

The origins of the current crisis trace back to the 1960s when economic development under the auspices of the Central American Common Market and the Alliance for Progress expanded the middle class and the urban working class, at the same time stimulating political mobilization in the countryside. These changes led to the rise of reformist political parties—especially the Social Democrats and Christian Democrats, who joined together to win the presidential elections of 1972. The election was stolen by the armed forces, which then unleased a reign of terror against its opponents that lasted for most of the next decade.

The suppression of the reformist challenge to the regime produced a radical opposition composed of several guerrilla groups and the "popular organizations"—militant grass-roots groups dedicated to pressing demands for reform through mass demonstrations and civil disobedience. This radical opposition gained strength rapidly and, by the late 1970s, began to pose a serious challenge to the survival of the regime.

In October 1979, a coup led by reformist military officers and moderate civilians created a government promising social reform, political democracy, and reconciliation with the radical left. Unfortunately, the resistance of the oligarchy and rightists within the officers corps led by Defense Minister José Guillermo García paralyzed the new regime. After an unsuccessful showdown with the rightist officers in December, the civilians resigned. Many of them subsequently joined the opposition, and the spiral toward civil war resumed.

The Christian Democrats rejoined the government and then split in March 1980 over whether to remain in it. José Napoleón Duarte's wing of the party stayed in the government, which then embarked on a policy of "reform with repression"—a strategy of combining limited socioeconomic reforms with an intensification of the war against the Left. Through 1980 and 1981, rightist elements within the government successfully marginalized the moderate elements so that little progress was ever made on agrarian reform or human rights.

Despite the efforts of the United States, particularly during the Carter administration, real political power in El Salvador remained where it had been for half a century—in the officers corps. Rightist officers led by General García consolidated their control by removing from positions of authority the reformist officers who had launched the October 1979 coup. This process was completed in late 1980 when the leader of the reformist officers, Colonel Adolfo Majano, was removed from the governing junta, arrested, and sent into exile. The Christian Democrats who remained in the government were left with only nominal authority and were unable to press ahead with either of their main objectives—rapid implementation of the agrarian reform and a reduction of human rights abuses.[3]

The elections of March 1982 were intended to strengthen the position of civilian politicians, particularly the Christian Democrats, relative to that of the armed forces. In the United States, it was hoped that this would improve the prospects for reform, thereby increasing the legitimacy of the Salvadoran government both at home and abroad.

Nominally the result of the 1982 elections, El Salvador's Government of National Unity was actually an artificial coalition produced by the intercession of the United States Embassy and the Salvadoran armed forces. The unexpected electoral victory of the extreme right, led by Major Roberto d'Aubuisson's ARENA party, threatened to produce a government headed by d'Aubuisson and excluding the Christian Democrats.[4] Because such a regime was unacceptable to the United States Congress, the Reagan administration set aside the election results by appealing to the armed forces, which depended upon United States aid to fight the war against the guerrillas.[5] The military responded by imposing Alvaro Magaña, an apolitical banker, as president, by insisting that the Christian Democrats remain in the government, and by safeguarding the agrarian reform from efforts of the rightist-dominated Constituent Assembly to repeal it. In this way, the extreme right was prevented from capturing control of the regime, but the dominant political role of the armed forces was reinforced rather than reduced.

Deprived of electoral victory by the military, the extreme right moved to strengthen its position in the officers corps. D'Aubuisson's immediate target was Defense Minister García, who was both an astute politician and an important political ally of the United States. By 1982, García had become vulnerable because of his willingness to publicly back United States demands for progress on human rights and agrarian reform, even though actual progress was meager. This vulnerability was exacerbated by the army's inability, under García's leadership, to contain the insurgency. In early 1983, the extreme right assembled a broad enough coalition within the officers corps to force García's ouster. He was replaced by General Carlos Eugenio Vides Casanova, an officer more sympathetic to the extreme right than García; Casanova's succession was followed by promotions for officers long associated with d'Aubuisson.

Because it included parties with diametrically opposed policies (for example, ARENA and the Christian Democrats), the Government of National Unity was paralyzed from the outset. President Magaña had no political base of his own, but served at the de jure pleasure of the Constituent Assembly and the de facto pleasure of the armed forces. Realignments of party coalitions within the Constituent Assembly left it divided almost evenly between ARENA and the Christian Democrats, and hence deadlocked. Initially, Washington hoped that the 1984 elections would break this deadlock and have a stabilizing effect on the governing coalition. But the nomination of José Napoleón Duarte by the Christian Democrats and of Roberto d'Aubuisson by ARENA transformed the election into a polarizing process rather than a stabilizing one. Duarte was unacceptable to significant portions of the private sector and the armed forces, who regarded his "communitarianism" as equivalent to communism. D'Aubuisson was unacceptable to the Christian Democrats, to their peasant and trade-union followers, and to the United States Congress.

At first, Washington sought to defuse the potential political explosion of the governing coalition by backing the candidacy of the National Conciliation Party (PCN) nominee Francisco Guerrero. Had Guerrero been able to rebuild the traditional rural patronage network of the PCN with the help of CIA funds, he might have managed to eke out a victory over d'Aubuisson in the first round of the election and then, with the Right rallying to him, over Duarte in the runoff. The new government would have been a continuation of the Magaña regime without Magaña. Guerrero's third-place finish in the first round of the election dashed this hope, making the runoff a contest between the two most controversial leaders within the governing coalition. Preferring Duarte to d'Aubuisson, Washington covertly poured more than a million dollars into the Christian Democratic campaign, and Duarte won the runoff. The Right was so angered by the United States support for Duarte that associates of d'Aubuisson, and perhaps d'Aubuisson himself, initiated an abortive plot to assassinate the United States ambassador.[6]

The outcome of the 1984 Salvadoran election did not succeed at breaking the deadlock among the civilian political forces arrayed around the regime, let alone alter the historic concentration of real political power in the officers corps. Ironically, Duarte's victory appears to have healed the split among the rightist parties in the Constituent Assembly, who proceeded to hand Duarte three major legislative defeats within his first two weeks in office.

Within the military, three major political tendencies are visible. Between a quarter and a third of the officers are identified with the extreme Right, and therefore with d'Aubuisson. Like their civilian allies, they are strong right-wing nationalists, unhappy with the United States for its continued emphasis on human rights, agrarian reform, and the need to keep the Christian Democrats in the government. At least some of these officers would be prepared to forgo United States assistance and pursue a Guatemalan model of pacification.

A second faction is composed of more professional officers whose primary concern is winning the war. This group, which coalesced around Colonel Sigifredo Ochoa in 1982 in order to depose García and is now led by Chief of Staff Colonel Adolfo Blandon, is ideologically close to the extreme right, but also recognizes the necessity of maintaining United States support in order to prosecute the war.

The third faction is the least cohesive because it is composed largely of the remnants of factions defeated in earlier internecine battles—the young reformist officers allied with Colonel Majano who were defeated by García in 1980, the pro-Christian Democratic officers allied with Colonel Gutierrez who were defeated by García in 1982, and the Garcia faction itself, defeated in 1983.

In the immediate aftermath of the election, the main political conflict within the military was between officers aligned with the far right and the professional group supported by the remnants of the other factions. As of mid-1984, there were signs that the conflict was stalemated; Col. Nícolas Carranza and several other prominent rightists had been removed from their posts, but General Vides Casanova remained as minister of defense.

Assuming Duarte can maintain himself in office against the efforts of the extreme Right to depose him, what will he be able to acomplish? If the past is any judge, very little. He may be able to reverse the Right's campaign to strangle the agrarian reform through administrative sabotage by replacing the ARENA officials in the agencies charged with carrying out the reform. But he will be powerless to prevent a return to rightist violence and intimidation in the countryside—the strategy followed by the Right prior to the 1982 elections. He may be able to remove a few additional d'Aubuisson supporters from the high command of the military, but he will be forced to rely upon the professional military faction to keep him in office. Since this faction views human rights as an obstacle to effective prosecution of the war, Duarte will have little success in curbing human rights abuses by the regular military. Nor is he likely to make any progress reining in the death squads. They are so closely interwoven with the fabric of the armed forces that to move decisively against them would be to challenge the officers corps as a whole.[7] Submitting military officers to justice is, as it has always been, an issue on which the military stands united, whatever other ideological differences officers may have with one another.

Will Duarte open serious negotiations with the Revolutionary Democratic Front and the guerrillas in the Farabundo Martí Front for National Liberation (FDR/FMLN) to find a political solution to the war? This is probably the least likely outcome because all the political forces around the regime oppose such an initiative. This is the second issue on which the officers corps is united, except perhaps for the remnants of the Majano faction, and, of course, the United States is opposed to such an opening to the Left. Thus far, Duarte's public position has been no different from the previous regime's: the government will negotiate only after the guerrillas lay down their arms.

In short, a Duarte presidency in 1984 will closely resemble Duarte's presidency in 1981. He will not be able to make significant progress on the central issues of agrarian reform, human rights, or a politically negotiated settlement of the war. Of equal importance is the private sector's intense hostility to Duarte. During his first presidency, capital flight from El Salvador accelerated tremendously; in all likelihood it will again, inflicting another trauma on an already comatose economy.

The Opposition

Formed in early 1980, the Revolutionary Democratic Front/Farabundo Martí Front for National Liberation (FDR/FMLN) is a broad, ideologically heterogeneous coalition organized under the political rubric of the FDR and the military command of the FMLN. The FDR unites moderate political parties such as the social democratic National Revolutionary Movement (MNR) headed by FDR President Guillermo Ungo, the Popular Social Christian Movement (MPSC), which split from the Christian Democrats in March 1980, and the "popular organizations" of peasants, workers, and middle-class professionals formed during the late 1970s.

The FMLN unites five armed organizations: the Forces of Popular Liberation (FPL), an orthodox Marxist-Leninist guerrilla group founded in 1970; the People's Revolutionary Army (ERP), a formerly Maoist group founded in 1971; the Armed Forces of National Resistance (FARN), a more nationalistic and less dogmatic group that split from the ERP in 1975; the Communist Party of El Salvador (PCES), a small pro-Moscow party; and the Central American Workers Party (PRTC), another small group founded in 1979.

The political platform of the FDR/FMLN represents a compromise between the traditional reformist demands of the FDR's constituent parties and the revolutionary socialist demands of the armed groups. It calls for far-reaching socioeconomic changes that would break the economic dominance of the oligarchy, but promises a long-term role for the private sector. It calls for a pluralist political system, though it is clear that political parties in a governing coalition would have little role if the FDR/FMLN came to power by militarily defeating the armed forces. And it calls for a foreign policy of "nonalignment," though the precise meaning of this would depend essentially upon United States attitudes toward an FDR/FMLN regime.

Until his death by suicide last year, FPL leader Cayetano Carpio was one of the major obstacles to greater unity within the FMLN. As senior guerrilla commander in age and experience and head of the oldest and largest section of the guerrilla army, Carpio held considerable influence within the opposition. He was not, however, disposed to compromise with the other guerrilla organizations or to accept their proposal for a joint military command. Among the guerrilla commanders he was the least enamored of negotiations with the government.

By 1983, Carpio's position had become a minority view even within his own organization. He then reportedly plotted the assassination of his second-in-command in order to regain political control of the FPL. When the plot was uncovered, he committed suicide. The new leadership of the FPL adopted a position of encouraging greater unity among the five guerrilla organizations, accepting the creation of an overall military command head by ERP leader Joaquin Villalobos. In reaction to this, a small pro-Carpio wing of the FPL split from the FDR/FMLN to form the Cayetano Carpio Revolutionary Workers Movement (MOR). Its departure does not appear to have significantly affected the FPL's combat capacity, as demonstrated by its seizure of the El Paraiso garrison in December 1983.

The fundamental conflict in El Salvador is between the political forces arrayed around the regime and those united under the umbrella of the FDR/FMLN. Since 1981, the battlefield has been the principal arena in which that conflict has been fought out. Since the failure of its "final offensive" in January 1981, the military capability of the FMLN has improved dramatically. Its annual fall offensives in 1981, 1982, and 1983 proved successful beyond the expectations of either the Salvadoran government or the United States. Moreover, these gains were achieved despite substantial improvements in both the equipment and training of the Salvadoran armed forces, provided through the United States military assistance program.

The FMLN has pursued a classic guerrilla strategy of slowly building its forces, attacking the army in remote, exposed positions, gradually increasing the territory under its control and increasing the size of its operations. By most estimates, the FMLN effectively controls from 20 to 30 percent of the national territory, and an equal portion is "contested." The size of regular FMLN combat forces has increased from between four and five thousand in 1981 to between ten and twelve thousand by 1984. It is now capable of operating in units of battalion size and mounting attacks of a thousand to fifteen hundred men, complete with artillery support. Occasionally it engages the army in conventional formations.

The government's principal strategy for reversing the course of the war has been the San Vicente pacification project. It was based upon the presumption that by concentrating government forces in a single department for an extended period, the guerrilla presence there could be extirpated, and peace could then be maintained through a combination of small, highly mobile "killer" battalions and civic action. Main forces of army units would then mount similar operations in another department, proceeding one department at a time until the entire country was pacified.

During the summer of 1983, as the San Vicente operation got fully underway, it appeared that this strategy might enjoy some success. The FMLN chose not to engage the major concentration of government forces assembled in San Vicente, and for several months launched no significant operations elsewhere. However, the FMLN's fall 1983 offensive effectively dismantled the San Vicente plan by reinfiltrating the department, escalating operations in other theaters, and successfully resisting the initial pacification drive in Usulutan.[8] By early 1984, the position of the Salvadoran armed forces was once again tenuous, though the military situation seemed to stabilize in the spring and summer.

Despite a cyclical pattern of fighting, the Salvadoran military has been unable to make any headway in the war. The military initiative lies largely with the FMLN, which chooses when and where major engagements will occur. The inability of the army to stem the gradual deterioration of its military position has multiple causes. Political conflicts within the military have frequently diverted its attention from combat operations. During the tenure of Defense Minister García, provincial commanders of proven incompetence retained their commands because they were important allies in the army's internal political battles. Moreover, the Salvadoran officers corps operates more like a fraternal order than like a military command. Once initiated into the club by graduating from the academy, officers pursue a well-defined career path in which time-in-service is the *sine qua non* of promotion, and each higher rank opens broader opportunities for graft and corruption. It is not an institution designed to fight wars. Even today, the officer-candidates trained in the United States are viewed as interlopers among the fully initiated, and efforts of United States advisors to replace the current promotion system with one based on merit meets strong resistance.

Enlisted soldiers suffer serious morale problems and have recently shown a high propensity to surrender without a fight. In part this is due to the FMLN's practice of releasing prisoners almost immediately, and to the army's reluctance to return former prisoners to combat. But morale is also damaged by the military's occasional reliance on forced-draft recruiting and the tendency of some officers to embezzle their soldiers' pay. Finally, the average soldier has little or no idea why he is fighting, whereas the average guerrilla has a strong sense of political mission.

In light of all this, it is doubtful that the Salvadoran army will make any significant advances against the FMLN in the foreseeable future. While increases in United States military assistance may produce a larger and better-equipped military, it cannot solve the basic problems of the nature of the officers corps or the morale of the recruit.

The FMLN, for its part, still does not have the capacity to mount a successful "final offensive," so a short-term guerrilla military victory is unlikely. The most likely prospect is for continued stalemate in the war, with the FMLN continuing to gradually strengthen its relative position.

Despite the meetings in 1983 between representatives of the FDR/FMLN and the Salvadoran government's Peace Commission, the outlook for a negotiated end to the war is not bright. The government continues to insist that the guerrillas must lay down their arms to participate in elections organized and overseen by the existing regime and its military forces. The FDR/FMLN refuses on the grounds that such a demand amounts to surrender. It has no faith that the military would respect the physical security of FDR/FMLN candidates or supporters, or that it would be allowed to "share power" if it did well in a free election. There are good reasons for skepticism. The history of Salvadoran elections and of the military's human rights abuses does not inspire confidence.

The negotiating position of the FDR/FMLN calls for an interim coalition government to undertake a variety of tasks that would prepare the way for a free election. Chief among these tasks must be the reorganization of the armed forces and the removal of those officers responsible for human rights abuses.

The government refuses to even discuss the issue of FDR/FMLN participation in the regime, and will probably continue to do so as long as the current balance of political forces in the military remains constant. Thus the prospects for any negotiated solution are dim, especially since the United States continues to lend its weight in opposition to any "power-sharing" formula.

NICARAGUA

The Internal Situation

The National Government of Reconstruction, which took power in July 1979 after the fall of Anastasio Somoza, represented an unlikely alliance of conservative businessmen and Marxist guerrillas of the Sandinista National Liberation Front (FSLN). The partnership was fragile from the outset, resisted by people on both sides, but consummated by circumstances. The guerrillas needed the private sector's prestige and influence to legitimatize their revolution both at home and abroad; the businessmen needed the guerrillas' guns to defeat the dictatorship.

In the euphoria of a victory in which the entire nation rose up against Somoza, guerrillas and businessmen alike pledged to sustain their partnership, dedicating themselves to the task of rebuilding an economy devastated by war. Both the program and the composition of the new government were painstakingly negotiated and delicately balanced between the two partners. An essentially social-democratic program promised a mixed economy, political pluralism, and a foreign policy of nonalignment, but it remained purposefully vague on what these would mean in practice. The platform's ambiguity reflected its origins as a compromise between the radicalism of the FSLN and the conservatism of the private sector. It was not the product of a consensus for social democracy.

As in every postrevolutionary regime, the anti-Somoza coalition began to show signs of strain almost immediately. While formal power was shared— representatives of the private sector sat on the executive junta and predominated in the cabinet—it soon became clear that real power lay in the nine-member National Directorate of the FSLN. The businessmen, who had opposed Somoza because he froze them out of the government and encroached upon their business ventures, began to wonder if they had gained much. The Sandinistas seemed no more willing to share political power, and their commitment to improving the living conditions of the poor posed a serious threat to the private sector's wealth and income. Before the revolution had reached its first anniversary, most of the private sector had gone into opposition.

Through 1980 and 1981, the central dynamic of Nicaraguan politics was the struggle between the FSLN-dominated goverment and the private sector opposition for the right to define the nature of post-Somoza Nicaragua.

The FSLN's "popular project" is socialist. At a minimum, it entails a radical redistribution of wealth and income, and the creation of an extensive social welfare system. To this end, the government has conducted a national literacy campaign, made basic health care and education free, and begun an agrarian reform.[9] Beyond this basic program, however, the FSLN is divided over the shape of things to come. Pragmatists in the National Directorate hope to reach a lasting accommodation with the private sector in which it will contribute to economic development in exchange for the right to make a limited profit and the right to limited participation in politics. The pragmatists are motivated by necessity; they doubt the government has the technical capacity to run a nationalized economy, and they doubt that they can obtain needed financial aid from Latin America or Western Europe if they adopt a Cuban model of development.

Hardliners in the Directorate, who were in the minority during 1980 and 1981, do not believe an accommodation with the private sector is possible or desirable. They would resolve the conflict by doing away with the private sector and building Nicaragua in the image of Cuba. Ironically, it was the Cubans who cautioned against such a strategy in the early years of the revolution.[10]

The private sector, for its part, is searching for a way to regain enough political power to safeguard its basic economic interests. It, too, is divided into pragmatists who would settle for some form of accommodation with the FSLN based on democratic socialism, and hardliners who hope to see the Sandinistas overthrown.

In their battle with the opposition, the Sandinistas hold a near monopoly on political power. They control the state apparatus, including the armed forces; they command a broad network of organized supporters in the "mass organizations"; and perhaps most importantly, they enjoy the legitimacy that springs from having defeated a hated dictator. While the private sector contributed to the insurrection politically and financially, the FSLN contributed in blood, fighting and dying at the barricades. Four years of economic hardship and increasing authoritarianism have been a drain on this reservoir of legitimacy, but they have by no means dried it up.

The opposition to the FSLN has little political organization. It must rely on the same weapons it used to good effect against Somoza: control over 60 percent of the economy and enough foreign contacts to make or break the international reputation of the regime.

The Sandinistas have used their control of the state to try to bend the private sector into cooperating with the government's economic plans, offering tax incentives and cheap credit for compliance while threatening expropriation as the penalty for decapitalization. The private sector has tried to use its economic muscle to extract political concessions from the regime, warning that the "rules of the game" both economically and politically must be codified in law before business confidence will improve enough to spur production.

Through 1980 and 1981, this political tug-of-war erupted every six months or so into crisis as one side or the other sought to test the political will of its adversary. Yet neither side was willing to leap into the abyss by pushing one of these crises to the breaking point, since both had too much to lose. Each crisis subsided with the initiation of dialogue followed by limited concessions aimed at keeping alive the hope of eventual accommodation. But each crisis left in its wake the residue of higher tension and deeper polarization.

This pattern of confrontation followed by conciliation was ruptured in 1982 by the launching of the covert war organized by the CIA and conducted by exiles from base camps in Honduras.[11] As the contra attacks escalated, the Sandinistas' tolerance for internal opposition declined; opponents appeared too much like a "fifth column." In March 1982, the FSLN declared a state of emergency that included severe limitations on the rights of opposition parties to organize, and also instituted prior censorship of the press, particularly the newspaper *La Prensa*.

On the Atlantic Coast, the cultural insensitivity of the government alienated the native Indian population, particularly the Miskitos. In early 1982, as contra raids across the border intensified, the government forcibly relocated about nine thousand Miskitos from their homes along the Río Coco in order to prevent them from giving assistance to the contras.

The hardening of the internal political situation also led the hierarchy of the Catholic Church, particularly Archbishop Obando y Bravo, to join the chorus of critics of the FSLN. The Sandinistas responded in kind, thus setting off an ongoing polemical battle between the Church and government, and within the Church itself.

As the not-so-secret war against Nicaragua escalated, the pragmatists within the FSLN and the opposition lost ground to the hardliners in their respective camps. Leaders of the internal opposition who once held out hope for accommodation with the FSLN began looking more and more to the counterrevolution as their salvation.

In military terms, however, the counterrevolutionary forces of the quasi-Somocista Nicaraguan Democratic Force (FDN) and Edén Pastora's Democratic Revolutionary Alliance (ARDE) were unable to make significant advances against the Sandinista army. Despite combined forces of over ten thousand combatants, neither group was able to seize and hold a significant portion of Nicaraguan territory, or rally any real political following.

The FSLN, however, was able to improve its own political standing by rallying the population around a nationalist appeal to defend the homeland against a return of Somocistas backed by the United States—a powerful combination of enemies. Moreover, the existence of the counterrevolution enabled the FSLN to rationalize a tougher stand toward domestic opponents, a deepening military relationship with Cuba and the Soviet Union, and a deteriorating economy.

As the elections scheduled for November 1984 approached, the Sandinistas relaxed some of the limitations that had been imposed on political expression. The FSLN was expected to win the elections easily by virtue of their nationwide political apparatus and the legitimacy that came from their defeat of the Somoza dynasty. None of their political opponents could rival the FSLN's strength on either grounds, so there was some doubt as to whether they would join in an electoral process they were virtually certain to lose.

Nicaraguan Foreign Policy

While both the Carter and Reagan administrations have voiced concern over the issues of political freedom and human rights in Nicaragua since 1979, the fundamental issue for the United States has been the FSLN's foreign policy. President Carter's policy of constructive engagement with the Sandinistas was designed to avoid forcing the FSLN into an alliance with the Soviet Union. It was hoped that if the United States did not react to Nicaragua with reflexive hostility, the Sandinistas might limit their military relationship with the Soviet bloc and their active support of revolutionary movements elsewhere in Central America. Within limits, this seemed to work reasonably well until late 1980.

In the wake of Ronald Reagan's election, the Salvadoran guerrillas undertook a "final offensive" to present the incoming administration with a fait accompli. The Sandinistas, perhaps believing that the Reagan administration would be hostile to them in any event, abandoned the policy of limited support for the Salvadoran insurrection and allowed Nicaragua to be used as a major channel for arms smuggling to the FMLN.

For a brief period at the outset of the Reagan administration, it appeared that the earlier understandings might be reestablished—that the FSLN would refrain from playing any significant role in aiding the Salvadoran guerrillas in return for the maintenance of constructive relations with the United States. This effort, however, failed; by the end of 1981, the United States had adopted a policy of pressures against Nicaragua designed to coerce the FSLN into halting aid to the Salvadoran Left.

The public record regarding the extent of Nicaraguan aid is difficult to read. There is general agreement that Nicaraguan assistance was limited prior to November 1980, that it was substantial from November 1980 to February 1981, and that it was halted between February and April 1981. From that point onward, there is disagreement. The Reagan administration has contended that substantial aid has continued. Some members of Congress and former government officials who have seen the classified evidence find it persuasive; others do not. In addition, there have been repeated stories in the press quoting United States officials in Central America and in Washington to the effect that the flow of arms from Nicaragua is minimal.[12]

There is no doubt, however, that Nicaraguan reliance on military assistance from Cuba, the Soviet Union, and other allied nations has increased as the armed attacks from Honduras have escalated. The Nicaraguan military buildup, which began during 1980, increased sharply after the United States covert action program was put in place in 1982.[13]

The Sandinistas appear to be willing to negotiate about the two major elements of their foreign policy which have caused the greatest concern in Washington—aid to the FDR/FMLN, and relations with Cuba and the Soviet Union. What concessions they would be willing to make on these issues is uncertain, but they have at least committed themselves publicly to discussing them, both bilaterally with the United States and multilaterally through the Contadora process.

It is unrealistic to expect that Nicaragua will sever all ties with Cuba or the Soviet Union, but the Sandinistas have a clear incentive to abide by a Contadora agreement banning all foreign military bases from Central America and reducing the number of foreign military advisors. Similarly, the Sandinistas are not likely to forsake their support for the FDR/FMLN, but the nature of that support is probably an issue open for compromise.

HONDURAS

Despite a tradition of military rule and socioeconomic inequality, Honduras is the one country in Central America that has managed to avoid the political polarization and violence that have engulfed its neighbors. Ironically, this good fortune stems in part from the fact that Honduras is the most underdeveloped nation in the region; the social dislocations and political mobilization that accompanied rapid economic growth in the rest of Central America during the 1950s, 1960s, and early 1970s were milder in Honduras because the pace of change was slower.

At the same time, the landed elite in Honduras has been much less powerful than its cohorts in El Salvador and Guatemala, in part because the Honduran economy was founded largely on the banana sector owned by United States corporations. Consequently, the Honduran government was not simply the guardian of the landed elite; it also played the role of intermediary between the foreign corporations and Honduran society.

Though the military ruled Honduras from 1963 to 1981, it was less intolerant of demands for reform and less brutal in its suppression of dissent. It allowed organized political opposition from political parties, trade unions, peasant leagues, student groups, and the press. It did not respond to challenge with indiscriminate official violence, "disappearances," or death squads. In fact, in the early 1970s the military government undertook limited reforms, including land distribution, in order to avert the growth of unrest among the peasantry.

As Nicaragua, El Salvador, and Guatemala were engulfed in civil strife, Honduras seemed to be the one nation of the northern tier where efforts to promote a peaceful transition to a democratic government of moderate reformists might actually succeed. With the support of the United States, Honduras held free elections in 1980 and 1981 that produced a restoration of civilian rule under President Roberto Suazo Cordova.

But democracy in Honduras was not so easily consolidated. As the price of a return to civilian politics, the military insisted that it retain control over certain key elements of national policy, particularly national security in both its internal and international dimensions. As the war in El Salvador intensified and the covert war against Nicaragua was launched, Honduras was increasingly swept up in the politico-military conflicts of its neighbors. The behavior of the United States tended to aggravate this problem. Both the Carter and Reagan administrations saw Honduras as an island of stability in a sea of turmoil. Both sought to increase the United States military presence there and to recruit Honduras as a partner in United States policy toward Nicaragua and El Salvador. Honduras was enlisted to provide sanctuary for the counterrevolutionary forces engaged in the covert war against Nicaragua, and the Honduran military was enlisted to provide combat support along the frontier with El Salvador during government drives against the FMLN. The effect of these developments was to push national security issues to the forefront of the Honduran political agenda, overshadowing the issues of social and economic reform that the civilian politicians had promised to address. This, combined with the massive increases in United States military aid, shifted the internal political balance toward the military, to the point that the head of the armed forces, General Gustavo Alvarez, emerged as the most powerful figure in the government.[14]

The subordination of the civilian politicians to General Alvarez met with internal resistance, mostly from opponents of the government but also, in muted fashion, from within the government itself. The small Christian Democratic party, the social democratic faction of the ruling Liberal party (ALIPO), the press, and others criticized the apparent impotence of the civilians.

The military's response was ominous; human-rights violations, including disappearances, began to rise. The instances numbered in the dozens rather than in the thousands as in El Salvador or Guatemala, but Honduras had been free of such abuses. Moreover, General Alvarez undertook a sophisticated campaign to weaken various civilian political institutions that stood as potential obstacles to the consolidation of power. From the trade unions to the university and the political parties, Alvarez promoted rightist challenges to existing moderate leadership. Even when Alvarez's allies failed to gain control of these institutions, they generally succeeded in dividing them and thereby rendering them weaker.

Though the civilians proved unable to mount any effective resistance to Alvarez's drive to consolidate power, his ambition provoked sufficient unease with the Honduran military that he was finally arrested, deposed, and sent into exile. With a sigh of relief, the civilians endorsed his removal as a strengthening of the democratic process.

A number of factors contributed to the internal military coup against General Alvarez, but one of the major ones was resistance to Alvarez's eager willingness to steer Honduras along a course charted in the United States Embassy. His successors appear less happy with Honduras's role as sanctuary for the Nicaraguan contras and training camp for the Salvadoran armed forces, but the momentum of policies already embarked upon will not be easily overcome. In all likelihood, the armed forces will continue with the basic policy initiated by Alvarez, albeit pursued with less zeal. The major threat to Honduran democracy will remain the danger that the nation will be caught up even more directly in the wars of its neighbors.

GUATEMALA

Since 1954 when the government of Jacobo Arbenz was overthrown by the CIA's "Operation Success," political stability has been elusive in Guatemala. Though the coup enabled the Guatemalan oligarchy to reestablish its dominion on a new foundation of military rule, the political mobilization of the population that occurred during the ten years of populist democratic government was not so easily reversed.

Demands for social and political change have come in waves, and the intransigence of the regime has made guerrilla warfare a virtually permanent feature of Guatemalan politics. A major guerrilla challenge was mounted in the mid-1960s, with substantial organized support in the urban areas. It was temporarily defeated between 1968 and 1972 by a campaign of official state terror in the cities and counterinsurgency in the countryside that took the lives of some twenty thousand people.

Like its neighbors, Guatemala experienced the rise of reformist political movements in the early 1970s. In 1974, the Christian Democratic party mounted a serious presidential campaign by nominating a moderate military officer, Efraín Ríos Montt, in the hope that his military background would make him an acceptable candidate to the armed forces. It did not. The military delivered the coup de grace to the reformist movement by fixing the election. As in El Salvador, the defeat of the reformist option triggered a renewal of gerrilla opposition that grew in strength throughout the 1970s.

The depth of the Guatemalan elite's intransigence was revealed by the military government's decision in 1977 to forgo further United States military assistance rather than have its human rights practices scrutinized by the United States. Nevertheless, the pressures brought to bear on Guatemala by the Carter administration's human rights policy did have some initial effect. In 1978, there was a fleeting move toward political relaxation when the armed forces sought to bring the Christian Democrats into the government in order to broaden its appeal and refurbish its international image.

The Christian Democrats obtained no real political influence, but even this small opening stimulated other opposition forces. The reaction of the Right was swift; the political opening closed, and in the first three months of 1979 the two most popular civilian leaders of the moderate opposition, Alberto Fuentes Mohr and Manuel Colom Argueta, were assassinated by death squads.

Over the next four years, the regime of General Lucas García earned its reputation as one of the bloodiest dictatorships in the world. Death squads operating at the direction of the president and under the guidance of his brother became the principle mechanism for containing urban political opposition. In the rural areas, the military unleashed a reign of indiscriminate terror against the Indian population.

Although the death squads were relatively successful at preventing the growth of organized urban opposition to the regime, the level of violence in the countryside proved to be counterproductive. Guatemala's earlier guerrilla insurgencies had failed because of their inability to appeal to Guatemala's Indians. The Indians, a majority of the total population and the only mass base available for rural insurgency, remained politically inert during the 1950s and 1960s. The terror visited upon them by Lucas García succeeded where the guerrillas had not—during the late 1970s, the Indian communities began organizing for self-defense.

Two of Guatemala's four major guerrilla organizations, the Guerrilla Army of the Poor (EGP) and the Organization of the People in Arms (ORPA), took the lead in organizing rural Indian communities. By early 1982, this campaign had been so successful that the guerrillas controlled substantial portions of the countryside, and many observers were convinced that they had seized the military initiative from the army.

The deteriorating military situation produced serious strains within the regime that culminated in the March 1982 coup that brought General Ríos Montt to power. A number of factors came together to produce the coup. The Reagan administration, blocked from resuming military aid to Guatemala by congressional resistance, was angered by Lucas García's unwillingness to allow even cosmetic changes in its human-rights practices. The oligarchy was angered by the electoral fraud of early March 1984 that they believed had stolen victory from Sandoval Alarcon's extreme rightist National Liberation Movement.

Within the armed forces, the grievances against Lucas García were many. He had alienated the United States and thus cut the military off from the flow of United States assistance. He was losing the war. And, perhaps most importantly, he and his cronies were becoming wealthy through corruption while younger officers were fighting and dying in the countryside.

Thus the coalition that united in the March 1982 coup to depose the Lucas regime was a heterogeneous one, composed of Sandoval's civilian and military allies, young officers of uncertain ideology, and the United States as passive and silent partner. Ríos Montt came to head the new regime almost by accident. The young officers who carried out the coup needed a senior officer to lead their new government, and they sought out Ríos Montt because of his reputation for honesty and loyalty to the military institution. Within a few months, Ríos Montt had displaced many of those who made the coup, establishing himself as undisputed head of the government.

Death-squad activity in the urban areas ended almost as soon as Lucas García was ousted, confirming that he had been directly responsible for it. The resulting calm was hailed by the Reagan administration as proof of the new regime's concern for human rights and as cause for resuming military aid. The situation in the countryside changed as well, but for the worse. Ríos Montt, who had been involved in the counterinsurgency operations of the early 1970s, undertook a major effort to defeat the new insurgency of the 1980s. He called it "Beans and Rifles."

Modeled in part on the strategic hamlets program used by the United States in Vietnam, Ríos Montt's pacification program was explicitly designed to deprive the guerrillas of the "sea" in which they swam—the rural population. During the summer and fall of 1982, the Guatemalan army endeavored to depopulate the rural areas where the guerrillas had demonstrated significant strength. Entire villages were massacred, others were subjected to aerial bombardment designed to drive the inhabitants either into Mexico or into areas more easily controlled by the regime.

People relocated from guerrilla areas were then herded together into the Guatemalan equivalent of strategic hamlets, formed into Civil Defense units, and sent out to fight the guerrillas. The human toll of Ríos Montt's counterinsurgency program is difficult to estimate; as many as twenty thousand people may have been killed, and tens of thousands were driven into refugee camps in Mexico. By the beginning of 1983, as many as a million people may have been internal refugees in Guatemala itself.[15]

In military terms, "Beans and Rifles" was a qualified success. The guerrillas were dealt a major setback, being deprived of their base of logistical support. Unlike the Salvadoran guerrillas, who operate in highly mobile columns of combatants and either take their logistical support with them or rely upon the density of population to provide logistical support wherever they are, the Guatemalan movement was much more territorially tied. Most of its columns operated in the immediate vicinity of the villages in which they lived. The extermination of those villages left the guerrillas with no means of support. Nevertheless, the number of guerrilla combatants killed in Ríos Montt's campaign was relatively small. The pace of the war slowed considerably as the guerrillas sought to regroup.

In August 1983, Ríos Montt was overthrown by more traditionally minded military officers led by General Mejía Victores. Once again, the coup coalition was diverse. Ríos Montt's evangelical fervor and his attempt to use the government to proselytize for the Church of the Word offended the Catholicism of many officers, and his bizarre behavior came to be seen as an embarrassment. His insistence that the oligarchy be required to accept sacrifices in order to stabilize Guatemala's economy earned him the enmity of the civilian Right. And his failure to obtain a restoration of United States military aid made his eccentricities all the more intolerable. As the coup plot was formulated, the United States once again gave tacit approval by doing nothing to head off the conspirators. In Washington, it was hoped that perhaps yet another new Guatemalan regime might provide the opportunity to convince Congress that a restoration of military aid was appropriate.

Mejía's government was as much a traditional Guatemalan military regime as

Ríos Montt's was unusual, displaying the sort of right-wing nationalism that came to be an ideological hallmark of the Guatemalan military in the late 1970s after United States military aid was halted. Despite United States proddings, Mejía has not been enthusiastic about Guatemalan participation in the revival of the Central American Defense Council (CONDECA). Thus, despite their anti-communism, Guatemala's officers are unlikely to enlist as partners in the Reagan administration's broader plans for regional military cooperation. This reluctance might be overcome if the Reagan administration were able to convince the Congress to resume security assistance to Guatemala, but the Mejía regime shows no signs of making any concessions on the human-rights issue that might make such a change feasible.

The Mejía regime promised to hold elections in 1984 and 1985 to begin a transition to civilian rule, but it was virtually inconceivable that the Guatemalan army would surrender its hold on political power. Over the past two decades, the army has developed a direct and substantial interest in the Guatemalan economy—largely by dispossessing Indians of their land. As an economic elite, the military now rivals the traditional oligarchy. To protect these interests, the military will not surrender substantive political power to civilians of any ideological stripe. None of this, however, rules out the possibility that the regime may allow "elections" for international consumption.

The Mejía Victores regime, like Ríos Montt's before it, is inherently unstable. The political factionalism of the Guatemalan officers corps was so thorough and almost institutionalized that any military regime had to be constantly on guard to maintain a minimum winning coalition among the various factions.

In early 1984, there were reports of renewed guerrilla operations in various parts of the country. Though it is too early to gauge how much strength the guerrillas retain, there is little doubt that the short-term and medium-term prospects are for an intensification of the war. Such a development would place serious stress on the regime, making further shifts in governing personalities all the more likely.

COSTA RICA

Unlike the rest of Central America, Costa Rica has a long tradition of stable democratic politics and state-supported social welfare programs. These have by no means brought universal equality or prosperity to Costa Rica's underdeveloped economy, but they have provided the existing order with great legitimacy, which in turn has prevented the emergence of violent political opposition.

Despite these strengths, Costa Rica is not immune to the turmoil swirling around it. Costa Ricans harbor two main fears for the future of their democratic society. The first is that they will be drawn against their will into the conflicts of their neighbors; the second, that their own internal economic difficulties will erode the foundation of legitimacy that has supported their democracy.

The most immediate concern is with Nicaragua. The presence of anti-Sandinistas operating from Costa Rican territory has turned the border with Nicaragua into a war zone. Without an army, Costa Rica is unable to either expel the guerrillas or protect its border against Sandinista "hot pursuit."

The conflict along the border has also produced some polarization within Costa Rica itself between those, both in and out of government, who support the guerrillas and would passively allow them to continue operating from their Costa Rica bases, and those who would take an active stance to maintain Costa Rican neutrality. In addition, Costa Ricans fear Nicaragua's arms buildup and the possibility of Nicaraguan support for terrorist activity inside Costa Rica, several instances of which have already come to light.

Another way in which Costa Rica could be swept up in the Central American conflict is through the outbreak of region-wide war, triggered either by interstate war between other nations in the region, or by United States intervention in Nicaragua or El Salvador. The regionalization of the conflict would almost inevitably spill into Costa Rica no matter how intently the government there sought to avoid entanglement.

These fears, serious as they are, remain secondary to the danger that economic difficulties may undermine Costa Rican democracy from within. Costa Ricans see unsettling parallels between their current plight and what happened to the "Switzerland of South America"—Uruguay. Like Costa Rica, Uruguay built its democracy upon the legitimacy provided by an advanced social welfare system atypical for an underdeveloped nation. Like Costa Rica, it was a predominantly middle-class society thought to be immune to the depredations of military intervention in politics. The descent of Uruguay into brutal dictatorship was triggered by an economic crisis that demolished its elaborate social welfare system, undermined the legitimacy of its political institutions, and gave rise to insurgency.

Costa Rica's current economic difficulties are every bit as difficult as those that precipitated Uruguay's collapse. The austerity required in any program of economic stabilization will inevitably mean reductions in social spending that will damage the standard of living of the poor and thereby reduce their stake in the existing order.

For Costa Ricans, the main item on the political agenda is how to safeguard their democracy against these dangers. The Monge government has been divided in its views since it came to office. Some have argued that close association with the United States and cooperation with United States policy in Central America offer the best guarantee of stability, for they will assure the continued flow of economic assistance necessary to ease the economic stabilization program. Others have argued that associating Costa Rica with the United States will inevitably draw it deeper into the conflicts of its neighbors since United

States policy has emphasized a military approach to those problems.[16] People who take this view point to Honduras, where the close partnership that evolved between the United States and General Alvarez led to substantial Honduran involvement in the conflicts of both Nicaragua and El Salvador, and to a strengthening of the military's influence in Honduran politics. Washington has done nothing to ease this dilemma for Costa Rica. It has aimed to enlist Costa Rica as a more active participant in the United States regional strategy for continuing the rolling back of communism.[17]

THE REGIONAL SEARCH FOR PEACE

As Central America's wars escalated and United States military involvement in them deepened, other Latin American nations, particularly those with interests of their own in the region, became increasingly fearful that direct United States intervention was the ultimate and logical outcome of the process underway. These fears produced a variety of diplomatic efforts aimed at reducing regional tension and beginning the search for negotiated political solutions to the conflicts in El Salvador, and between Nicaragua and its antagonists in Honduras and in Washington.

Mexico has taken the lead in this search for diplomatic alternatives in part because Mexico, more than any other Latin American nation, sees Central America as its own zone of influence. Moreover, since Mexico has a vital interest in its bilateral relationship with the United States, no Mexican government could relish the prospect of seeing Mexican nationalism enflamed against Washington by a direct United States intervention in Central America. Finally, the Mexicans' own political tradition, both in domestic politics and in international affairs, leads them to believe that social and political change, even revolutionary change, is unavoidable in Central America and efforts to resist it only increase the likelihood that it will take extreme form. Mexico has no interest in seeing the emergence of additional Cubas in Central America, but its vision of how to avoid this runs counter to Washington's.

One of the earliest Mexican diplomatic initiatives on Central America was prompted by reports in late 1981 that the United States was contemplating direct military action in Nicaragua, El Salvador, or against Cuba. Mexican President José López Portillo requested that Secretary of State Alexander Haig visit Mexico to consult on the Central American crisis, and it was on that visit that Haig met secretly with Cuban Vice-President Carlos Rafael Rodríguez. Although these meetings produced no discernable diplomatic progress, they may well have been a factor in the new policy tone that soon emerged in Washington—that the United States would not take unilateral actions in Central America, but rather would seek multilateral action through the Inter-American system.[18]

In March 1982, with the Salvadoran elections approaching and the United States in the midst of a major political offensive against Nicaragua, Lopez Portillo announced a new diplomatic initiative calling for negotiations to ease the three major "knots" of tension in the region. He proposed Mexico's good offices in beginning dialogue between Nicaragua and the United States, Cuba and the United States, and between the government and FDR/FMLN in El Salvador.

Cuba, Nicaragua, and the FDR/FMLN accepted the Mexican offer immediately. The Salvadoran government flatly rejected it, thereby dooming any change of untying that particular knot. The United States reacted coolly to the proposal at first; only after the proposal had achieved wide public support in the United States and abroad did the Reagan administration agree to it. The discussions with Cuba proved to be entirely perfunctory. General Vernon Walters traveled to Havana for secret talks with Fidel Castro, but no effort was made to follow up on Cuba's repeated declarations, both public and private, that it was willing to discuss with Washington all issues having to do with Central America.[19]

Washington's dialogue with Nicaragua was more drawn out, but never advanced to the point of actual negotiations. Nicaragua and the United States exchanged a series of diplomatic notes setting out agendas for discussion, but the United States continued to refuse to take the next step of actually discussing the issues outside simple ambassadorial contacts. By August, even the exchange of diplomatic notes had come to a halt.

During July and August 1982, Nicaraguan exiles launched a series of major attacks from their base camps in Honduras. As rumors of war between Nicaragua and Honduras swept the rgion, President Herrera Campins of Venezuela and Lopez Portillo appealed to Nicaragua, Honduras, and the United States to take swift diplomatic action to avert the outbreak of war. The Mexican-Venezuelan initiative was the first joint effort of the two nations in support of diplomatic solutions to the Central American conflict, and it marked a change in Venezuelan policy, which had theretofore been generally supportive of the United States. The initiative proposed measures to reduce border tensions between Nicaragua and Honduras, and urged the United States to upgrade its contacts with Nicaragua to actual negotiations.

Washington's response was as cool as it had been to the López Portillo initiative earlier in the year. In his letter of reply to Herrera Campins and Lopez Portillo, President Reagan reiterated existing United States policy rather than responding directly to the substantive proposals that had been made. Much of Reagan's letter echoed proposals that had been advanced through another diplomatic track that the United States had been promoting as an alternative to the efforts of Mexico.

In 1982, the United States had taken the lead in organizing the Central American Democratic Community (El Salvador, Costa Rica, and Honduras) as a mechanism for regional cooperation designed to counter the alleged threat from Nicaragua. The United States participated in the initial meeting of CADC and signed its declaration. In part because it was too transparently an instrument of United States policy—its initial declaration repeated almost verbatim the United States position—the CADC never got off the ground. In mid-1982, it was succeeded by the Central American Forum for Peace and Democracy, which was also largely a creation of Washington.

Despite the various failures of diplomatic initiatives, the escalation of the wars in El Salvador and against Nicaragua in late 1982 and early 1983 produced a great sense of urgency in the region and among neighboring nations. In January, Panama and Colombia joined Mexico and Venezuela in the Contadora Group (named for the island where their foreign ministers met initially) to search for negotiated solutions to the region's conflicts.

Costa Rica withdrew from the Forum for Peace and Democracy, effectively killing that organization, and launched an effort to bring together the Central American countries with the Contadora Group. The basic thrust of this endeavor was to convene a regional peace conference of the five Central American states mediated by the good offices of Contadora. In effect, it was an attempt to merge the two existing diplomatic tracks—that of the Latin American nations surrounding the region, particularly Mexico and Venezuela, and that of the Central American nations themselves.

Initially, there was great skepticism about the prospects for success, given the failures of so many prior efforts, the apparent intractability of the regional conflicts, and the record of United States hostility toward any diplomatic initiative that did not fit exactly with United States policy. Despite numerous meetings among the Contadora foreign ministers, some of them with the foreign ministers of the Central American nations, little was accomplished during the first six months of the effort. There were two major stumbling blocks. The United States insisted that negotiations must be region-wide and must deal with all the issues simultaneously; peace could not be negotiated in parts. Nor could Contadora press for internal negotiations in El Salvador, but rather had to limit itself to dealing with interstate conflicts. Though the United States did not participate in these meetings, its position was faithfully echoed by Honduras. On the other side, Nicaragua insisted that Contadora should promote bilateral negotiations to reduce regional tensions—particularly between Nicaragua and its various antagonists.

This deadlock was broken in July when Nicaragua agreed to proceed with multilateral negotiations, dropping their insistence that bilateral accords take precedence. By September, the Contadora process had made astounding progress; the Central Americans agreed upon twenty-one principles covering a range of social, economic, political, and security issues. In January 1984, these were spelled out in greater detail, and working groups were formed to draft formal, verifiable accords putting the principles into practice.

That, of course, was no easy task. Among both the Contadora nations and the Central Americans, there were differences in expectations and objectives, and the attitude of the United States toward the whole process remained a key factor in the probability of its eventual success.

Mexico has been and remains a main motivating force behind the Contadora initiative. It has long believed that the escalation of conflict in Central America endangers its own interests, and that the policies of the Reagan administration have done little but fuel the region's wars. From the outset, Mexico has sought to use the Contadora process to defuse the regional crisis. Since the inauguration of President Miguel de la Madrid, conservatives within Mexico have pressured him to de-emphasize Mexico's differences with Washington on this issue, lest the United States take retribution by making Mexico's economic crisis more difficult to resolve. On several occasions, there have been reports that at least some in the Reagan administration favor such an approach.

Venezuela entered the diplomatic fray in Central America largely because the Christian Democrats were defeated in the 1982 Salvadoran elections. Duarte, a personal friend of Herrera Campins since his exile in Venezuela, has always been the favorite of COPEI (the Christian Democratic party), and Venezuelan support of United States policy in El Salvador was basically support for the Salvadoran PDC. A second objective has been to push Nicaragua toward a Venezuelan-style multiparty state rather than merely toward a Mexican-style one-party system.

The defeat of COPEI in the last election has several implications for Venezuela's role in Contadora. Its attitude toward Nicaragua is likely to remain unchanged, but the Democratic Action Party, a member of the Socialist International, is likely to look more favorably upon a negotiated solution in the El Salvadoran war. Like Mexico, however, the new Venezuelan government is under considerable pressure to focus its attention on the domestic economic situation rather than on foreign affairs.

In Colombia, the election of President Belisario Betancur marked the beginning of a new and unprecedented activist foreign policy. On the issue of Nicaragua, Colombia appears to stand somewhere between Mexico and Venezuela. On the issue of El Salvador, Betancur's enthusiasm for negotiations will be tempered by his success or failure in reaching accord with the Colombia guerrilla movement, the M-19.

Panama's position is difficult to fathom largely because of the internal political uncertainty around the 1984 elections. The new commander of the guard, General Manuel Antonio Noriega, has appeared to be sympathetic to United States military policy in Central America, and Panama's predominant interest is still the smooth implementation of the Canal treaties. Among the Contadora nations, this makes Panama the most sensitive to Washington's attitude.

Among the Central American states, Costa Rica has been the most unambiguously supportive of the Contadora process. It sees a diplomatic solution to the region's wars as the best and perhaps only way to extricate itself from the dilemma of staying on good terms with Washington while at the same time avoiding being drawn into conflicts not of its making.

At the other end of the spectrum, Guatemala has been the least supportive. The rightists who dominant the Guatemalan military believe the solution to Central America's problems lies in military victory over the FDR/FMLN in El Salvador and the extermination of the Sandinista regime in Nicaragua. If Contadora derails such a program, Guatemala is unlikely to support it. On the other hand, the Guatemalans are not prepared to commit their own forces to seeking such a military solution without a clear and substantial *quid pro quo* from the United States. Since this has not been forthcoming, Guatemala has not played an active role either for or against Contadora's progress.

Nicaragua entered the Contadora process at Mexico's urging, and has remained cautiously supportive of it because the Sandinistas have come to see it as the main bulwark against direct United States intervention. The Sandinistas appear to be prepared to give up their material support of the FDR/FMLN in exchange for guarantees of their own security. They are not likely, however, to make many additional concessions on internal pluralism. Nor have they been prepared to rely solely on Contadora, taking their case repeatedly to the United Nations when opportunities have arisen. The Nicaraguans feel politically outnumbered at least three to one among the Central American states, and that they can rely only upon Mexico among the Contadora nations themselves.

El Salvador would be happy to see a Contadora agreement that halted Nicaraguan support of the FDR/FMLN, but it would clearly have difficulty with an agreement that required the withdrawal of United States military advisors from Central America since they have become so central to the Salvadoran regime's war effort. If Contadora should turn its attention to the issue of negotiations between the Salvadoran government and the FDR/FMLN, El Salvador's support for Contadora would evaporate.

The Honduran role in Contadora has been particularly important. During the tenure of General Alvarez, Honduras held Washington's spot at the table, faithfully articulating United States policy. In private conversations, Alvarez made no effort to hide his cynicism about Contadora, describing it as a necessary exercise prior to solving the Nicaraguan problem militarily. It is not yet clear what impact the removal of Alvarez will have on Honduras's role in Contadora.

Ultimately, nothing is more important for the success or failure of the Contadora process than the attitude of the United States. Few of the participants are prepared to confront the United States directly, and none believe that the process will succeed if Washington actively opposes it.

The attitude of the Reagan administration toward Contadora has been ambiguous. Verbal support has been rendered when requested by the participants, but a number of United States actions have contradicted its basic objective of reducing regional tension. The Kissinger Report, which articulates the rationale for the Reagan administration's policy almost to the letter, damns the Contadora process with faint praise.[20]

In retrospect, it appears that the ambiguity of the United States attitude is more than just a rhetorical facade required by the broad support Contadora has garnered both within the United States and abroad. Washington's support for the process seems to wax and wane depending upon how successfully Washington believes it can control the process and bend it into an instrument of the administration's overall regional strategy.

Thus the initial attitude of the Reagan administration was rather cool, as it had been to earlier initiatives. It warmed somewhat when it seemed that Contadora would avoid the difficult issue of negotiations in El Salvador, focusing instead upon interstate tensions. It warmed further when Nicaragua agreed to a multilateral approach, thus giving Honduras (and hence Washington) effective veto over any eventual agreements. If Honduras is no longer willing to continue in its role as surrogate for the United States, one may expect Washington's attitude toward Contadora to turn more frigid. Yet one element of the Reagan administration's approach has been consistent. It has never let the existence of the Contadora process inhibit its military moves in the regions, even when these have flown in the face of what Contadora has been trying to achieve.

UNITED STATES POLICY

Since the turn of the century, Central America has been a de facto protectorate of the United States. Although the social and political changes that swept the region over the past two decades have reduced the ability of the United States to control events in Central America, it is still true that nothing has a greater impact in the region than policy decisions made in Washington.

The policy of the Reagan administration has been remarkably consistent. The new administration came to office intent upon halting the spread of "communism" in Central America; it interpreted turmoil as primarily a product of subversive activities by the Soviet Union and Cuba. It sought to achieve its goal primarily by military means, vastly expanding United States military assistance to El Salvador and Honduras, trying to resume military assistance to Guatemala, and eventually mounting a massive covert war against Nicaragua.[21]

Central American reality has proven much more intransigent than the United States anticipated. The Reagan administration's initial hopes for a quick military victory in El Salvador have been dashed by events, and even the seemingly more realistic objective of gradually increasing the combat capacity of the Salvadoran army has met with little success. On the political side, Washington's hopes of promoting the fortunes of the moderate center and controlling the depradations of the Far Right in order to build a political base of support for the existing regime have not been met. The Right has shown itself to be stronger and more intractable than anticipated. Despite major increase in the commitment of United States resources, Washington's strategy for settling the war in El Salvador is farther from fruition than it was three years ago. The paucity of results raises serious questions as to whether the continuation of the current policy, at whatever level of resources, will produce any greater success.

In Nicaragua, the Sandinistas have proven to be militarily stronger and politically more durable than the United States expected. The contras have been unable to make any significant military headway or establish any serious military presence within Nicaragua, despite the fact that their number has grown far beyond original plans. Politically, the growth of the covert war has produced a result opposite of what was intended. Though the contras have inflicted serious damage on the Nicaraguan economy, political unrest due to economic hardship has been far outweighed by the Sandinistas' ability to rally popular support to the regime on the basis of an appeal to Nicaraguan nationalism.

In Honduras, Washington's effort to transform that formerly peaceful nation into a forward base of military operations has succeeded but at the expense of the development of civilian control over the military, and therefore at the expense of Honduran democracy.

The Reagan administration's reliance on military means of dealing with Central America's problems has produced international criticism, congressional resistance, and wide public opposition in the United States. These pressures have forced the administration to present at least the facade of willingness to see the region's conflicts resolved by negotiations. There is even some indication that more moderate policymakers within the administration would truly prefer negotiations as an alternative to deepening United States military involvement. But despite oft-repeated claims of seeking "political solutions" to the Central America crisis, the Reagan administration has approached negotiations in the region with little enthusiasm or seriousness.

If the administration is not prepared to support negotiations, the prospects for peace are bleak. After three years of escalating costs and deepening military involvement, the administration's policy has been strikingly unsuccessful in defeating either the FDR/FMLN or the Sandinistas. There is no reason to think that this trend will suddenly reverse itself.

Eventually then, the Reagan administration (or its successor) will be forced to confront the basic choice of whether it is prepared to "lose" in El Salvador or to commit United States forces to combat. This eventuality has not gone unanticipated, despite numerous administration protestations that it has no intention of sending United States forces to Central America; the military buildup in Honduras has been explicitly designed, at least in part, to establish the infrastructure necessary to support a large-scale United States involvement in a Central American war.

The Reagan administration has declared itself determined to halt the march of "communism" in Central America. It has declared that this is a necessary policy because vital national security interests are at stake. It has created, in short, a logic to justify current policy that leads inexorably towards a direct United States role, if that is what is necessary to avert defeat.

NOTES

1. The debate over the extent of Cuban and Nicaraguan military aid to the Salvadoran guerrillas has been a long and heated one. The administration led off with the White Paper, *Communist Interference in El Salvador,* Special Report 80, February 23, 1981 (Washington, DC: U.S. Department of State). This document was subjected to withering criticism by both the *Wall Street Journal,* June 8, 1981, and the *Washington Post,* June 9, 1981. Subsequently, the administration continued to claim it possessed evidence of arms flows from Nicaragua and Cuba to El Salvador, but refused to release it on the grounds that sources would be compromised. But unidentified U.S. government officials in Washington and Central America said repeatedly that the evidence was actually sparse (see, for instance, the *Boston Globe,* June 10, 1984). In June 1984, a former CIA analyst stated publicly that no substantive evidence existed (see the *New York Times,* June 11, 1984, and the *Washington Post,* June 13, 1984). Among members of Congress who have seen the evidence that the administration has, some find it persuasive and some do not.

2. Thomas P. Anderson, *Politics in Central America* (New York: Praeger, 1982), p. 64.

3. The Reagan administration, of course, insists that great strides have been made on both agrarian reforms and human rights. Space does not allow a full review of the arguments and evidence on this issue. Those interested in such a review should consult the congressional hearings held on the administration's semiannual certification of progress in these and other areas, and the detailed rebuttal prepared semiannually by America's Watch and the American Civil Liberties Union.

4. Though the PDC won a plurality of the vote and 24 of the 60 seats in the Constituent Assembly, the rest of the seats were divided among four rightist parties: ARENA with 19; the old military-dominated National Conciliation Party (PCN) with 14; the small, personalistic Salvadoran Popular Party (PPS) with one; and a small party of moderate industrialists, Democratic Action (AD) with two. After the election, ARENA, PCN, and PPS formed a majority coalition to freeze the PDC out of the government and to elect d'Aubuisson provisional president. For accounts of this period, see the *Washington Post,* April 17 and 23, 1982.

5. For a detailed account of U.S. efforts to prevent d'Aubuisson from becoming president, see the *Washington Post* and the *New York Times,* April 23, 1982. A year later, U.S. Ambassador Deane Hinton commented that the only drawback to the presidency of Alvaro Magaña was that "one had to resort to the military" to install him in office (the *Washington Post,* April 28, 1983).

6. The CIA's involvement in the 1984 Salvadoran election is described in the *Washington Post,* May 4 and 13, 1984. The plot to assassinate Ambassador Thomas Pickering is described in the *New York Times,* June 26, 1984.

7. On the relationship between the Salvadoran Armed Forces and the death squads,

see the account of a former head of Salvadoran military intelligence in the *New York Times*, March 3, 1984, and the *Washington Post*, April 8, 1984; a five-part investigative series, "Salvadoran Rightists: The Deadly Patriots," by Craig Pyles, *The Albuquerque Journal*, December 18–22, 1983; Alan Nairn, "Behind the Death Squads," *The Progressive*, May 1984, pp. 20–29; and the *Christian Science Monitor*, May 8, 1984.

8. On the failures of the San Vicente plan, see the *Washington Post*, November 6, December 13 and 18, 1983; and the *New York Times*, November 4 and December 18, 1983.

9. For a good collection of articles on various aspects of the Nicaraguan revolution, see Thomas W. Walker (ed.), *Nicaragua in Revolution* (New York: Praeger, 1981).

10. *Washington Post*, November 9, 1980.

11. For a discussion of the development of the covert war, see William M. Leo-Grande, "Nicaragua and the United States," in Thomas Walker (ed.), *Nicaragua in Revolution*, 2nd ed. (New York: Praeger, forthcoming).

12. See note 1 above.

13. Details of the Nicaraguan military buildup are provided in the State Department background paper, *Nicaragua's Military Buildup and Support for Central American Subversion* (Washington, DC: Department of State and Department of Defense, June 1984). This document, like others before it, presents the Nicaraguan buildup as an offensive threat to Nicaragua's neighbors. In 1982, the House Intelligence Committee criticized the administration for such a portrayal since it ran against the intelligence community's (classified) assessment of the intent behind the buildup. See *U.S. Intelligence Performance on Central America*, Staff Report of the House Permanent Select Committee on Intelligence, September 22, 1982 (Washington, DC: mimeographed, 1982).

14. On General Alvarez's role and the reasons for his ouster, see the *New York Times* and the *Washington Post*, April 4, 1984, and the *New York Times*, April 4 and 24, 1984.

15. On Ríos Montt's counterinsurgency campaign, see Amnesty International, *Guatemala: Special Briefing Paper*, July 1982.

16. For details of the debate inside Costa Rica during 1983 and 1984, see the *Washington Post*, May 14, 1983; May 21, 1984; and the *New York Times*, May 16, 1984.

17. For instance, the CIA supported guerrilla forces operating against Nicaragua from base camps in Honduras, thereby increasing border tensions. The administration also urged Costa Rica to accept a U.S. plan for transportation infrastructure development in the border area, a plan similar to one underway in Honduras, and having obvious military potential. Finally, the U.S. urged Costa Rica to begin a military buildup alien to Costa Rican political tradition.

18. See, for instance, Haig's address to the Organization of American States, the text of which is printed in the *New York Times*, December 5, 1981.

19. Wayne S. Smith, "Dateline Havana: Myopic Diplomacy," *Foreign Policy*, no. 48, Fall 1982, pp. 157–174.

20. The Kissinger Report, touted as a bipartisan consensus, did nothing to allay congressional opposition to Reagan's policy. For an extended discussion of the Kissinger Report, see William M. LeoGrande, "Through the Looking Glass: The Kissinger Report on Central America," *World Policy Journal*, no. 2, Winter 1984, pp. 151–184.

21. The Reagan administration always points out that its economic aid to Central America is about three times as great as its military aid, as if this were somehow proof that the core of its policy is not the pursuit of military objectives. In fact, most of the "economic" aid being sent is Economic Support Funds (ESF)—not development aid, but simple budgetary support to keep the recipient economies afloat until the regional conflict can be ended.

Chapter 4

DEFENDING DEMOCRACY

James Michel

IT IS UNFORTUNATE that so many discussions of Central America seem to start with a maze of myths and misconceptions. There are important issues of policy that should be the subjects of informed debate. It is both necessary and possible for the United States to approach Central America on the basis of some consensus as to what those problems are.

Once again, however, serious consideration of the issues is impeded by the need to insist first upon a more objective appraisal of the factual setting in which these issues arise. Dr. LeoGrande's paper is riddled with exaggerations and omissions. Its analysis is incomplete and sometimes simply wrong.

Dr. LeoGrande's basic assertions are two:

—that "the situation in Central America has deteriorated greatly since 1981" (p. 19);
—that "the paucity of results raises serious questions as to whether the continuation of the current [United States] policy, at whatever level of resources, will produce any greater success" (p. 45).

A calmer appraisal of these points suggests different conclusions:

—First, except for Nicaragua and its continuing support for the guerrillas in El Salvador, considerable progress has been made toward the gradual democratization of Central American life—particularly in El Salvador;
—Second, United States policy has contributed significantly to this progress. If the Congress now completes action on the President's program embodying the recommendations of the National Bipartisan Commission on Central America, this progress can be consolidated and Cuban-Soviet activities countered.

These comments address first the region and its dynamics, then United States policy.

CENTRAL AMERICA

If one is to analyze Central America from the standpoint of its own dynamics rather than the United States political calendar, the best reference point is five years ago instead of three. It was in 1979 that Central America's traditional order broke down.

- —At this time five years ago, on May 29, 1979, a Sandinista column headed by Edén Pastora invaded Nicaragua from Costa Rica to begin what proved to be the decisive campaign against General Anastasio Somoza.
- —At this time five years ago in El Salvador, General Carlos Huberto Romero's government was paralyzed by its own ineptitude and repression and by the terrorism of young radicals who were amassing substantial popular support.
- —In Guatemala, the government of Romeo Lucas García had been implicated in assassinations of moderate politicians and was in increasingly open conflict with the Catholic church; the countryside was prey to armed bands from left and right.
- —Honduras was more peaceful, but it, too, had a military president, a suspended constitution, and a simmering conflict with El Salvador.
- —Only democratic Costa Rica was free of violence.

Today, the traditional dictators are gone. But the pendulum could now swing all the way from right-wing dictatorship to Communist totalitarianism.

- —General Somoza is gone. But his self-appointed successors have so repressed their people that many, including Pastora, have again taken up arms, this time against the communization of their country.
- —General Romero is gone. El Salvador has just completed its third successful national election in two years, but the relentless guerrilla assault supplied and managed from Cuba and Nicaragua continues.
- —General Lucas is gone. Although his successors have also been generals, Guatemala held Constituent Assembly elections on July 1, 1984, and is preparing national elections for 1985.
- —Honduras has a restored constitutional order and a strong civilian president. It has made peace with El Salvador but now faces a constant threat from Nicaragua.
- —Costa Rica remains vibrantly democratic. But it, too, feels itself threatened by Nicaragua.

Dr. LeoGrande's paper reads for the most part as if none of this had happened.

Dr. LeoGrande writes about El Salvador as if it were the semifeudal state of the pre-1979 era. In fact, his treatment of El Salvador implies that the government and military have not changed since 1932. Dr. LeoGrande's primary mistake is to view El Salvador's travails through the lenses of the past.

During the last four years, El Salvador has had three popular elections. Its governments have implemented, with military support, a land reform so radical that a quarter of El Salvador's arable land has been redistributed to the benefit of half a million peasants and the detriment of thousands of landowners. Despite a guerrilla war that continues—though perhaps less widely than Dr. LeoGrande suggests—violence has declined markedly.

El Salvador has a new constitution and a strengthened civilian executive. Its judicial system has begun to enforce the law against members of the military. And the military itself has been transformed from a defender of the past into a protector of the future.

Dr. LeoGrande dismisses these changes either by ignoring them or denying that they have taken place. He ignores totally the work of the Constituent Assembly, the strengthening of judicial processes, and the Magaña government's amnesty program and persistent widening of the political center.

Of course, Dr. LeoGrande wrote most of this paper before the popular election of Napoleón Duarte as president of El Salvador on May 6, 1984. And it is also true that he wrote before a Salvadoran jury returned a guilty verdict against five national guardsmen accused of killing four American churchwomen in 1980. But an uninformed reader of this paper would never imagine that the proceedings of the trial in Zacatecoluca had been broadcast, live, to the Salvadoran people for sixteen hours.

It is, in fact, at least four years since the government and military in El Salvador could properly be characterized as serving as "guardian[s] of the landed oligarchy" (p. 20). In 1971, over 40 percent of the nation's farmland was controlled by less than 1 percent of the population. Eleven percent of the land was owned by absentee landlords and worked by sharecroppers or tenant farmers. Fifteen percent was organized into large plantations, worked by hired laborers and, during peak seasons, migrant workers. This inequitable distribution caused rural poverty and sparked social unrest.

Overall, the government's land reform program now has benefited more than 550,000 persons or almost 25 percent of the rural population. Over one-third of the farmland is now in the hands of the *campesinos* (farm workers) who worked as tenants and sharecroppers on land they could not hope to own before the reforms. These are not facts to be dismissed with a reference to "the Right's campaign to strangle the agrarian reform" (p. 23).

In short, Dr. LeoGrande denies the cumulative effect of four years of reform, political action, and institutional change.

One explanation for this blind spot may lie in Dr. LeoGrande's vision of what he calls "the fundamental conflict . . . on the battlefield" (p. 25).

Dr. LeoGrande gives a detailed, nuanced account of political groups associated with the guerrillas. Yet he omits any description of the political forces that have been willing to go before the Salvadoran people. Indeed, he inexplicably dismisses the 1982 elections as "a victory of the extreme right" that "the Reagan administration set aside" (p. 21). Yet these elections produced a Constituent Assembly that promulgated on December 15, 1983, a constitution that:

—guarantees freedom of expression, assembly, and religion;
—explicitly protects agrarian reform;
—affirms the apolitical nature of the armed forces;
—outlaws an "official" party;
—strengthens the legislative branch;
—strengthens the judicial branch;
—guarantees *habeas corpus* and legal presumption of innocence;
—mandates public health and education;
—increases worker rights and expands these rights to include peasants.

The bias in Dr. LeoGrande's political assessment is suggested by his treatment of the 1980 split in Christian Democracy. At the March 1980 congress, seven delegates resigned and eleven were expelled. Yet Dr. LeoGrande calls the remaining 134 delegates "a faction" backing the government. He similarly exaggerates the guerrillas' military strength and avoids discussing their external support in the context of Salvadoran politics.

Dr. LeoGrande does discuss Nicaraguan support for the guerrillas in El Salvador. In doing so, however, he commits an error that obscures one of the fundamental realities faced by both Salvadoran democrats and the United States. On page 31, he writes: "in the wake of Ronald Reagan's election, the Salvadoran guerrillas undertook" their January 1981 "final offensive." The fact is that the Salvadoran guerrillas began planning the offensive with Cuban help in the spring of 1980—just as the government of El Salvador, with help from the United States government, was launching the agrarian reform. Salvadoran Communist party leader Shafik Handal left Havana for Moscow and the bloc on May 30, 1980. From June 2 to July 22, 1980, he visited the USSR, Vietnam, the German Democratic Republic, Czechoslovakia, Bulgaria, Hungary, Ethiopia, and then Moscow again to procure arms for the guerrillas. To ignore this chronology is to miss a critical link in the causality of the conflict in El Salvador and Central America generally.

Dr. LeoGrande's treatment of Nicaragua is better. He recognizes that Nicaragua is no longer as it was in mid-1979: newly liberated from the Somoza dictatorship, pledged to the world and its neighbors to be democratic, nonaligned, and nonaggressive. As in El Salvador, however, he gives a lengthy account of differences within the Far Left, in this case the Sandinistas, but makes little mention of the conflicts between the Sandinistas and the church, the various Indian groups, or labor.

Since 1979 the FSLN has lost most of its former anti-Somoza allies. By asserting that this split is the product merely of the opposition's unwillingness to accept the "economic hardship and increasing authoritarianism" that Nicaragua's social revolution requires, Dr. LeoGrande badly misrepresents the San-dinista's policies. As is documented most recently in the Nicaraguan Episcopal Bishops' Conference *Pastoral Letter on Reconciliation* (April 22, 1984) and the AFL-CIO's *A Revolution Betrayed* (March 1984), the split between the Sandinis-tas and Nicaraguan business, labor, and the church has come about largely because of the Nicaraguan government's systematic oppression of these groups.

His paper also downplays the fact that Nicaragua's military buildup gives the Sandinistas military power unimagined in the annals of Central America. Table 4.1 compares Central American armed forces in 1977 and 1983 according to data published by the International Institute for Strategic Studies in London. Somoza had three tanks and twenty-five armored vehicles. As detailed in the July 18, 1984, Department of State Background Paper, *Nicaragua's Military Build-Up and Support for Central American Subversion*, the Sandinistas today control the largest and best-equipped military force in the region. With about 240 tanks and armored vehicles as well as 80 multiple-rocket launchers, Nicaragua has a firepower that easily dwarfs any other in Central America. With Soviet and Cuban encouragement and resources, the Sandinistas have turned Nicaragua into a general headquarters for thousands of guerrillas throughout the isthmus. Ironically, this buildup began the day the Sandinistas moved into Somoza's bunker, even as the rest of the world was prematurely celebrating the end of Nicaraguan militarism.

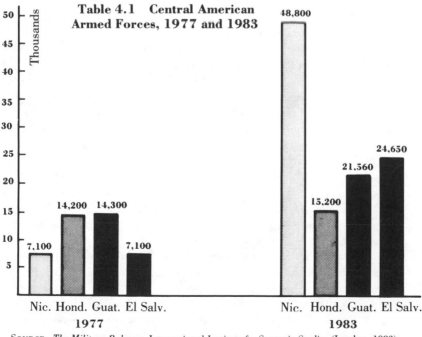

Table 4.1   Central American Armed Forces, 1977 and 1983

SOURCE: *The Military Balance*, International Institute for Strategic Studies (London, 1983).

Similar lacunae are evident in the paper's treatment of Honduras (where President Suazo is never mentioned); Guatemala (where the wellsprings of change over the last two years are missed); and Costa Rica (where differing viewpoints among Social Democrats are presented with the same misleading evenhandedness accorded El Salvador's Christian Democrats).

UNITED STATES POLICY

Dr. LeoGrande's references to United States policy consist mainly of assertions that the United States is seeking a "military solution" to Central America's problems, is failing in efforts to promote political reform and human rights, and opposes peace or at least has a "record of . . . hostility towards any diplomatic initiative that does not fit exactly with United States policy" (p. 41).

Dr. LeoGrande does not discuss United States economic assistance, which accounts for some 70 percent of the resources we are providing Central America. Table 4.2 gives some idea of the amounts involved.

Dr. LeoGrande also dismisses the report of the bipartisan commission in one sentence, saying that it "damns the Contadora process with faint praise" (p. 44). This is unfortunate, for the Kissinger Commission Report's treatment of the search for peace in Central America is one of the main chapters in the report. It addresses El Salvador and Nicaragua as well as the Contadora process. And it identifies a framework for regional security that addresses the substance of such questions as sovereignty, human rights, subversion, foreign military presences, force levels, verification, democracy, and development. Those are the issues that are at the heart of the Contadora process. They are specified in the Contadora Document of Objectives. And they have the support of the United States.

Today, were it not for the United States, the struggle between the advocates of democracy and their armed Communist enemies would be desperately unequal. This is not because of numbers, for an overwhelming majority of Central Americans have always supported democracy when given the chance, but because Nicaragua's neighbors would be unable to preserve a balance if they could not count on the United States. Costa Rica has no army. Honduras, even now, has but sixteen light tanks and a dozen armored vehicles. And across the Gulf of Fonseca from Nicaragua, guerrillas are using the military technology and supplies they receive through Nicaragua to fight democratic reforms supported by an overwhelming majority of Salvadorans.

Like so many other observers, when assessing United States policy toward Nicaragua Dr. LeoGrande disregards the recent history of United States–Nicaraguan relations—especially the chronology of that history. His paper correctly notes the United States shift from a policy of "constructive engagement" during 1980 and 1981 to a policy of more direct pressure during succeeding years. In his assessment, however, Dr. LeoGrande ignores the fact that the United States abandoned "constructive engagement" only *after* it became appar-

Table 4.2
U.S. Economic Assistance (Direct Appropriations) to Central America
(Belize, Costa Rica, El Salvador, Guatemala, Honduras, Nicaragua, and Panama)

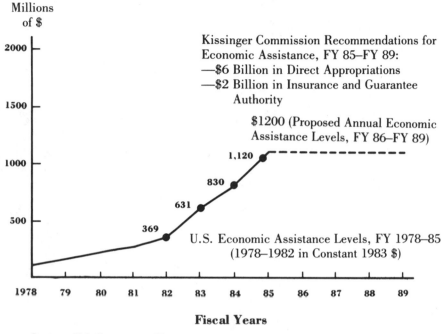

Kissinger Commission Recommendations for Economic Assistance, FY 85–FY 89:
—$6 Billion in Direct Appropriations
—$2 Billion in Insurance and Guarantee Authority

$1200 (Proposed Annual Economic Assistance Levels, FY 86–FY 89)

U.S. Economic Assistance Levels, FY 1978–85 (1978–1982 in Constant 1983 $)

Fiscal Years

SOURCE: U.S. Department of State.

ent that this policy was not compelling the Sandinistas to end their support for the Salvadoran insurgency.

We have had five years to determine what is happening. It is obvious that the overwhelming majority of Central Americans want democracy. They are clearly capable of working and even fighting for it. Equally, Cuba and the Soviet Union are attempting to turn Central America's travails to the disadvantage of both Central America and the United States. The distinguished and independent bipartisan commission reviewed the evidence and provided a blueprint for a long-range solution. The administration has accepted that blueprint.

We have, in short, a coherent policy that addresses the need to help strengthen democratic institutions and to lay the basis for equitable economic growth in a more secure environment. There are no quick or easy solutions, but a little patience and balance would help.

Chapter 5

A CENTRAL AMERICAN TRAGEDY

Viron P. Vaky

THE TWO PRECEEDING papers reminded me of President Kennedy's wry question to the briefers returning from Vietnam, "Did you guys visit the same country?"

The more papers I read and the more seminars I attend the more impressed I am at how convoluted, multidimensional, and difficult the Central American situation really is, and how easy it is to get lost in the trees. I find myself being continually pushed back to simple, basic points.

So let's start with a basic point. That is that Central America is a foreign-policy problem, and is in the headlines, because of the security dimension posed by the Soviet-Cuban involvement. If it were not for that we would not have had this conference; as a nation we would not really be as involved or as concerned about Central America's situation as we are. Now it is true that the security dimension interacts and is intertwined with a larger local dimension of serious and difficult problems and strains, inequitable social and political systems, and a long history of poverty, injustice, repression, and the savaging of the innocent. It is essential that one understand the history and sociopolitical context of the region. As our panel moderator, Robert Leiken, has written elsewhere, when you travel to Central America you travel in time as well as in space.

The real policy problem then, is, how do you relate these apples and oranges—these two discontinuous dimensions? You cannot rationally and accurately focus on any *one* dimension, either one, without getting into difficult problems. They do affect each other. Yet the fact of the matter is that the security question is beginning to drive everything else.

The current administration has from the beginning subsumed the Central American situation under Cold War categories. The president has been very clear, very consistent, very simple about this. He said, using his own words very recently, "Central America is a Soviet-Cuban power play, pure and simple." What has happened then, is that in executing policy, the administration—as all administrations have the power to do—has in effect defined the terms of the policy debate. Certainly in this country, the policy debate is driven by, or turns on, the security question and the two issue clusters that compose it: First, how does one define or conceive of the threat, how does one assess it? Second, what are the cost-benefit ratios of the various alternatives for dealing with that threat?

There is virtually unanimous agreement—there certainly is bipartisan agreement—that Soviet-Cuban military bases or combat military presence in the isthmus would be an intolerable threat. The question that gets debated is, "Is there anything less than that that is intolerable?"

The basic argument in official circles is that the threat is not confined to Soviet military bases, but that even conventional forms of relationships with the USSR and Cuba are threatening because they have the possibility of facilitating intelligence activities, or they may provide the platform for future aggression. Some even argue that the threat rests in the Marxism, or the revolutionary ethos of these groups, because, first, that ideology and ethos may *require* them to export revolution, or because even if not specifically aligned with Moscow they could be susceptible to future Soviet support.

One of the conceptual problems, therefore, is that in approaching Central America "from the top" this way one's policies and tactics inevitably become shaped by extraregional purposes, that is, with an eye on Moscow and Havana—even though they have local cost, local impact, local content. Other problems and objectives begin to be placed in one's conception in reference to this East-West problem. In fact, that is what is happening in the policy debate. What one thinks one ought to do about human rights, about conditioning military aid to El Salvador, about the conditions or requirements for extending or receiving economic aid, all get debated in terms of how these things affect or relate to the security question. Arguments in the Congress and so on aren't really debated on *whether* we ought to extend economic aid, or *whether* we ought to support democracy, but *how* to do these things, and *how* they affect the security question.

So when all is said and done I am driven back to the question that Bill LeoGrande asked at the end of his presentation. The central question in Central American policy centers on Nicaragua. The central questions that seem to be driving everything else are: Can we coexist with the Sandinistas in their present configuration? Are there any circumstances or conditions under which we would be prepared to live with that regime? Can one establish a *modus vivendi* with regard to instrumental and tactical questions like cross-border subversion or foreign advisors? Or must the regime change its nature?

These questions point to the second problem cluster—what are the ways for handling what one perceives of as the threat? How do you calculate the costs and benefits? There is, after all, a very definite and constant interplay between positing an objective and the cost of achieving it. One keeps affecting the other.

The problem here again is that the administration is caught in a dilemma.

The ascendant administration view, as I see it, is that the Sandinistas are irredeemable and implacable. The situation is a zero sum game. A year ago the president said (despite the rhetorical vows to the four Ds of democracy, development, defense, and dialogue), in response to a newsman's question, "I have never trusted the Sandinistas from the time they took power, and you shouldn't either." Only a couple of days ago, in an Irish TV interview, he said the Sandinistas have no honor and no honesty. How does that relate then to these other concepts? The implications are pretty clear. If no settlement or *modus vivendi* is deemed tolerable that permits the Sandinistas to survive (or the guerrillas to survive in El Salvador), do you really have any alternative but military force? But at that point the domestic costs of a military solution force the planners back around the mulberry bush to search for something in between.

The problem is that the conceptualization of Central America as a zero sum game points the administration *away* from negotiation. A lot depends on what one means by "negotiation." I have a hard time perceiving the administration as prepared to accept negotiation in the sense of a compromise, or *modus vivendi*. For example, I think that no agreement on cross-border subversion, or military strength, or foreign advisors, is likely to be achieved except at the price of permitting the Sandinista regime to survive. Probably no reduction in foreign military advisors is going to be achieved without symmetry, that is, without United States withdrawal as well as Cuban withdrawal. Now, if these kinds of deals are not acceptable, then "negotiations" are not acceptable. "Negotiations" are turned into something else—a continuation of confrontation by other means.

Americans have a hard time understanding negotiations with "enemies." Very often we require as *preconditions* the very sorts of things one should be negotiating about, so that it becomes a non-starter in which what one is really talking about is the terms of surrender.

We have said, for example, with regard to both the Contadora process and the twenty-one objectives, that we needed a comprehensive settlement all at once. We have insisted not only on changes in Sandinista *external* behavior in terms of security questions, but also on changes in the *internal* nature of the regime. Now the first might be negotiable. But the question of changing the internal political and social order is not easily achieved by negotiation. It is perhaps better suited to a long-term diplomatic strategy of pressure and incentive.

One of the problems, then, is, how does one sort out objectives? It is not that you have to abandon these objectives. But how do you sort them out in terms of time frames and appropriate strategies? The secretary of state's report to the Congress of March 15, 1984, on efforts to achieve peace said that we believe that pressure in Nicaragua should be reduced or removed only after Nicaragua undertakes real changes in its external and internal policies that will contribute to regional peace. So what's left to negotiate? If we insist on wrapping up all these demands in one package we make negotiation impossible, and we leave confrontation as our only alternative.

This kind of dilemma leads one into several problems: First, it leads one into sophistry and cynicism, and, worse, into self-deception. One tries to lull critics, evade restrictions. Images are presented in simplistic and often mistaken ways. There is no doubt that the administration's rhetorical presentation of its policies, objectives, and programs is full of sophistry. And when one continually presents a selective analysis for the purpose of persuading, these images soon become "the way things are." No doubt these simplistic images are sincerely believed by many.

Second, it leads to contorted policies and to "the worst of all worlds" strategies. If one posits an objective that proves too costly to pursue outright, but one refuses to abandon the objective, then one resorts to all kinds of "in-betweens" in the hope that the goal can still be reached on the cheap and on the sly. That is why we fell into the covert gambit. The problem is that these "in-betweens" seldom work, and we either worsen the situation or go down a slippery slope. Above all, it tempts us into the "fallacy of the last move," i.e., an assumption that the situation is closed-ended with the level of our input the only variable. We look at El Salvador, for example, at any given moment and say we can take care of this situation with X more resources. But the situation does not stay the same; our effort induces escalation on the other side requiring still further input by us.

Third, policies can be self-fulfilling. If one acts as if Central America constitutes a full-blown East-West confrontation, it soon will be. Our own policies may in fact soon make negotiations an impossibility. We seem to be inadvertently—or purposefully—turning Ché Guevara's theory on its head: If the objective conditions for justifiable intervention do not exist, then one tries to *create* them.

I have to end by saying that I view Central America with pessimism. I do not think we will realistically negotiate. We will continue to exert pressure on Nicaragua with a potential for inducing spreading conflict. The war in El Salvador will not be ended by reconciliation; it will go on until one side or the other prevails. We will stimulate polarization within Costa Rica, and our massive military presence will affect internal dynamics in Honduras. We will also position ourselves on a slippery slope. If we choose, in effect, to resolve the problems by force—defeat the Salvadoran insurgents and force the Sandinistas to cry "uncle"—we will have to get much more deeply and overtly involved. We will not overthrow the Sandinistas on the cheap with the contras; the Salvadoran army will not defeat the insurgents by themselves.

I can only conceive of Central America as a classic Greek tragedy in which all the actors on all sides act out their nature and so roll toward further tragedy. What we are likely to see, then, are greater tests of will, spreading conflict, more bloodshed, and more savaging of the innocent.

Chapter 6

RAPPORTEUR'S REPORT

Craig VanGrasstek

INTRODUCTION

ROBERT LEIKEN OF the Carnegie Endowment moderated a panel discussion that featured William LeoGrande, James Michel, and Viron Vaky. (The papers and comments of the panelists are presented in this volume as chapters 3, 4, and 5 respectively.)

William LeoGrande argued that the situation in Central America has deteriorated greatly since President Reagan assumed office, and this deterioration will continue unless current American policy changes. He then analyzed the status of each country in the region.

Real political power is still in the hands of the Salvadoran armed forces, and newly elected President Duarte serves at their pleasure. Although there is currently a stalemate between the right wing and moderate forces, LeoGrande sees little chance for improvement in human rights, reinvigoration of the nation's land reform program, or a negotiated solution to the civil war.

LeoGrande characterized Nicaragua's internal political dynamics as an uneven struggle between the Sandinistas (FSLN) and the private sector. The Sandinistas will overwhelmingly win the elections in November, given their own natural advantages and the disorganized state of the opposition. Meanwhile, the armed opposition—the so-called contras—cannot beat the Nicaraguan army in the field.

He described Honduras as "the Cambodia of Central America," where United States military and political pressures seem to be forcing the nation into direct involvement in the Central American crisis. He sees a similar phenomenon taking place in Costa Rica, where the Costa Ricans oppose further involvement but are too dependent on United States economic assistance to fully resist American pressures.

Finally, LeoGrande observed that the Contadora initiative is not going to succeed in bringing peace to the region unless the United States allows it to do so. He stated that it is demonstrable that the United States supports Contadora only in word and not in deed, and that current American policy makes it virtually impossible for Contadora to make meaningful progress.

James Michel disputed most of the points made by LeoGrande, arguing that there is much more cause for hope in Central America. This is most apparent in El Salvador, where there has been an encouraging process of democratization since the elections of 1982. He offered praise for President Magaña's work, the ratification of the new Salvadoran constitution, increased reliance on the legislative process (e.g., the passage of the amnesty law, the renewals of the agrarian reform), and the reorganization of the Salvadoran armed forces.

Michel criticized the Nicaraguan electoral plans for the absence of guarantees for full media access, the provision allowing sixteen-year-olds to vote, and the short campaign period. He agreed that the Sandinista leaders are likely to win, but pointed out that there is always the possibility of surprises in elections.

He disputed LeoGrande's contention that the United States is using Honduras as a staging area for possible military intervention. While there has been some growth in the Honduran military over the past few years, this has been minor compared to the expansion of the Nicaraguan forces.

Michel defended American policy toward the Contadora initiative. He stated that the United States fully supports the Contadora efforts, and that there has been encouraging progress in this area recently.

INTERVENTION AND COEXISTENCE

Ambassador Viron Vaky served as the panel's discussant, and began by noting the importance of examining the essential nature of the Central American crisis. This area of the world would not be a major United States foreign policy concern if it were not for the Soviet-Cuban connection. The Reagan administration has subsumed the other aspects of the problem under the security dimension and the East-West conflict, and this has determined the tone of the subsequent policy debate. As a result of this dominance of extraregional issues, both the administration and its critics have tended to view "local" problems in terms of their effects on the security question. In Ambassador Vaky's view, the Reagan administration has so deep-seated a distrust for the Sandinistas that the very existence of their regime is deemed unacceptable, and there is little room left for negotiation or compromise.

Vaky highlighted the precarious nature of current United States policy by pointing out that one can understand the argument for a full military intervention, just as one can understand the argument for negotiation and compromise, but it is difficult to articulate or understand a policy that occupies an undefined middle ground between these two alternatives. The purpose of covert assistance to the contras and the overt military aid to the Honduran government is unclear, and while the present policy does not inevitably lead to American intervention it does force United States policy down a rather slippery slope. The graduated military option induces an escalation.

This theme was taken up by other conference participants. *William Leo-Grande* stated that current United States policy leads to bleak choices. In El Salvador, the United States can either encourage the Duarte government to negotiate a solution with the rebels, or it may have to send United States combat troops to achieve a military solution. The United States faces a similar problem in Nicaragua, where the administration may have to choose between seeking a *modus vivendi* with the Sandinistas or dispatching troops to oust them from power.

Other participants pressed James Michel to clarify the administration's position vis-à-vis coexistence with the Sandinistas. *Ted Moran* of Georgetown University asked if coexistence with the Sandinista regime as it is now is possible.

Michel responded that the words "as it is now" are central. The United States neither should nor will make its decisions based strictly on ideological considerations; policy should be based primarily on behavior. Whether a change in behavior is a change in nature is a question for philosophers to answer.

Michel stated that he could foresee the United States living with a Sandinista regime in Managua, but there are four points of contention that must first be addressed:

1. The Sandinistas must diminish their military relationship with Cuba and the USSR.
2. There must be some equilibrium established among the armed forces of the Central American states.
3. Nicaragua must cease its support for subversion in other countries.
4. The Nicaraguan people must be provided with fuller opportunities for political participation.

Michel noted that all these conditions are related to Nicaragua's behavior rather than its ideology. The People's Republic of China is an example of a socialist state with which the United States has full and even cooperative relations, and these relations are made possible by China's behavior: the Chinese do not attempt to subvert democracies.

Viron Vaky asked whether these four objectives could be separated and prioritized. Until now, the United States has attempted to treat them as a seamless web. By dealing with them one at a time, the matters of immediate concern (e.g., cross-border subversion) can be handled early on and the other problems can wait. Michel responded that partial solutions do not guarantee that the problem will not reappear, and hence are not satisfactory.

Alan Berger of the *Boston Globe* posed the question of the offensive that the Salvadoran rebels are expected to launch during the United States presidential campaign. He asked what the likely United States military/political reaction would be to this offensive. Michel responded that the claims of a coming offensive are common, as are rebel and Sandinista claims that the Reagan administration intends to intervene in El Salvador or Nicaragua following the United States elections in November ("standard FMLN talking point #17"). There is no reason for any new rebel offensive to be more successful than previous efforts. The United States does not have to think about the possibility of armed intervention in either Nicaragua or El Salvador because neither situation is out of control.

NICARAGUA'S TIES WITH CUBA AND THE SOVIET UNION

Wayne Smith of the Carnegie Endowment commented that the four enumerated goals of United States policy are all sensible, and three at least can reasonably be accomplished. He asked Mr. Michel to explain, however, whether the real goal of United States policy was a *reduction* in Nicaragua's security ties with the Soviet Union or *severance* of these ties altogether. Assistant Secretary of State Langhorne Motley has called for complete severance of these ties, and senior State Department officials have privately acknowledged that the United States has no intention of allowing a Marxist regime to stay in power in Central America.

Michel answered that severance would be an optimal goal for the United States, although there could certainly be some level of Nicaraguan connection with the USSR which would not be objectionable to the United States. There is still a definitional problem involved: At what point does one cross the line between reduction and severance? Michel declined to speculate over where that line should be drawn.

Wayne Smith noted that if our demand is for *severance* of Nicaragua's security ties with Moscow and Havana rather than their reduction, then there is no possibility at all of coming to terms with the Sandinistas.

Several participants warned that if we fail to view the present crisis with a sense of historical perspective, the mistakes of the past could well be repeated. The United States may be making the same errors today that it did with Cuba a generation ago, and the Sandinistas could be forced into ever tighter dependence upon the Soviet Union to guarantee their security. This could result in a far more serious security problem for the United States in future years.

THE OPPOSITION AND ELECTIONS IN NICARAGUA

In response to a question from *Bruce Cameron* of Foreign Policy Advocates, LeoGrande stated that there has been an active and even raucous dialogue between the Sandinistas and their domestic opposition (including the Church) over the past few years. This exchange now centers on the terms of the coming election in November of 1984, with each side trying to set conditions that will maximize their showing at the polls. The FSLN currently has a strong advantage, and this is magnified by the law that mandates a short campaign and suffrage for sixteen-year-olds.

Michel and LeoGrande differed over the openness and fairness of the upcoming Nicaraguan elections. Michel challenged LeoGrande's assertion that the elections will probably be at least as open as was the recent presidential runoff in El Salvador. LeoGrande responded that he has no doubt that the United States State Department will announce the day after the Nicaraguan balloting that the elections were a fraud.

Arturo Cruz, Jr., of the Johns Hopkins School for Advanced International Studies complained that the views expressed by American opinion leaders concerning elections in Central America are based more on political utility than on objective analysis. American liberals are likely to applaud the Nicaraguan elections and find fault with those being held in El Salvador, while conservatives will do just the reverse. American conservatives still use the clichés of the 1950s, and American liberals resort to the slogans of the 1960s. In the end, both are wrong. They do not see that the Central American nations are not static societies, but dynamic countries caught up in violent change.

Cruz noted that the real intent of the elections in his own country— Nicaragua—is commonly misunderstood in the United States. The elections are not designed to reach national political reconciliation, but rather will seek to establish a *primus inter pares* among the Sandinista *comandantes*. It is the internal bargaining within the Directorate that will really determine the immediate future of the revolution.

POLITICAL AND SOCIAL PROGRESS IN EL SALVADOR

LeoGrande and Michel disagreed over the meaning of the 1982 election and its aftermath. Michel took issue with LeoGrande's characterization of the elections as a victory for Roberto d'Aubuisson's ARENA party and his charge that this showed that little progress was actually being made in Salvadoran democratization. The feared rightist takeover did not materialize in 1982, and the government of President Alvaro Magaña has helped to move the country toward democracy. LeoGrande responded that while ARENA had not in fact taken power, this was only prevented by an American-backed intervention by the Salvadoran armed forces.

The actual state of social justice in El Salvador was discussed at length by the participants. *Leonel Gomez*, a former Salvadoran agrarian reform official, disagreed wholeheartedly with Michel's assertion that significant reforms were being made in his country. He described how in the course of his own work in the agrarian reform he had received no fewer than eight death threats in 1980 alone, and how his agency's director was assassinated along with two officials from the American Institute for Free Labor Development (AIFLD). These were only a few of the three hundred killings that his agency followed in 1980, and not one has yet been brought to the courts.

Another obstacle to an effective agrarian reform is massive fraud within the agency itself. Gomez stated that he and his associates had uncovered proof that more than $40 million had been embezzled before 1979, but no investigation has been initiated and no arrests have been made. Between the death threats and the fraud, there is little if any progress being made by the Salvadoran land reform.

HUMAN RIGHTS VIOLATIONS BY THE SALVADORAN ARMY AND GUERRILLAS

LeoGrande and Michel differed sharply over the reform of the Salvadoran security forces and their human-rights abuses. In addition to disagreeing over whether or not the actual level of abuse has fallen in recent years, they expressed opposing views on the allegedly better record of the Salvadoran National Police. Michel said that the national police are a more disciplined and professional force than other security forces, whereas LeoGrande stated that there was no evidence that they are any less brutal.

Leonel Gomez argued that there had been no meaningful reform of the Salvadoran armed forces. *Jiri Valenta* of the Naval Postgraduate School asked if the armed forces have a monopoly on brutality, or if the guerrillas are just as guilty of human-rights violations. Gomez responded that there have indeed been numerous cases of guerrilla brutality, and that five of the eight death threats that he received in 1980 were made by the guerrillas. Cayetano Carpio, leader of one of the main guerrilla groups, ordered the assassination of his own second in command, who was stabbed to death with an ice pick. He later committed suicide after his involvement became known. There have been many other cases of threatened or actual murder by the guerrillas. Nevertheless, Gomez emphasized that the Salvadoran army is unmatched in its brutality.

Bruce Cameron asked how the reappointment of Vides Casanova as minister of defense in El Salvador related to Michel's assertion that progress has been made in reforming the Salvadoran army. Vides Casanova was cited in the Tyler Report—a report issued by Judge Tyler following his investigation of the murder of four American churchwomen in 1980—for possible complicity in the cover-up following the assaults.

Michel responded that although the Tyler Report states that it is possible that Vides Casanova acquiesced in the cover-up, he did order the arrest of the accused national guardsmen and turned them over to the civilian courts. The Tyler Report acknowledges there is no evidence that Vides Casanova actually did participate in the cover-up. He comes from the older generation of Salvadoran officers, but he has made progress in reducing the army's human-rights violations by removing officers who have been suspected of association with death squads, issuing internal orders against human-rights abuses, and speaking out against human-rights violations.

Susan Kaufman Purcell of the Council on Foreign Relations raised the question of the Salvadoran military's connections with the oligarchy. She said that there are many cases in the history of Latin American military-civilian relations in which the armed forces have severed their connections with the oligarchy and allied themselves with the middle or lower classes. The armed forces usually break their alliance with the oligarchy when they recognize that failure to do so will threaten their survival. This process may be going on in El Salvador today, and, in fact, there are several signs of it already.

Leonel Gomez took up this point, arguing that the alliance between the army and the oligarchy is economic in nature rather than political or social. The army officers have found it convenient to serve the interests of the fourteen families who have traditionally controlled the wealth of El Salvador because it has offered them the opportunity to get rich from kickbacks and other payments. It is not a question of anticommunism, but one of millions of dollars. Unless and until this economic connection can be broken, there is little chance that the army officers will break with the fourteen families.

The American Strategic Debate

Chapter 7

THE NATURE OF THE CRISIS

Edward N. Luttwak

THE PECULIARITY OF the Central American crisis is the disproportion between its modest scale and great complexity. The territories in question are not large, and neither is the number of soldiers, policemen, guerrillas, and terrorists active in each country; nor are the present or prospective amounts of United States military assistance of any size by global standards—armed intervention would be a matter of battalions, not divisions. Against this, there is the intricacy of struggles that (1) proceed concurrently in the realms of internal politics, regional diplomacy, and the global East-West competition, including the worldwide propaganda war; (2) comprise both (rural) guerrilla and (urban) terrorist phenomena as well as the confrontations of regular armed forces; and (3) are governed by interactions (themselves very complicated) between violence in all its forms and the political, social, and economic circumstances of each country.

As a result, in Central America it is not the magnitude of American resources that is being tested but rather the realism of our political and policy perceptions, the consequent harmony of congressional and administration priorities, and the degree of "milieu adaptability" of the civil and military departments of the executive.

There is a like contrast, just as sharp, between the modest dimensions of any outright military threats now emanating from the region, and the gravity of the actual and potential repercussions of the Central American crisis upon the strategic interests of the United States.

THE GLOBAL STRATEGIC LEVEL

A critical factor in the ability of the United States to sustain a tolerable balance of power on the global scene at a manageable cost has been the inherent security of its land borders, which have required neither frontier defenses nor any garrisons for their protection. This strategic advantage obtained by a restrained statecraft offsets an otherwise crippling disadvantage that derives from the unalterable facts of geography. Because the United States is so far removed from the chief geostrategic zones of Europe, the Middle East, and northeast Asia, its security commitments in those theaters impose a double burden: the United States must provide combat and supporting forces as any adversary in place must also do, but in addition it must also maintain and reinforce those deployments at the far end of transoceanic lines of communication, whose protection is almost as costly as the forces themselves.

Until now, this permanent strategic disadvantage has been offset by the immunity of the United States to any overland threat. In a crude approximation, it might be said that the long-term equilibrium of United States strategy has relied on the sufficiency of rather small ground forces, which permits the upkeep of rather large naval forces: the ground forces can be small because the land borders need not be guarded; the naval forces must be large to avoid strategic isolation.

At the level of global strategy, therefore, the ultimate penalty of a failure of statecraft in Central America would be the need to garrison the southern borders of the United States. That would compromise the entire structure of United States global strategy, imposing an unhappy choice between the abandonment of important deployments overseas and a permanent increase in the scale of the defense effort. Certainly from the point of view of the Soviet Union nothing could be more productive than to outmaneuver the United States on a truly global scale by imposing the burden of landward defenses in addition to the inherent burden of protecting the transoceanic lines of communication.

In the context of the generally defensive American strategy, long-term dangers to be avoided set the goals rather than opportunities open for exploitation. In viewing Central America the magnitude of the danger impels some to action while its remoteness from present conditions has the opposite effect. If the present danger already manifest in the form of a Nicaraguan regime allied with the Soviet Union could be contained effectively, the two perspectives could be reconciled, but that is not the case.

Why Containment Is Not a Valid Option

As it is, any significant deployment of United States forces in Central America would be very costly in geostrategic terms: the ground forces in being, numbering less than one million in both the United States Army and Marine Corps, are already overstretched in fulfilling prior commitments in Europe, the Middle East, and East Asia. For this reason alone, it is impossible to view with equanimity the emergence of any new perimeters of containment in need of an active defense.

But in fact the suggestion that the United States should cope with the emergence of a Leninist Nicaragua allied to the Soviet Union by a long-term and indeed permanent strategy of containment is fundamentally flawed for quite other reasons, which would remain compelling even if there were American forces in abundance.

The entire experience of the postwar period shows that containment can only be effective when United States military power is only needed to complement and guarantee the forces of local allies in meeting overt military threats. When there are stable allies fully capable of coping with internal conflict and self-sufficient in defeating attempts at subversion from without, the United States can help to assure deterrence by contributing forces in place, or merely by strategic guarantees.

Where, on the other hand, a state of internal insecurity is chronic, where local efforts do not suffice to cope with external subversion, a strategy of containment would require the permanent deployment of United States forces in the role of surrogate policemen. In such conditions, the strategic guarantees that are in fact the chief instrument of containment could scarcely suffice and might well remain totally irrelevant.

One cannot therefore dispose of the strategic problem created by the emergence of a Leninist Nicaragua allied to the Soviet Union by advocating a policy of long-term containment. No facile analogy can be drawn between conditions in postwar Europe in the wake of the Second World War and the present circumstances of Central America.

This applies as much to the broader suggestion that would combine a classic strategy of containment with United States efforts to encourage and finance measures of political, social, and economic amelioration, whose stabilizing effects are in turn supposed to make a strategy of containment feasible. Though there is no doubt about the desirability of political, social, and economic progress quite independent of this or any other strategic purpose, there is no congruence in time between the two halves of such a combined approach. Even under the most optimistic assumptions, many years must pass before political, social, and economic conditions will in themselves provide immunity from external subversion and internal strife. Containment on the other hand would be needed as of now, for the Leninist regime of Nicaragua is already in place and has already been most active in subversion.

The Threat to the Oceanic Lines of Communication

One geostrategic threat already manifest in the Central American region affects very directly an important part of the network of United States transoceanic lines of communication. Under present plans, a large proportion of the shipping tonnage required for the reinforcement of the European front, a slightly smaller part of the tonnage required for a full-scale Central Command (rapid-deployment force) contingency, and a not inconsiderable part of the tonnage required by a major Korea-Japan contingency would have to transit out of the Gulf of Mexico and through the Caribbean–Central American zone to reach its destination. In addition, much of the shipping from all United States ports required for a Central Command or Korea-Japan contingency would have to transit through the Panama Canal.

The transoceanic lines of communication are already in need of protection. But until now, the antisubmarine and antiaircraft forces required to protect those lines of communication could be reserved for the already vast ocean areas that constitute the approaches to Western Europe, the Persian Gulf, and the northwest Pacific respectively. The ocean areas adjacent to the United States, including the Central American–Caribbean zone, could, by contrast, be regarded as relatively safe. This assumption set a limit to the very costly forces required to protect the transoceanic lines of communication. Even the emergence of a well-armed Cuba closely allied to the Soviet Union did not fundamentally change the situation, although it did impose the necessity for some countervailing deployments of considerable cost in the long run.

Now, however, there is the added threat of an entire new set of potential bases for Soviet forces in Nicaragua, a country that is uniquely well placed in that regard, for it has both a Pacific and an Atlantic coast. Nicaragua, moreover, already serves as a base of subversion that can affect the entire region, Panama included. Under the new Panama Canal Treaty, Panama is gradually assuming full responsibility for the security of the canal; this means that any threat to the political security of Panama and to the upkeep of friendly relations between Panama and the United States automatically constitutes a strategic threat.

In this regard, it is worth noting that Cuba's island geography did not favor either the sponsorship of subversion or a strategic role in Soviet sea-denial plans. The impossibility of sustaining subversion and insurgency by the overland infiltration of people and supplies has been a very great impediment to the many and varied Cuban attempts to export revolution; Nicaragua, by contrast, suffers from no such limitation. Similarly, the ease with which Cuba can be blockaded and its very proximity to Florida reduce its value as a Soviet basing area as compared to Nicaragua.

THE IMMEDIATE PROBLEM: INSURGENCY IN EL SALVADOR

It is fitting and appropriate for the citizens of the United States to apply undiminished standards in evaluating the political, social, and economic circumstances of countries such as El Salvador. In neighborly regard, we may deplore poverty, social inequities, and also the many imperfections of a belated democratization by no means universally welcomed. When confronted with such conditions, many conclude that the organized violence of an insurgency is merely a natural consequence of poverty, social inequity, and authoritarian rule. From this a prescription follows just as naturally: it is not the guerrillas that should be fought but rather the conditions that are believed to have caused the insurgency itself. Often enough, those who offer this prescription also assume that if they emerge victorious from their struggle, the guerrillas themselves will readily find solutions for the political, social, and economic problems that supposedly motivated their insurgency.

But in fact this chain of reasoning is based on a fallacy of composition. By whatever standards we choose to apply, whether levels of income or criteria of income distribution, whether measures of political participation or the analysis of political structures, it becomes immediately apparent that El Salvador is not uniquely unfortunate among the poor countries of the world. If wretched political, social, and economic conditions sufficed in themselves to evoke insurgency we should therefore find insurgencies in a great many other countries as well. In fact political, social, and economic circumstances are merely the necessary and not the sufficient conditions of insurgency.

Except where separatist motives are present, the true determinant of insurgency is, in almost all cases, the active role of external powers whose motives vary from the ideological to simple expansionism or even religious solidarity, but which in any case are relying on internal war as a substitute for overt aggression. If external powers provide the propaganda support that is psychologically so important for guerrillas otherwise isolated in the remote countryside, if they provide a sanctuary where guerrillas can occasionally recuperate from the travails of protracted war, and if they provide such arms and supplies as cannot be obtained locally, then there is an insurgency. By contrast, in the absence of such external support even the harshest political, social, and economic conditions need not result in more than sporadic violence or merely mute suffering. Certainly the present insurgency in El Salvador would not have arisen in ideal conditions; but it is just as certain that insurgency of equal or far greater dimensions would arise in many other countries if there also guerrillas could obtain the support of countries with the aptitudes and resources of the Soviet Union, Cuba, and Nicaragua.

It follows directly that to seek the remedy for insurgency in political, social, and economic amelioration alone is a prescription fatally incomplete. Even with the best efforts of all concerned, even if very great progress is made very rapidly, conditions are not likely to improve fast enough to outpace the tempo of an insurgency already well established, as is the case in El Salvador. The democratization of society, the diffusion of legality, the removal of structural inequities, and the improvement of economic conditions are necessary and urgent but will not suffice: it is also necessary to cut off the external support that has in fact made the insurgency possible, and to defeat the guerrillas already in the field.

Are the Guerrillas a Solution Rather Than the Problem?

There is, of course, the expectation of some that the guerrillas themselves would remedy the conditions that are necessary for insurgency. If this were indeed plausible, then the entire problem of defeating the guerrillas would be moot, for they would no longer be a problem but rather the solution. Unfortunately, neither the history of the many Latin American insurgencies of the past that were in fact successful, nor the recent experience of Nicaragua under the Sandinista regime suggests that there is any basis for optimism.

Just as the regimes created in the past by insurgent oligarchs were oligarchies, just as the regimes created by successful bandits were merely kleptocracies, just as military coups have resulted in military autocracies, so also the regimes created by totalitarian guerrillas can only be totalitarian. In Central America as elsewhere, totalitarian regimes can be expected to expand their armed forces very rapidly, as Nicaragua has already done; they can be expected to develop sophisticated agencies of internal repression and external subversion, as Cuba has done; and they can be expected to be quite successful in external propaganda and, for a while, in internal propaganda as well. The distribution of land and accumulated capital confiscated from private ownership provides each new totalitarian regime with a seemingly most successful start; and the measures of political mobilization meant to assure totalitarian control can most usefully be associated with much-needed literacy and hygiene campaigns.

All this can generate a genuine popularity for the new regime, and an atmosphere of hope and goodwill in which the measures already underway to suppress all dissenting voices seem of small consequence. But after that initial phase, the inherent incapacity of totalitarian systems to sustain real economic progress makes itself increasingly manifest. That has of course been the fate of Cuba, whose gross national product has not kept pace with that of other Latin American countries. (The Cuban share of the total planetary product declined from 0.22 percent in 1960 to 0.16 percent between 1960 and 1980; whereas during the same period the non–oil producing countries of Latin America increased their share from 4.98 percent in 1960 to 6.57 percent; other, more conventional, terms of comparison are even less favorable.) Thus it seems that misgovernment and mismanagement, adverse terms of trade, particular forms of exploitation, and general thievery are all less harmful to economic progress than totalitarian controls.

Likewise, a new social hierarchy of party officials, policemen, propagandists, and senior military officers gradually emerges to claim all the privileges of status. Meanwhile, any hopes of democratization are explicitly barred, and even within the ruling party political participation is more and more restricted as power is increasingly centralized within its highest councils. This process has been witnessed through its diverse stages in too many countries too diverse in all their circumstances to allow room for any hopeful expectation should the totalitarian guerrillas of El Salvador emerge victorious. They too, like the oligarchs and the bandits, the military men and their Nicaraguan counterparts, are destined to create a regime in their own image.

THE MODALITIES OF COUNTERINSURGENCY

The United States is obviously at a disadvantage when confronted by insurgencies such as the one now manifest in full force in El Salvador because it cannot itself carry out the broad-spectrum action that is required to defeat a well-established insurgency and to eliminate its stimulants within civil society. The United States government cannot provide its own civil servants to implement directly political, social, and economic reforms; it cannot itself collect taxes and administer justice; it cannot gather political intelligence in each village and town; and it cannot supervise the conduct of each soldier and policeman in his dealings with the population at large. For all these things, the United States government must rely on the assisted government and all its agencies. As a result, the United States is saddled with responsibility for the actions of the assisted government and all its soldiers, policemen, and civil servants without having any commensurate degree of executive control over their activities. There is, of course, no jurisprudential basis for such an attribution of responsibility, but the latter is a fact of life both in El Salvador and in the United States, and also on the worldwide diplomatic scene.

Even in providing military assistance, to enhance that one dimension of a broad counterinsurgency effort, the United States labors under a structural disadvantage. Strategy offers two alternative methods in resisting insurgency: one, traditional, brutal, and cheap; and the other, modern, humane, and very expensive. In the traditional method, insurgency is controlled by the passive defense of productive areas combined with intermittent massacre-sweeps of the rest of the territory, in order to disrupt "liberated areas" and dissuade participation in the insurgency; as a result, a gendarmerie and foot infantry suffice. In the modern method, the insurgents themselves must be found and defeated without harming the innocent population at large, and the insurgents are elusive and low-contrast targets; as a result, timely intelligence and fast-moving forces of good quality are required, and both are very expensive.

The United States obviously cannot condone, let alone support, the traditional method of counterinsurgency practiced by all the empires of the past, by the Soviet Union in Afghanistan even now, and also by a number of regimes in the recent history of Central America. In particular the United States cannot countenance the crucial ingredient of the mass reprisals. Historically, such reprisals, along with the static guard of cities, towns, and key installations, as well as the occasional ambush of betrayed insurgents bands, have proved capable of preserving colonial rule and unpopular governments for a very long time, even centuries.

By contrast, the methods of counterinsurgency developed over the last generation by the armed forces of the United States specifically exclude the use of violence against innocent civilians. Such violence is seen as counterproductive in a strategy designed to win the allegiance of the population at large rather than to terrorize it into obedience.

Though the modern United States counterinsurgency methods stress the primacy of political, social, and economic amelioration in a broad-spectrum effort, they require two forms of military action, to be carried out in fact by two distinct sets of forces, one regular and one not. First, a countrywide popular militia must be formed to prevent the insurgents themselves from using terror to extract obedience; this obviously calls for a mass force with whatever minimal training is feasible and with only the simplest weapons, to provide some form of defense for each locality. The localized militia cannot, however, be expected to resist any sustained guerrilla attack on its own; it certainly cannot seek out and destroy the guerrilla forces.

To provide prompt assistance for village militiamen under attack, and to actually reduce the guerrilla forces in the field, United States counterinsurgency methods also require well-trained and very well equipped regular forces in adequate numbers. Such regular units must be amply provided with efficient communications and suitable transport, notably helicopters, to enable them to provide prompt help for village militias under attack and to allow them to employ sophisticated tactics to ambush guerrilla bands on the move and achieve surprise in attacks against guerrilla encampments.

When the training and equipment requirements of modern United States counterinsurgency methods are estimated in the context of El Salvador and then compared to the assistance actually given, it is immediately obvious that only a fraction of the requirements are being provided under current aid levels.

Thus on the one hand, by its very presence on the scene, the United States precludes the use of the traditional method of counterinsurgency; but on the other, the United States fails to provide the training and the relatively great quantity of modern equipment required by its own more humane method.

For this reason, most criticisms of the tactics of the Salvadoran army in the field are quite inappropriate: criteria of evaluation that assume implicitly the availability of helicopters in abundance, of excellent communications, and of all required supplies. These criticisms are being applied to an army that must move mostly on foot with no mechanical transport whatever, let alone helicopters; that is very short of radios, and that does not even have field rations for its troops.

Within the complex of larger choices to be made for the region as a whole, a specific choice must also be made in regard to United States military assistance for the government of El Salvador: the present level of military assistance does not correspond to any valid operational requirement. It is certainly far too low to enable the armed forces of El Salvador to use the modern and humane methods of counterinsurgency. On the other hand, the total denial of United States military assistance is quite likely to precipitate a reversion to the traditional method, with all its brutalities. In fact the likely consequences of an interruption of United States military assistance are already presaged in the conduct of some Salvadoran police units, which receive no United States assistance. In the armed forces, it is now fully understood that human rights violations endanger the flow of United States assistance. In the police organizations, on the other hand, there is no such competition with the patronage of those who actually promote human rights violations. However laudible its intentions, the legal prohibition against the provision of training and material aid to police organizations is now very clearly counterproductive.

CONCLUSION

The United States is paying a very high political and diplomatic cost for its policies in Central America. The political progress no longer deniable in El Salvador entails the possibility that the support of its elected government against the insurgents will evoke a wider degree of acceptance both at home and abroad, but the campaign against Nicaragua is fated to remain unpopular. In both cases, moreover, to persist at the current level of activity offers no assurance of success, to say the least.

One theoretical alternative is to increase very greatly the magnitude of United States assistance to the government of El Salvador to enable it to carry out counterinsurgency in the modern style. Concurrently, the campaign against Nicaragua would have to be greatly intensified, to remove the present regime from power. To defeat the Salvadoran insurgents would avail little if the Nicaraguan regime endures, for its fate and program are to serve as the promoter of insurgency throughout the region.

Another theoretical alternative is to abandon the struggle and rely on the self-protective instincts and domestic resources of the Mexican establishment to resist the spread of insurgency.

The midpoint of political compromise that delimits current United States policy does not correspond to either one of these valid strategic options.

Chapter 8

REDEFINING THE STRATEGIC CHALLENGE IN CENTRAL AMERICA

Robert Pastor

IN A MAJOR address to a joint session of Congress on April 27, 1983, President Reagan defined the strategic challenge he perceived in Central America:

> The national security of all the Americas is at stake in Central America. If we cannot defend ourselves there, we cannot expect to prevail elsewhere. Our credibility would collapse, our alliances would crumble, and the safety of our homeland would be put at jeopardy. [In defending Central America] we have a vital interest, a moral duty, and a solemn responsibility. . . .

In his chapter, "The Nature of the Crisis," Edward Luttwak approaches his subject with the same fervor and the same reason as President Reagan. Both start with the "big picture"; their attention is concentrated on the strategic contest with the Soviet Union. All other international objects or subjects are considered only to the extent that they relate to this strategic challenge. Luttwak's chapter therefore reads more like a memoir of a global strategist's most surprising journey to the backwater of Central America than like a description of the region's crisis.

Luttwak acknowledges that the intensity of concern seems disproportionate to the size of the countries and their problems, but he argues that the threat justifies the concern. Failure to reverse the Nicaraguan revolution, according to Luttwak, would eventually lead to catastrophic consequences for the United States, however remote these appear today. "The ultimate penalty of a failure of statecraft in Central America would be the need to garrison the southern border of the United States. That would compromise the entire structure of United States global strategy. . . ."

Max Weber once wrote that "world images that have been created by ideas have, like switchmen [on a railroad] determined the tracks along which action has been pushed. . . ." Following Weber's insight, one method for discerning the direction of administration policy toward Central America is to understand the world image of its theoreticians. Luttwak's world image as it relates to

81

Central America can be reconstructed in his answers to three sets of questions: (1) What is the origin of the crisis in the region? (2) What interests are at stake? and (3) What is the best policy to address the crisis and protect and advance United States interests?

In this essay, I will describe and evaluate Luttwak's answers to these questions as well as his critique of an alternative world image. I will suggest why neither the theory Luttwak advances nor the one he disparages is adequate to the task of addressing the crisis in Central America. And finally, I will redefine the national security challenge in the region in a way that integrates the strategic imperative, which is the essence of Luttwak's argument, with regional opportunities and local realities.

ORIGIN OF THE CRISIS

Two world images provide rather simple and coherent explanations to the origin of the crisis in Central America. Both have the virtue of being elegant and provocative, but also the drawback of being inadequate and therefore wrong as the all-encompassing theory, which each pretends to be. For want of better terms, the world images can be referred to as "social-democratic" and "strategic-conservative." Luttwak's analysis effectively demolishes the first, and then falls victim to the fallacies of the second.

The "social-democratic" theory holds that the crisis in Central America is due to decades of poverty and social injustice. However, as Luttwak correctly points out, El Salvador—the country ravaged by the region's worst insurgency—is considerably more advantaged than its more pacific neighbor, Honduras. More broadly, Central America—writhing in crisis—sits comfortably in the middle class of the developing world. Moreover, the "social-democratic" theory fails to explain why the crisis is occurring today, *after*, rather than before, two decades of extraordinary economic growth and substantial progress in education and health. As Luttwak notes, poverty may be a necessary explanation for some insurgencies, but it is not sufficient for explaining any.

The "conservative-strategic" theory holds that the crisis, in the succinct phrase of President Reagan, is "a Soviet-Cuban power play—pure and simple." In moderately more sophisticated language, Luttwak agrees that "the true determinant of insurgency is, in almost all cases, the active role of external powers. . . ." In the case of Central America, the problem is the Soviet Union, Cuba, and Nicaragua. But under closer scrutiny, this explanation proves to be a prejudged assumption rather than a substantiated conclusion. If Soviet-Cuban support is crucial, why have they chosen El Salvador as their target rather than a country with as many problems but with greater intrinsic wealth and power like Mexico, or why not the United States? If Nicaraguan support through the transfer of weapons is so crucial to the insurgency in El Salvador, and if the administration has devoted as much attention and resources to interdiction as it has claimed in testimony before Congress, then why has there not been one significant interdiction of arms since early 1981? While it is necessary to interdict all the arms to stop the flow, it is necessary only to find some to prove that it exists.

If support by a contiguous country is as important to a successful insurgency as Luttwak claims, then why did the revolution on the island of Cuba succeed, and why have decades of revolutionary insurgency in Guatemala and Colombia endured without overland support? Nicaraguan support for the Salvadoran guerrillas may be helpful, but there is no evidence to suggest that it is crucial, and many signs point to other, more important, explanations.

To understand the crisis in Central America, and to respond to it effectively, one needs first to discard prejudices and evaluate assumptions critically. Rather than stagnation, the region's current crisis originates in dramatic—though uneven—progress. Between 1950 and 1978, the six nations of Central America averaged an annual rate of growth of 5.3 percent, doubling the real per capita income during this period. If the population had remained stable instead of tripling (from 8.3 million to 23 million), real per capita income would have quintupled. Primarily an exporter of bananas and coffee in 1950, Central America multiplied its trade by a factor of eighteen during this time and diversified its economies.

The region's problems stem from the rapid population growth; the poor distribution of the benefits of growth internally and between the Central American nations; and the obsolete political-military institutions that blocked the path to political power by representatives of the emerging middle and working classes. In the late 1970s, the world economy shifted into reverse, with serious consequences for the small and vulnerable economies in Central America. New groups pressed for power, but the military and entrenched interests responded with intransigence and repression. Civil wars—or "revolutions," as they are more commonly called—spread and deepened. Viewing the United States as the supporter of the military and the status quo, the revolutionaries sought friends and models among the enemies of the United States—the Soviet Union and Cuba. There is no denying the close ties between Central America's revolutionaries and Cuba, but the suggestion that the region's rebels are taking orders from Cuba is an unwitting betrayal of ignorance of the crisis. More importantly, the mind-set that leads policymakers toward exclusive preoccupation with such questions leads them away from effective policy. The guerrillas could hardly survive, let alone threaten a government, if their leaders were lackeys. The key question is not who gives instructions to the guerrillas, but rather what drives Christian and Social Democrats to ally with the violent Marxist left. In replacing the first question about command and control centers with the second about defecting democrats, the United States would move two steps closer to forging a sensible policy.

Interests

If the problem is poverty, then United States interests could be interpreted as promoting development and assisting those who would change oppressive social structures. United States security interests would only be affected if the United States identified with the oppressive structure and fought the forces of change, compelling revolutionaries to ally with Cuba and the Soviet Union.

If the problem is the spread of Soviet-sponsored communism, then, as President Reagan repeatedly declares, the very security of the United States is at stake. Luttwak's analysis of the security interests at risk rests on the premise that a Leninist regime in Nicaragua or El Salvador would jeopardize the sea-lanes of communication (SLOC), which are vital to the United States economy and the defense of Europe, and would make the United States vulnerable to land-based attack. These are two rather significant interests, but however desirable it might be to prevent the overthrow of the Salvadoran government or to see a democratic evolution in Nicaragua, it requires a considerable leap to believe that these two interests would be jeopardized if these desires were not realized.

In World War II, without any bases in the Caribbean, and with a submarine fleet considerably smaller and less sophisticated than the current Soviet fleet, the German navy wreaked havoc on Allied shipping in the region. There is little reason to doubt that if a war between the United States and the Soviet Union remained conventional for an extended period, the Soviets would have similar success paralyzing United States and Allied shipping. But it is not clear that they need Cuba, much less Nicaragua, and indeed, one could argue that the Cubans and Nicaraguans would have a compelling reason not to be used. During the last twenty-five years at different points in time, the United States has looked for pretexts to punish the Castro regime; if Cuba, Nicaragua, or any other country in the region were to interfere with United States shipping, that would constitute a legitimate justification for action, not just a pretext. In brief, the Soviets have ample naval capability without the need for Cuban, let alone Nicaraguan, naval bases, and small nations in the region have a compelling security interest in not making war against the United States and in not being used for that purpose. Therefore, it is hard to see how the sea-lanes could be threatened by a change in regime in Central America.

Another security truism is that minimal defense of the United States border permits us to use our defense resources in other theaters. To leap from that, however, as Luttwak does, to the proposition that the maintenance of the Sandinista regime "would require the permanent deployment of United States forces in the [region in the] role of surrogate policeman," and that the United States would need to garrison its southern border, is a leap from logic. There are alternative mechanisms to deter a conventional attack by Nicaragua on its neighbors, and if substantial evidence could be marshaled to prove Nicaraguan support for insurgency outside its borders, there is good reason to believe that the OAS would respond as it did when Venezuela brought compelling evidence of Cuban intervention in its internal affairs to the OAS in 1964. The Organization sanctioned Cuba and effectively excluded it. Unlike Cuba, Nicaragua would be severely affected by isolation from the hemispheric community, precisely because it is not an island. Nicaragua's many efforts to maintain relationships with Latin America and Europe and to avoid isolation are eloquent enough testimony to their recognition of their more precarious position, which is made even more tenuous by the evident uninterest of the Soviet Union in financing a second Cuba. In brief, Luttwak's assertion that maintenance of the Nicaraguan regime requires that the United States act as a surrogate policeman is groundless.

While an invasion of the United States across the Mexican border is certainly a vital security preoccupation, the probability of its occurring is infinitesimal. A far more likely need for the stationing of United States troops on the border would be to curtail the flow of Mexicans illegally crossing it in search of work or peace as a result of serious political or economic instability in Mexico. Of course, these would be Mexicans seeking opportunity, not Communist armies seeking conquest, and the National Guard and state police units could cope with this contingency without diverting resources from NATO.

The Mexican example is a good one for illustrating the limitations of policy analysis that proceeds automatically from a cataloguing of interests. Precluding instability in Mexico is certainly an interest of the United States, and one that it shares with Mexico. Moreover, both governments recognize there is a relationship between instability in Central America and instability in Mexico. At this point, however, the path divides, with the Reagan administration seeing the relationship in terms of dominos and prescribing a very different approach to the region's problems. Though the United States strategy implies the need for United States military intervention as an option to prevent the Marxists from coming to power in El Salvador or consolidating it in Nicaragua, Mexican leaders, by and large, believe that Mexico is far more likely to be destabilized by United States intervention than by the victory of guerrillas.

Luttwak does not show how the two security interests he identifies are endangered by any likely scenario in Central America; he also fails to show how these interests relate to policy. The Mexican case suggests that an interest, however defined, is not much of a guide to policy. Indeed, in that case, a shared interest has led toward diametrically opposite strategies to reduce instability in Central America.

Policy

Although the definition of United States security interests does not offer a guide to effective policy, it does offer a clue to the policymaker's intentions when the interests are described in apocalyptic terms. If one believes that the origin of the crisis is the Soviet Union, and the very security of the United States is at stake, then one does not hesitate to use all means available to protect United States interests. Luttwak is not at all inhibited at following the logic of this argument to its conclusion, and in criticizing those who do not. He argues that containment of the Nicaraguan revolution is "a flawed strategy"; we should not settle for anything less than reversing the revolution by whatever means necessary. It is refreshing, if not illuminating, to read his criticism of the Reagan administration's strategy, which he describes as a timid compromise between what the situation requires and what the politics demand.

However, President Reagan's statements parallel Luttwak's argument, and it is at least conceivable that without congressional or political constraints in a possible second term, President Reagan's actions would follow the logic of his words. In his televised address to the nation on May 9, 1984, President Reagan reiterated that the United States had vital interests in defending Central America because of proximity ("San Salvador is closer to Houston than Houston is to Washington") and the need to keep open the sea-lanes. "This communist subversion poses the threat that 100 million people from Panama to the open border of our south could come under the control of pro-Soviet regimes." The problem in Central America, according to President Reagan, is "the Communist reign of terror" in Nicaragua, but he concludes that "Communist subversion is not an irreversible tide." It can be rolled back if the United States unites behind his strategy. Thus far, however, he argues: "We've provided just enough aid to avoid outright disaster but not enough to resolve the crisis. . . ."

President Reagan was bolder in outlining the policy he would most like to follow in the region during a press conference on July 24, 1984. He first noted that a Soviet general had bragged a couple of years before that the Soviets had bases in Cuba, Nicaragua, and Grenada. "Well," President Reagan then said, "they don't have one in Grenada anymore. And I think it is the responsibility of this government to assist the people of Nicaragua in seeing that they don't have one in Nicaragua."

Clearly, both Reagan and Luttwak believe that the only solution to the crisis in Central America is reversing the Nicaraguan revolution, using whatever means necessary. Since the various Nicaraguan guerrilla groups appear to lack the capability to overthrow the regime, and the other Central American countries (through CONDECA, the Central American Defense Council) seem hesitant to try, that leaves United States intervention—indirect if possible, direct if necessary—as the only instrument to attain a change in Nicaragua.

Such intervention, however, will create so many new and serious problems that the current situation would look good in comparison. A military intervention by the United States would most likely dislodge the Sandinistas from the major cities of Nicaragua, but would probably lead to a long-term guerrilla war, necessitating a sizable, lengthy, and costly—in human as well as financial terms—United States military occupation. The reaction in the United States would be so serious as to prompt people to think of the Vietnam demonstrations and the race riots of the late 1960s as little more than a prelude. In Europe, the Alliance could very well shake as governments try to preempt and outflank proliferating and invigorated peace movements. In Mexico and Venezuela, the popular reaction would be hard to contain, and United States embassies throughout Latin America might very well find themselves in hostagelike situations. And, of course, condemnation at the United Nations would be nearly universal. In sum, the costs of such an action exceed any reasonable calculation of benefits.

AN ALTERNATIVE

Just because the security interests as described by President Reagan and Edward Luttwak seem more a reflection of their preoccupation with the Sandinistas than a guide to a sensible policy, this does not mean that the United States has no security interests in the region. It clearly does. The United States has important security interests in reducing the possibility that Marxist-Leninists, who are hostile to the United States and friendly to our adversaries, come to power violently. (In the event that Marxists do come to power, the United States interests are in limiting their government's military relationship with the Soviet Union.) Stating this interest, however, does not help us to propose policy anymore than does stating the interest in dire strategic terms. But there is a difference. The end-of-the-world interests implicit in the conservative-strategic perspective encourage the policy analyst to look to the global picture and to enter a struggle without limits. The alternative definition above—to reduce the chance of a Marxist takeover—encourages the policy analyst to focus on the balance of local and regional forces and to set limits on the use of power, recognizing that the use of all measures could result in a worse outcome than the one it is intended to prevent. So a definition of interests can help to sketch and shade options, and it can lead the policy analyst to concentrate on certain issues and ignore others, but it is not helpful in proposing specific policies.

In formulating policy, using this alternative definition, there are three strategic levels to recognize and address: local, regional, and international. The war is fought at the local level, and it is there that victory or defeat will be felt most intensely. The United States is the most powerful of all international actors in Central America, but United States power does not mean control, and of course, in the case of Nicaragua, United States influence is, at best, negligible, and frequently counterproductive.

United States policy ought to weigh every word and action in terms of its effect on the local struggle and on the actors who are crucial in determining who will win, and what local interests will be served. The Reagan administration's strategy has been backwards, reflecting more concern on how developments in Central America affect Soviet perceptions than about how its statements on the Soviet Union affect local politics in El Salvador. By declaring the crisis an East-West struggle in which United States interests were vitally engaged, the administration unwittingly strengthened the hands of rightists in every Central American country. These right-wing leaders believe that the Communists—which they define broadly enough to include many Christian and Social Democrats—are behind all the unrest in the region, and that they, the leaders, are fighting the good fight on behalf of President Reagan. In short, an obsession with the Soviet dimension led the administration to adopt a strategy that weakened local democrats, providing opportunities to the Soviets that they would not normally have had.

The second strategic level is the regional level. Fortunately for the United States, our security interests are not unique. As Mexico, Venezuela, and Colombia extend their economic and political reach, they become more aware of the adverse consequences to *their* countries of the spread of Cuban communism. It appears that Nicaragua fears possible isolation from these countries more than possible intervention by the United States. Our strategic interests, however, lie in working closely with Latin American democracies while encouraging them to assume greater responsibility for their own security interests. The worst thing the United States could do is what it is apparently doing: leaving the Latin American leaders with a distinct impression that we do not trust their instincts and strategy and are prepared to pursue our own policy, unilaterally if necessary.

The final level is the Soviet-Cuban level. Policy analysts need to understand but avoid concentrating solely on the broader strategic implications of the spread of Marxism in the region.

The essence of the national security challenge for the United States in Central America today is not how to parry the Soviet Union, but how to influence sociopolitical change in a sensitive Third World environment. The strategic perspective is necessary to fix the wandering attention of the United States on Central America, but it is not helpful in addressing the crisis. At times, as in the last four years, the strategic perspective may even lead to counterproductive policies. To influence change in the region, knowledge of the local landscape is infinitely more useful than divining Soviet intentions, which we can assume are malign anyway.

Secondly, United States policy should be built on an awareness that United

States security interests in the region are not unique, but neither are they identical with those of our friends. Venezuela, Mexico, Colombia, and other middle powers share an interest in containing Soviet expansionism, but they also have an interest in reducing the region's heavy political, economic, and psychological dependence on the United States. While the latter interest could lead these countries to embrace occasionally those who are anti-American, still it would be wise for the United States to remember Dean Acheson's definition of United States security interests: "to maintain as spacious an environment as possible in which free states might exist and flourish." John F. Kennedy talked similarly of a world safe for diversity.

If United States policy recognizes the interest of the United States in diversity and in devolving some of its powers and responsibilities to middle powers in the region, then that will involve on the part of the United States more tolerance for disagreement and criticism. The outcome of a strategy based on respecting diversity and encouraging devolution will not resemble the administration's dreams, but it stands a better chance of succeeding and enduring.

Schopenauer once wrote: "Every man takes the limits of his own field of vision for the limits of the world." The successful pursuit of United States national security in Central America requires a fundamental reassessment of the conservative-strategic perspective, which has so limited our nation's vision as to endanger our interests. The time has come to expand the vision to include new landmarks as well as old land mines. Only then, by redefining our strategic challenge, will we put ourselves in a position where we can influence change in a manner compatible with our interests rather than be surprised by change and impelled to contain or prevent it.

Chapter 9

MUDDLING THROUGH

Stephen Rosenfeld

I CHOOSE NOT to address the question of the day as a strategic problem. My objection to that approach is not that it has no strategic aspect, but that the attempt to impose a strategic design imposes at the same time what I consider distortions, perhaps not distortions of truth (of that history will be the judge), but certainly distortions of political feasibility. Instead of considering the strategic aspect, I think the main thing we have to recognize is that we are the inheritors at this moment of a problem with a short-range and a long-range past to it, which is not amenable to large, strategic, macro direction. It is a problem that, furthermore, has something going for it in terms of our American approach to it, which has not been adequately recognized in this discussion.

By that I mean that there is in the United States something of a rough consensus on how to deal with this problem. It is the congressional muddle. It coincides with neither of the larger intelligent designs offered by the two previous chapters, but the congressional muddle nonetheless has some consistency to it, and it has some continuity to it. It consists more of a set of instructions to some of the players, namely to our own government, but the implications are there for instructions to the other players as well. The consensus is easy to see. "Help Duarte—he looks like a decent guy. He's not Thomas Jefferson, but within the context he's better than any of us have a right to expect. He's dealing with formidable problems in controlling his own military and doing A, B, and C." The congressional consensus is to help him and to find the best way to help him, and on that there can be an argument, which we're having. That's number one.

Number two is Nicaragua. There the congressional muddle reflects an ambivalence between a reluctance to intervene and a reluctance not to intervene. We have been teetering back and forth on the CIA votes for a couple of years— no doubt that will continue. You can find inconsistencies in the congressional approach. You can say, as the administration now does, "Why give Duarte aid with one hand but deny him the great help that a CIA operation in Nicaragua would give?" Nonetheless, a Congress that reflects a broad constituency is prepared to live with inconsistencies. Strategists find inconsistencies difficult to live with, but I think they had better learn to live with them.

We have a couple of other factors that I think are going to affect this Central American situation. Our 1984 election will be an election on Central America. Much of the argument that we are having in our society right now (I say *much* of it, not *all* of it) is going to be removed by the elections. If we have a Democratic victory, a policy closer to the Left than the Right will be installed. The election will be a very large factor which will influence the next four years far more than any single strategic consideration.

The larger issue, at least on the foreign policy side of our elections, is going to be the Soviet-American relationship. Our choice as a nation on that is also going to preempt much of our current strategic discussion and lead us into certain regional choices in Central America and elsewhere.

Now, I'm aware of the limitations in policy terms of accepting the political consensus as something sacred, or something desirable, as something with its own sovereign right to be followed. The people are certainly unintellectual, not anti-intellectual, in their approach to foreign policy. They are not guided entirely by any one set of considerations, strategic or otherwise. The people like to change their minds from time to time. Nonetheless, the Central American problem is one with which the political society has been engaged intensively for four-plus years right now. The political society is literate on the subject. The choice that it makes will be, I believe, a ragged one—all choices by political societies that are not left to strategists are ragged ones—but I nonetheless think it reflects the raggedness in a context where nothing better is available, where there is no consensus for something cleaner, and it has the virtue of enlisting some continuity over a period of time. I do not submit to Edward Luttwak's despair, "All right, you Mexicans, you asked for it, we're going to kick it into your laps." I'd like to believe that Bob Pastor's readiness to turn to the Contadora fellows is going to somehow pull our chestnuts out of the fire down there, but I find myself full of misgivings about the Contadora members and about the Contadora process. I am nonetheless prepared to accept the decision of our political society. It is a muddle, it is a raggedness, but I will go with it.

Chapter 10

RAPPORTEUR'S REPORT
Michael Clark

EDWARD LUTTWAK INTRODUCED the session, which *William Maynes* moderated, with a summary view of the importance of Central America in United States global strategy. What is important in Central America, Luttwak argued, is what isn't there—namely, a contiguous threat to the continental United States. In the absence of such a threat to the continent, the unique geographic position of the United States represents a fundamental strategic advantage; the unexampled security of frontiers has been the condition of our freedom of action outside the hemisphere and has enabled us to avoid the fate of strategic isolation. Should revolutionary upheaval in Central America continue to spread, however, and eventually include Mexico, the long-term equilibrium of American strategy would be completely undermined. An expanded Soviet naval presence in the hemisphere and, in the extreme, the destabilization of Mexico would be the ultimate consequences of a failure to halt the spread of subversion in Central America, and would force a withdrawal of American forces from other theaters in order to protect vital American sea-lanes and defend the southern border of the United States.

To avoid this, the United States might attempt to *contain* the insurgent threat; that is, after all, what we have done for forty years. In essence, containment is a simple proposition; all it requires is that we provide additional guarantees to reasonably strong allies. Yet containment has failed historically when our allies have faced strong internal challenges aided and abetted by an external power.

Too much attention has been paid to the failings of the Salvadoran government, Luttwak insisted, and not enough has been given to Nicaraguan support for the insurgency. Excluding the exceptional circumstance of regional or ethnic separatism, the common ingredient in long-standing local insurgencies is the element of external support. Nicaraguan support for the insurgency in El Salvador enters invisibly and cannot be contained by technological means. Only a structural change in the Nicaraguan regime, Luttwak argued, will eradicate the conditions of El Salvador's insurgency.

There are but two counterinsurgency alternatives to the containment approach. The traditional method of dealing with insurgencies involves a "high content of massacre," the function of which is to "interrupt the generational continuity of the insurgents" or, again in Luttwak's words, "to prevent guerrilla babies from growing up." For obvious reasons, Americans find this sort of behavior intolerable. The modern method is extremely expensive, however. The technological requirements of an effort to fight an insurgency while respecting the distinction between guerrillas and innocents are demanding: extensive training, rapid transport (especially helicopters), and sophisticated communications and intelligence are all necessary. As a partner, the United States is ill-equipped to fight insurgencies since it prohibits resort to traditional methods as a condition of aid, and then fails to provide adequate means for the modern method. Worse, allies are subjected to relentless (and demoralizing) moral scrutiny. In El Salvador, the United States has attempted to restrain the military while refusing to supply the material means essential to success.

The alternative to a counterinsurgency strategy is to call it quits, withdraw, and leave Mexico to its own devices. Only through a more or less abrupt disengagement, Luttwak concluded, might the Mexicans be permitted to sense the full significance of events in Central America.

Robert Pastor challenged Luttwak's conceptions of the origins of the Central American crisis, the interests at stake, and the strategic alternatives available to the United States. First, he asserted, the role of Nicaragua in El Salvador's insurgency has been generally overstated. United States efforts to interdict the flow of arms from Nicaragua have failed to turn up even a single significant shipment since early 1981. Nor is it the case, Pastor added, that insurgencies have only succeeded or been maintained when supported by a contiguous power. Revolutionary movement succeeded in Cuba without a direct lifeline, and insurgencies continue in Guatemala and Colombia without overland access to Nicaraguan arms. Finally, and most importantly, an exaggerated emphasis on the Nicaraguan role leads one to ignore the internal dimensions of the Salvadoran insurgency.

Second, Pastor took issue with Luttwak's depiction of the threat posed by revolutionary movements in Central America to American security interests. The Cubans are well aware that under seven different administrations the United States has been looking for a pretext to pummel the Cubans; interfering with shipping or providing bases for that purpose would provide not only a pretext, but compelling justification for such action. In short, the Soviets don't need Cuba, and the Cubans would risk everything if they supported the Soviets in a general conflict.

With respect to the possibility of an overland threat to the United States, one must ask whether such a scenario is at all likely. The most plausible circumstances requiring stationing of large forces on the southern border would be related to instability in Mexico. The Mexicans themselves, however, feel their stability more endangered by the prospects of a United States intervention in Central America than by a regime change in El Salvador.

Third, turning to the question of American strategy, Pastor argued that the consequences of an effort to reverse the Nicaraguan regime by military means would make the *status quo* look good by comparison. Neither the contras nor the Central American Defense Council (CONDECA) is capable of doing the job; and, while United States intervention could certainly dislodge the Sandinistas from Managua and other major cities, we would find ourselves dragged into a long-term occupation and guerrilla war. The results could prove unsettling to the CONDECA countries and would spark a domestic reaction in the United States. In addition, our European allies are more likely to be shaken by a long-term occupation and war in Central America than by almost any other resolution of the conflict in El Salvador and Nicaragua.

In sum, Pastor concluded, an excessive focus on the Soviets as the problem in Central America has led us to strengthen unwittingly forces which are in fact hostile to peaceful, democratic change, and thus our interests. Moreover, because Nicaragua is so small, there has been a presumption that the quick use of military force would be effective. The threat of force could be effective if coupled with a balanced negotiating strategy. Unfortunately, the administration's approach has been all force and no negotiations. In Central America, the most effective approach would be one that gave the Contadora nations a stake in the security arrangements by relying on them much more than has been the strategy of the Reagan administration.

Finally, *Stephen Rosenfeld* addressed the topic of American strategic perspectives, as a matter not of strategy but of political feasibility. There are dangers to be avoided in yielding to popular opinion, he noted, but Central America is an area of foreign policy about which our political society is literate. The raggedness of the current consensus is in part a reflection of the fact that it is a political and not a strategic consensus. But in a context where nothing better is available, the "muddle" at least elicits continuity over time while avoiding either the unwarranted despair or optimism of Luttwak and Pastor. American domestic politics do and will continue to exert a large influence over United States policy in Central America, Rosenfeld concluded.

In the subsequent discussions conference participants questioned Luttwak's appraisal of the insurgent threat and, more pointedly, challenged his policy prescriptions. Several participants suggested that an effective response to the Central American crisis would require greater sensitivity to local circumstances, and that the range of options available to the United States is broader than had been suggested. In concluding, they discussed the likely reactions of United States allies, particularly in Europe, to alternate outcomes of the Central American crisis.

AMERICAN SECURITY: A NARROW VIEW

Against Luttwak's broad view of the threat posed to United States security by the emergence of revolutionary regimes in the Caribbean Basin, *Morton Halperin* and others argued that United States interests might be better served by tolerating a certain degree of objectionable behavior—including anti-American rhetoric, authoritarian politics, and even some support for subversion—and focusing instead upon what would truly constitute a direct threat to the security of the United States, the establishment of Soviet bases.

Current United States policy, these critics charged, is marked by an excessive emphasis on the nature of the Nicaraguan regime. A certain degree of anti-American rhetoric has to be expected from revolutionary regimes, *Anibal Romero* observed. It is simply a fact of life in countries where the United States must live down a long history of involvement in support of notoriously repressive regimes. And although democratic institutions are to be preferred over authoritarian ones, American efforts to impose democracy from without are usually counterproductive. In Nicaragua, *Robert Pastor* noted, the effort to draw middle sectors into the counterrevolutionary camps sucked out the most important democratic forces from the country. Finally, *Halperin* added, Nicaraguan support for subversion is nominal, in material terms. To be sure, the example of Nicaraguan defiance, like that of Cuba, exerts a powerful influence in regional politics. Revolution in Nicaragua frightens military leaders and gives a moral boost to the insurgency. But this moral support would amount to nothing were it not for internal conditions in El Salvador and elsewhere.

Luttwak responded, first, that efforts to come to terms with the Sandinista regime were bound to fail. The initial United States response to the Sandinistas had been anything but hostile. The Carter administration suspended aid to Somoza, thus preordained his fall, and then helped the people who came to power. Despite this, and long before the contras were organized, the Sandinista leadership had adopted the view that "good relations with the United States would mean the revolution had gone wrong." Second, to restrict American security concerns to the establishment of Soviet alliances as manifested by the installation of Soviet bases is to discount the significance of both Nicaragua's own military buildup—Nicaragua recently added fifty tanks to the eighty-five it already has, in a region where there are no other tanks—and of the advantages to the Soviet Union of mere access to facilities in Nicaragua.

Michel Tatu added that postponing a forceful response to the moment of overt alliance might be imprudent. In the first place, once a Marxist regime is consolidated it is no longer possible to influence that regime's behavior with economic incentives. In the second instance, without a high degree of United States sensitivity to Soviet involvements in Nicaragua there will be a series of step-by-step increases as there have been in Cuba. Nicaragua will always be prepared to justify any buildup—in the last resort as its sovereign right. But by waiting until the Sandinista leadership overtly allies with the Soviet Union, it may be too late or too costly to respond. Finally, even if it is admitted that 90 percent of Nicaraguan aid is moral, and the remaining material aid is virtually insignificant, this moral support, Mr. Luttwak argued, is vital to the Salvadoran insurgency. The most important support a guerrilla, at night in the field, can receive is propaganda support which dampens the fear that he is nothing more than a solitary presence.

REVOLUTIONARY REGIMES: IRREVERSIBLY HOSTILE?

In his prepared remarks and in subsequent exchanges, *Luttwak* observed that except in one respect, the record of revolutionary regimes is one of unmitigated failure; the exception is in the area of social control. While Communist governments adopt economic and political policies that are "programmed to fail," they are remarkably adept at building large military and police forces. In the end, all totalitarian governments have one common quality: they cannot be removed except by external force. In Central America, this means that once guerrilla movements consolidate power, we have to remove them. When *Jiri Valenta* observed that anti-Americanism is not a necessary feature of Marxist-Leninist regimes, Luttwak replied that in Central America, the hostility of revolutionary regimes is a product of geography, not regime. Yugoslavia and China are near the Soviet Union; but any government in Central America that dreams of independence must, because of the imminent and crushing presence of the United States, necessarily be anti-American. Thus it is regime and geography together that make revolutionary governments in Central America implacably hostile.

Robert Pastor agreed that the hostility of the Sandinista leadership was a cause, not a consequence, of United States policy since July 1979, which has grown increasingly belligerent, but also agreed with *Morton Halperin* that United States covert operations against the Sandinistas served to mobilize popular support to their regime. Hostile United States military actions against Nicaragua guarantee that Sandinista leaders, who *are* anti-American, can more easily make their case for anti-Americanism to the Nicaraguan people, who are *not*. *Jiri Valenta* further observed that, as the recent case of Grenada demonstrates, the process of Leninization is not irreversible. In Nicaragua, it may be possible to play the Borge faction against the Tercerista faction with an eye to either splitting—as in Grenada—or moderating the regime.

SEA-LANES

Michael Harrison challenged Luttwak's view of the strategic role of sea-lanes in American defense of Europe. Harrison questioned whether Luttwak really believed in the plausibility of a ninety-day-plus strategy for the resupply of allied forces in the event of the outbreak of war on NATO's central front. If so, our allies must be surprised to learn that the United States plans rely heavily on a long-term conventional defense of Europe. But even if this scenario is thought plausible, Harrison added, it is not at all clear what advantages Nicaragua, in addition to Cuba, supplies to the Soviet Union.

In response, *Luttwak* noted that strategists concerned with the defense of Europe focus upon the "divisional count" as the most significant measure of the relative balance of forces in the continent. American cargo ships are essential to maintaining NATO forces in the event of war, and yet the number of those ships has declined dramatically at the same time that the Soviets have established a large interdiction force. At one time it was possible to counter the expansion of the Soviet fleet by increasing the number of flows. Now it is possible that the Soviets, by sinking the initial flow of cargo, might postpone the resupply of Europe by some two to three months, approximately the time it would take the United States to recover. In the event, given the precarious balance of forces existing in the world today, it would be impossible to postpone nuclear war for months, or even two to three weeks. Thus, because access to bases in Nicaragua would more than double the range of Soviet responses to United States defensive countermeasures, the conflict in Central America uncovers "one of the major fault lines of American strategy."

EL SALVADOR: A STRATEGIC LOGIC?

Joseph Joffe suggested that the effort to reconstitute Salvadoran society in the midst of a counterinsurgency war would necessarily prove counterproductive. Since the military forces, at whom the bulk of any reform effort must be directed, are also those whose cooperation is essential to the defeat of the insurgency, it would prove impossible to twist arms without endangering the more fundamental effort to avoid military defeat. Thus, Joffe asked, isn't it the case that American policymakers are forced to accept the strategic logic imposed by circumstances, namely, that it is not possible to improve the Salvadoran military forces, and therefore you must resort to military power in order to defeat the guerrillas and preserve a friendly government?

Stephen Rosenfeld replied that the record of progress in El Salvador completely undermined Joffe's point. *Robert Kennedy* added that congressional recalcitrance provided the United States with leverage in El Salvador to strengthen the hand of civilian over military leaders. Because Duarte received congressional support during his recent visit to Washington, the Salvadoran military has been more willing to cooperate with him. *Robert Pastor* was less optimistic, insisting that although many of the actions taken by the Salvadoran government are significant—in particular, the transfer of the head of the notorious Treasury Police, Nícolas Carranza, as well as the recent conviction of the National Guard soldiers accused of murdering four American churchwomen—these actions tend to come in bursts in order to pressure Congress for more military aid and are in themselves insufficient to create the climate in which social democrats in favor of reform can afford, without extreme risk of life, to abandon armed struggle and alliance with the guerrillas. Reform, Pastor argued, is not simply the fetish of human-rights-minded liberals, but is essential even if one's only objective is to prevent the extension of Cuban/Soviet influence in Central America. Moreover, reform is advanced by not providing a blank check to the local security forces, that is, by making them less secure, not by making them more so.

In a subsequent exchange *Edward Luttwak* argued that United States aid is essential to the reform process, but that reform is not required for successful counterinsurgency. Because of a little-known congressional restriction, United States officials are prevented from providing aid or training to the police forces of foreign countries. Yet in El Salvador, it is not the military, who receive United States aid and training, but the police who are most notoriously involved in the violation of basic human rights. In the countryside, poorly paid police and national guardsmen are easily bought off by large landholders. In order to professionalize these forces, it is necessary for the United States to enter this "market relationship" and outbid the oligarchy for the services of local officials. Even so, Luttwak later observed, reform is unnecessary for successful counterinsurgency, as the case of Guatemala demonstrates. The Guatemalans took the "precaution" of shooting local leaders, priests, and well-connected intellectual journalists in front of the United States embassy, thereby ensuring that they would not get inadequate United States aid and then find themselves in the no-win situation described earlier. Having resorted to traditional methods, Guatemala has proven their effectiveness, and is now, Luttwak asserted, a model of successful counterinsurgency.

AMERICAN STRATEGY: THE MILITARY OPTION

Roy Gutman questioned whether the United States had a strategy in Central America, and suggested that at best what is being pursued, inconsistently and without steady attention, was a policy of strategic denial. *Robert Pastor* disagreed. The administration does have a coherent strategy. In El Salvador, the aim is to defeat the Left militarily by two methods: to give the civilian government political legitimacy, and to strengthen the counterinsurgency through military-to-military channels. Toward Nicaragua, the view is that the regime can be changed only by military force—and this objective will be more actively pursued after our own elections. But can the present strategy succeed? *Pastor* felt that only a change in strategy could succeed. *Luttwak* said that at present levels of United States involvement and funding it cannot. *Luttwak* insisted, however, that military victory in El Salvador could be achieved without direct United States involvement. But since the modern methods of counterinsurgency are quite expensive, American financial commitments would have to be expanded considerably. Asked by *Alan Berger* to put a price tag on a successful military effort, *Luttwak* estimated that full support for the counterinsurgency in El Salvador would amount to $300 million per annum. No estimate was given of the cost of an effort to remove the Sandinista regime.

A VENEZUELAN MODEL

Several participants challenged the view that a desirable resolution of the Central American crisis could be achieved by military means alone. Far from being a model, Guatemala was seen as a negative example of a tolerable resolution of the conflict. The relative calm of Guatemala, *Rodolfo Silva* warned, is artificial—it is the calm of a time bomb ready to explode. Democratic nations, like the United States, Colombia, Costa Rica, and others in the region, share responsibility for not having found ways to support legitimate popular protests against oppression and corruption. Scores of moderate leaders, like Enrique Alvarez Meza in El Salvador, Alberto Fuentes Mohr in Guatemala, and Pedro Joaquín Chamorro in Nicaragua, have been murdered, together with thousands of politicians, trade union leaders, students, intellectuals, and even priests. As a result, the mantle of legitimate revolution has been allowed to fall into the hands of the Communists. Opposed to the extremist military solutions of both the Right and Left, democrats must find ways jointly and collectively to promote respect for legitimate rights.

Perhaps what is needed, *Silva* suggested, is not a military strategy but a political strategy. Opposed to the Guatemalan strategy that "worked by killing everybody in the center" is the strategy pursued by Venezuela. After the overthrow of the Pérez Jimenez dictatorship, Venezuela had the good fortune of having two men of courage and vision in Admiral Larrazabal and in Romulo Betancourt. The first, as military leader, allowed and promoted the return to democracy and free elections, rather than the usual model of staying in power. Betancourt, as elected President and under attack by leftist guerrillas supported by Cuba in the early 1960s, did not use this as a pretext to destroy the political opposition and eliminate moderate leaders. Rather, the Venezuelan leadership strengthened the political center and supported the democratic process, thus isolating subversion. The result is twenty-five years of political stability, democratic elections, and alternation in office of the two main political parties. The success of the Venezuelan strategy, Silva concluded, contrasts sharply with that of Guatemala, and one can only surmise that had the Guatemalan strategy been applied in Venezuela, Venezuela would also find itself in the same condition as Guatemala.

Robert Pastor drew two additional lessons applicable to El Salvador from the Venezuelan case. First, the example of Venezuela underscores the usefulness of combining a negotiating strategy with an electoral process. And second, the ensuing stability of Venezuela illustrates the importance of delegitimizing the political role of the armed forces. Without a serious effort to rein in the security forces of El Salvador, the apparent stability of that nation will remain a deception.

Edward Luttwak maintained, however, that the example of Venezuela was not appropriate to Central America. Venezuelan President Romulo Betancourt enjoyed the benefits of a more stable and developed society, oil wealth, and substantial United States economic assistance. Moreover, the United States had a presence in Venezuela that was far more dynamic, active, and effective than is generally recognized—at a time when American power was still perceived as invincible. Guatemala, which received no United States militiary aid, is struggling in far less favorable circumstances. Finally, despite the atrocities involved in the Guatemalan counterinsurgency, the situation since has improved greatly as the guerrilla threat has been removed.

EUROPEAN VIEWS

Finally, *Andrew Pierre* asked whether United States credibility as a global power was challenged by outcomes in Central America, and whether this posed special problems for the Atlantic Alliance. *Edward Luttwak* took issue with Robert Pastor's earlier assertion that United States intervention in Central America would provoke a sharp reaction in Europe, and insisted that the political price of United States policy in Central America is already being paid. In bureaucratic terms, as a share of the Pentagon budget, the cost of the war is virtually insignificant, but it is a "$100 billion war in terms of what it is costing us in Europe." In many European minds, Luttwak noted, there is a quasi-equation: Soviet Union in Afghanistan equals United States in El Salvador. The strongest criticism of our Central American policy can be made on this point, namely, that it forces us to pay the full political price of being there without our realizing the purposes of our presence because of inadequate means.

Michael Palliser, on the other hand, noted that there are as many views in Europe of the Central American crisis as there are in the United States. Most Europeans, he suggested, are content not to interfere, and indeed even to toe the American line, on an issue that the United States clearly regards as vitally important—provided the Europeans know what the line is and have some assurance that it will not change every four years.

Global Impact

Chapter 11

STRATEGIC IMPLICATIONS OF THE CENTRAL AMERICAN CRISIS

Zbigniew Brzezinski

THIS ESSAY TOUCHES on four issues in the current Central American crisis, namely, and first, the Central American problem as an issue in the American-Soviet relationship; second, in that context, the Central American problem as a military issue; third, as an issue in hemispheric and regional relations; and finally, as a domestic issue in American politics.

In addressing myself to this issue I am very conscious of the fact that the Central American problem poses for the United States a particularly anguishing dilemma. All countries, democracies included, deviate from time to time from the norms to which they are committed. That certainly has also been true of the United States in its international conduct. But I think that it is a fair judgment to say that in Central America the Unites States has deviated from its internal norms more consistently and for a longer period of time than in any other part of the world. American political and economic domination of this region has been extensive, and by and large it involved forms of behavior and consequences not altogether compatible with the norms to which we subscribe.

If that is all that one could say on the subject, in a way the remedies would be self-evident: they would be derived from the principles that guide us, and the self-corrective mechanisms of the American system would probably move us in the right direction. I am reminded when I think of the problems of Central America of the very basic changes that did transpire in the United States– Mexican relationship as recently as in the thirties, at the time of expropriation of American property and so forth, and the United States was able to adjust to that.

What clearly makes the Central American problem much more difficult for us is its relationship, whether we like it or not, to the American-Soviet rivalry. The existence of Cuba, in fact the Marxist cast of much of the Central American revolution, automatically makes the Central American problem part of the larger American-Soviet confrontation. That complicates not only the political ramifications of the problem, but indeed even ultimately moral judgments regarding that problem. For one can no longer confine oneself to the relatively simple and categorical statements that I made about the American deviation from its internal norms when one is compelled to ask also what would be the long-range consequences of unfavorable developments, if these turns of events are associated with the larger American-Soviet confrontation.

Insofar as that confrontation is concerned, it is my judgment that currently for the Soviet Union the Central American issue is at best a secondary front. It is a relatively minor objective at this stage; it does not constitute a central area of competition with the United States. To be sure, for the Soviet Union there are certain benefits to be derived from the existence of the problem and—from the Soviet point of view—from its negative unfolding. The United States is likely to be more isolated internationally, and that is clearly in the Soviet interest. Indeed if things go in the wrong direction, without my spelling out what that may mean, the Central American problem could produce a crisis of the Western Alliance for the United States, if you will, a kind of Suez 1956 in reverse for the United States, where the United States embarks on an adventure that isolates it in the international community and which fragments the Alliance itself. Beyond that, for the Soviet Union, there is the more specific interest in preserving revolutionary gains, which means making certain that neither Cuba nor Nicaragua is jeopardized.

The Soviets in their attitude are clearly aware that there is a fundamental asymmetry between the American and the Soviet stakes in the region. Without defining specifically such terms as victory or defeat, one can nonetheless postulate that for the Soviet Union something amounting to historical victory in this region would be a genuine strategic triumph. However, a Soviet defeat in the region would be only a tactical setback. Conversely, for the United States a victory in the region (still undefined) is only at best a tactical success. But a defeat for the United States in the region is a strategic calamity because of its linkage to the larger dimensions. That means that Central America is a serious problem for us—a very complicated problem—but it is essentially a low-risk opportunity for the Soviet Union. And that brings me to some comments on the military dimension of the issue.

From the military point of view the problem is clearly much more manageable for us and, in contrast, more complicated for the Soviets. For example, in stark contrast to the Vietnamese conflict, one has to conclude that the scale of the problem, its operational conditions, and the opportunities for operational leverage are much more advantageous for the United States than for the Soviet Union. Insofar as the scale of the problem is concerned, the size of the territory is smaller, the insurgency problem is smaller, the external backup and the capacity for the insertion of external force are infinitely smaller than was the case in Vietnam. Insofar as operational conditions are concerned, the distance from the United States in contrast to the distance from the Soviet Union is infinitely to the advantage of the United States in Central America, whereas it was not in Vietnam. There exists the Southern Command (SouthCom), and a very elaborate military infrastructure has lately been developed by the United States through a deliberate buildup in the last several years in Central America. The region is clearly accessible to the United States and relatively inaccessible to the Soviet Union, Cuba notwithstanding. In terms of operational leverage the area is clearly susceptible to effective military interdiction, and indeed, if necessary, it is susceptible to direct pressure and action on the source of the problem (however that source may be defined).

However, for the moment I think there are some indications that the United States in its military strategy is tempted to pursue an approach reminiscent of its engagement in Vietnam. The rather interesting strategic critic of the Vietnam War, Colonel Harry Summers, in a recent review of our strategy pursued in the Vietnam War, makes a number of points that struck me as suggestive. I quote:

> Our adoption of the strategic defensive was an end in itself, and we had sub-stituted the negative aim of counter-insurgency for the positive aim of the isolation of the battlefield.[1]

He goes on to say,

> In Vietnam such an adjustment was never made. Instead of focusing our attention on the external enemy, North Vietnam—the source of the war—we turned out attention to the symptom—the guerrilla war in the south—and limited our attacks on the North to air and sea actions only. In other words, we took the socio-political task (nation-building/counter-insurgency) as our primary mission, and relegated the military task (defeating external aggression) to a secondary place. The effect was a failure to isolate the battlefield, but because of the confusion over objectives this fact was not readily apparent.[2]

I think these comments are suggestive of some of the military dilemmas that confront us, and we do have some bearing on the kind of security policy that we are pursuing. However, any consideration of the logical implications of these assertions has to be assessed in the context of what I referred to as the hemispheric or regional issue in the Central American problem. The hemispheric and regional aspects of the problem clearly rule out, from the political point of view, a direct military intervention by the United States. The United States in a larger sense is now in the process of readjusting its traditional relations, both with Central America and with Latin America. Certainly the Panama Canal treaties are a reflection of the greater willingness of America as a society to temper the one-sided character of its previous relations with Central America and to readjust that relationship on a more equitable basis. More generally the relevance of the Monroe Doctrine has come to be questioned as a guiding principle for American policy, and more and more Americans realize that the Monroe Doctrine was interpreted altogether differently by North Americans and by our Latin friends of the south. By the United States it was viewed as an altruistic declaration of commitment to joint security; to most Latin Americans it was a document spelling out the justification for Yankee imperialism.

Since that adjustment is now underway, and has been underway for some decades, it is clearly more difficult in that context to countenance a solution that relies primarily or even exclusively on the use of military force, even though the objective conditions for the use of such force are more favorable than in many of the cases of post-World War II American involvement. The Central American issue nonetheless, enflames passions throughout the continent, and it could divide us from that continent on a massive and highly counterproductive scale. Moreover, it is quite evident that there is a fundamental dichotomy between our perspectives on this problem and the perspective of some friends, potentially affected parties and countries in neighborly relations with which we have a vital interest. It is enough just to read some key passages from speeches by President de la Madrid of Mexico and President Reagan to see how wide the gap in perspectives truly is. During President de la Madrid's May 1984 visit to the United States, he said:

> We are convinced that the Central American conflict is a result of economic deficiencies, political backwardness, and social injustice that have afflicted the countries of the area. We cannot therefore accept its becoming part of the East-West confrontation, nor can we accept reforms and structural changes being viewed as a threat to the security of the other countries of the hemisphere.[3]

In contrast the President of the United States put it entirely differently:

> For the United States the conflagration in Central America appears too close to ignore. Like a fire in one's neighborhood, this threat should be of concern to every nation in the hemisphere. . . . Complicating the situation and making it even more dangerous has been the intervention of a totalitarian coalition which has undermined what we had hoped would be a democratic revolution. These totalitarians have been pouring gasoline onto the fire by pumping massive supplies of weapons into Central America and encouraging tyranny and aggression. Thousands of Cubans and Soviet bloc military personnel have accompanied this flow of weapons and equipment into the region. Responsible governments of this hemisphere cannot afford to close their eyes to what is happening.[4]

This striking gap clearly should make any American policymaker extremely careful about relying primarily on the military dimension in dealing with the problem, for if such reliance were to lead primarily to military solutions, however surgical in their character, the entire fabric of America–Latin American relations would be endangered. In the shortest term, American-Mexican relations would be badly strained, thereby complicating even our own ability to help Mexico cope with its internal problems. Clearly the ability of our own polity to deal intelligently with Mexico's internal problems is in the vital security interest of the United States.

All that, in my judgment, underlines the importance of United States sensitivity to such formulas as those advocated by the Contadora Group in order to project an American willingness to compromise and to adjust and to project also some American recognition that the diagnosis offered by the Mexicans contains at least 50 percent of the truth. But beyond that there is the further problem of our domestic politics and how they impinge on the shaping of policy in the above context. We must remind ourselves of the fact that there is a striking domestic contrast between the early phases of the Vietnam War and the current political situation. The Vietnam War started in the setting of bipartisan support in the United States for the engagement, and it was only the war that destroyed bipartisanship in the United States, not to speak of bipartisan support for engagement in the war. The Central American conflict, and the need to shape a policy responsive to it, have started in a setting of partisan conflict, of intense partisan division. The question is, will the awareness of the stakes eventually generate a bipartisan response?

The initial move in that direction, such as the Bipartisan Commission's report, has not been politically too promising. It did not generate bipartisan support for United States policy. The contrast between President Reagan and President de la Madrid continues to be replicated domestically. When one reads the discussions of the Central American problem on the two sides of the political fence one can hear echoes almost word for word of the sharp disagreement between Reagan and de la Madrid. The Democratic party puts primary emphasis in its analysis of the problem on its socioeconomic roots, and presents it almost as a crisis generated by the imperatives of social reform. The administration in office clearly puts primary emphasis on the externalities of the conflict, merging, if you will, the possible consequences of a hostile victory with the causes of the problem.

Inherent in all this is the longer-range danger that domestic division and national fatigue will make the maintenance of an effective and balanced policy in that region impossible. It could indeed make Central America, which has not yet become the political equivalent of Vietnam, a highly divisive issue which then propels the United States into seeking urgent remedies by one or another extreme.

In the light of the above, my own bottom line is a set of propositions that I can summarize very quickly. The first is that the United States cannot afford to lose, because of its rivalry with the Soviet Union, and whether we like it or not that rivalry is a fact. A loss would have widespread ramifications for ourselves, for others, for perceptions of international affairs that intangibly merge (and inevitably so) with the realities of international politics. But, secondly, if the United States cannot afford to lose, it similarly cannot afford to win militarily and preemptively because of conditions in the hemisphere. That, thirdly, leads me to the view that the United States simply must stay on course, essentially on the two levels of its current engagement, which is to some extent military, to some extent socioeconomic. But to stay the course the United States, fourthly, must apply pressure directly on Nicaragua, since a prolonged conflict would be domestically too divisive and because the absence of direct pressure in Nicaragua means that the United States has little choice but to put primary emphasis on military counterinsurgency in El Salvador itself, as earlier in South Vietnam, at the expense of the longer-range sociopolitical economic priority in El Salvador.

In brief, it is my view that we have to exploit some of the military advantages we have external to El Salvador to try to effect positive political changes in Nicaragua internally, and to affect the external conduct of Nicaragua and perhaps Cuba. Through such pressure, the conflict will either peter out, or we will be in a better position to negotiate an accommodation that exploits politically the application of pressure on the adversary. That, in turn, will give us greater opportunity to pursue an enlightened socioeconomic political program internally in El Salvador. This is not an attractive conclusion to many Americans, but the other alternatives strike me as either unrealistic or as excessively dangerous.

NOTES

1. Harry Summers, Jr., "Defense without Purpose," *Society*, vol. 21, no. 1 (November/December 1983), p. 16.

2. Summers, "Defense without Purpose," p. 10.

3. "De La Madrid Rejects Latin Solution by Military Force," *Los Angeles Times*, May 17, 1984, p. 1.

4. "Excerpts from Remarks by the Two Presidents," *New York Times*, May 16, 1984, p. 24.

The View from Europe

Chapter 12

EUROPE, THE UNITED STATES AND CENTRAL AMERICA: A NEST OF MISUNDERSTANDINGS

Michel Tatu

ONE CANNOT EXPECT the Europeans to speak in one voice about Central America. There are, after all, not only different viewpoints from one country to another, but there are inside each country different "political sensibilities"—some people are more sensitive to one aspect of the problem, others to other aspects of the problem.

This paper offers one European view that does not pretend to encompass all other European views. It develops two particular cases that appear rather characteristic of the European mood regarding Central America. One is the Grenada affair, with particular emphasis on the British dilemma, and another is the French Socialist government's attitude since 1981 toward El Salvador and Nicaragua. The latter is rather representative of a certain attitude of one part of the European Left toward such problems. There are, however, some points that seem in the first approximation to be common to most European countries.

THE PROBLEM OF PERCEPTIONS

The first point is that any United States administration would be wrong if it expected unanimous or at least vigorous support of European governments and opinions toward its policy in Central America, whatever this policy is. Some statements by the Reagan administration are a little surprising, in the sense that American officials are sorry that the European governments do not support some of their actions as eagerly as the administration would like. Even in other circumstances, the troubles in Central America would be a nest of misunderstandings between Europe and the United States. The area belongs to the security zone of the American superpower (at least in the eyes of the White House, if not of Congress and the media), not to that of any European power, even those like France and Britain, which still have colonial possessions in the Caribbean. The security perception cannot be identical between any two countries in the world. Security has to be considered from an egoistic point of view, and one cannot simply transfer the perception from one side to another. So the Europeans cannot see Central America with the same eyes as the North Americans see it.

This is understandable. Cuba, for example, is far from Europe. Moreover, European nations have grown accustomed in recent decades to the presence of Communist powers at their doors—even, in the case of Germany, on their own territories. So the sensitivity to the security concerns of Washington about Cuba or Nicaragua cannot be the same on both sides of the Atlantic, even for a European who tries to look at the scene through American glasses.

Moreover, it is not an obligation, a commitment because of the Western Alliance, to support whatever the Americans do in such areas. We should not identify the Western Alliance with, for example, the Warsaw Pact or a Communist alliance where everything the Soviets do in other geographic areas has to be supported more or less enthusiastically, and the measure in which the Soviet position is supported is considered as a measure of their fidelity to the alliance. This must not be a criterion for the Western Alliance.

The only thing that the Alliance is obliged to do is not to be an obstacle to American policy in an area where Washington considers it has an important, imperative, significant problem. Whatever can be said about European policy in Central America, it has never been an obstacle, it has never really prevented the American administration from applying its policy.

The second point is that Europeans see the situation in Central America as a sort of test for American policy, but what kind of test depends on what I call the "political sensibilities." Some Europeans see this situation as a test for the United States of its capacity to handle North-South relations, to handle relations with Third World countries in an area close to the United States. This is important, as many Europeans pretend to have better sensibilities than the United States toward North-South problems and Third World developments. Whether it is true or not is subject to debate.

Central America is of particular concern to nearly all Western European nations. For Latin countries (notably Spain) the area is a sister area, with a common language and some common heritage. France adds to the Latin ingredient a cultural affinity (many Central and South American leaders have been educated at the Sorbonne, particularly those with Marxist leanings) and a congenial sympathy for the nationalist mood in the area and resistance to "Anglo-Saxon" domination. The same countries, plus the Netherlands, also maintain strong ties with some of their colonies there. Last but not least, all European countries see in Central America, after Africa, the best test case for deploying and implementing a generous and comprehensive "Third World" approach, in line with the "North-South dialogue" that most governments have tried to develop in the past ten years. It is not a coincidence that among the sixty countries involved in the two Lomé conventions (concluded in 1974 and 1980 by the European Community for trade preferences with Third World countries) eleven belong to the Caribbean zone, including nearly all the islands of the area (Cuba excepted).

Among the ten members of the European Economic Community certain countries are more active than others for political reasons, and have developed a cooperation of their own with friendly forces. The Federal Republic of Germany has been heavily involved in Central America along two competitive lines: the Social Democratic party, with its Herbert Foundation, helps Social Democrats in the area, and the Christian Democratic Union does the same with Christian Democratic parties and governments. As far as the French Socialist party is concerned, it has been involved, as we will see, in the conflicts in El Salvador and Nicaragua, if only because of the old and personal connections existing between its leaders and some of the figureheads of the leftist forces in those two countries.

There is another test, however, the test of the American capacity to handle very complicated problems, and to develop a long-term strategy that manipulates a variety of instruments—military, political, and social—to facilitate the local development of social justice while satisfying strategic considerations. This test is at the same time a test for the decision-making process in the United States. The results so far, as evidenced by the divisions within the United States, indicate that Europeans should not expect any real American strategy in Central America. There are so many different points of view that it is doubtful that this problem can be handled in this present state of nonconsensus in the United States.

One very interesting aspect of this dilemma is the role of Congress, which in my view is so important that it is very difficult to have real strategy toward a problem that is so complicated and demands a comprehensive approach. There is no parliament in the world, or at least in Europe, that has as much relative power as the United States Congress, except perhaps in the Netherlands or Denmark. The role the Congress has played in formulating foreign policy also supports my first argument. One should not expect the Europeans to be more American, that is to say, more sensitive to United States security interests, than the average United States congressman. So the divisions within the United States are such that they can only encourage Europeans to wait and see.

In the longer term, too, it is a test of the United States capacity to conduct military operations, whether covert or open. The United States performance to date has raised questions in some European circles. Whatever the political sensibilities about the United States capacity, to put it bluntly, to conduct military operations on the ground, one has the feeling that the United States is able to make some naval or air operations, but as soon as one American marine or soldier is committed in some operation on the ground this becomes an unmanageable problem for the United States. I say this at least but from a French point of view. In Chad we have had three thousand soldiers dug into the sand for a year or two. Even if one might question the utility of this deployment, we do not have in France the same problems of consensus about such military operations, despite criticisms about the role of these soldiers we have there.

This brings me to the third point, which is the question of moral conduct, a problem much discussed at this conference. Here we have it the other way around. Normally it is the Europeans who have been accustomed to receive lessons of political morality from the United States, and now Central America is an occasion for the Europeans to give lessons of morality to the United States. We might push it a little bit farther and say that some governments, maybe many, are happy to have the opportunity to put on a good face, a moral face, in front of immoral American conduct.

Now this brings us to the fourth point. Whatever the reactions are, one should distinguish in Europe different types of reactions to whatever happens in Central America. There is a short-term reaction; a sort of obliged reaction, an automatic, conditioned-reflex government reaction; and a long-term reaction.

Short-term reactions depend on political sensibilities, or political affinities, and they are usually critical of the American action. We add to that the "obliged reaction" of the governments, which means that governments have to take some distance from United States policy. One cannot expect governments, even the best people with the best feelings toward the United States, to support enthusiastically some operations that are at the limit of legality, or even farther than the limit, like the invasion in Grenada. Whatever Europeans think about the long-term result, and in fact about the success of the operation, they cannot support enthusiastically the actions of the United States. It is not possible for any government in the world to say "Oh, the United States government and the CIA were right in mining the ports in Nicaragua." This is not possible and, this paper will argue, some political leaders in fact supported decisively the invasion in Grenada. However, these same people would have taken another line if they had been in power.

Now we should add to that the long-term reaction, which is perhaps the only reaction that matters. The long-term reaction may be different from what is stated, and what is perceived in the first phase, because strategic considerations come into play. The following two examples illustrate more specifically these general observations.

AN EMBARRASSING CASE: GRENADA AND BRITAIN

Grenada was a bone of contention between Europe and the United States even before the invasion of November 1983. More than two years earlier, in April 1981, Washington had exerted pressure on the European Community to stop European assistance in the construction of Grenada's Salines Airport, which was built with significant Cuban labor but under the leadership of an English company. As a member of the Lomé convention, Grenada was entitled to receive credits from the European Development Fund and the Community contributed over six million dollars (out of a total of seventy) to the project. Though Great Britain, France (then under the government of Valéry Giscard d'Estaing), and West Germany were receptive to the American argument that the airport might be used not only for tourist purposes but for helping Cuba bring her troops to Africa, the European Commission continued funding to the Bishop government. At the same time, Europe undertook emergency food aid to El Salvador despite pressure from Washington, which feared that the help would fall into the hands of the Salvadoran insurgency.

But the invasion of Grenada by American forces in 1983 created a much bigger problem. Three embarrassing factors were involved for European powers, two of which affected particularly Great Britain. London was sensitive, as any other nation, to the violation of international law which might be argued on this occasion. In addition, Grenada was a member of the Commonwealth, one of the sixteen countries in the world that recognize Queen Elizabeth as their nominal head of state. Furthermore, London, still cultivating a special relationship with Washington, felt the need to be more closely associated than other European capitals with American decision-making and to have in return a better understanding of American motivations. This special relationship explained, among other considerations, the heavy support London received from Washington during the Falkland crisis a year earlier.

But these factors had a contradictory effect on each other: the need not to condone a violation of international law went against a special role of Britain in the area, and London's desire not to be involved was out of line with the special relationship with Washington. All this explains the great embarrassment of the British government in the whole affair, the extreme prudence of Mrs. Thatcher herself (who spoke very little on the subject), and the criticism of that attitude by a parliamentary inquiry commission, which mentioned in April 1984, despite a majority of Conservative members of Parliament in its ranks, the "lethargic approach" of the government. As Sir Geoffrey Howe said later, London had expressed its "doubts" about an invasion of Grenada to the American government on October 21, 1983, just one day before President Reagan signed the order for the operation. But this being done, the British government refused to do more, and even preferred not to know what was in preparation. As the *Times* put it on April 6, 1984, "It was a reasonable assumption for Washington to make that the British passivity indicated a reluctance to get involved." But in the eyes of public opinion, American behavior was criticized as unfair. According to the parliamentary commission, the British government "reacted passively to the events entirely on the advice received from Washington, which in the event proved to be unreliable advice." Denis Healey, the Labour spokesman, put it more bluntly: "The lack of candour shown by the American President amounted to deceit of a favorite ally."

This is not to say that the event created a crisis in Anglo-American relations. The British government refused to condemn the intervention in Grenada and abstained, unlike France, when the Security Council voted a United Nations resolution that "deeply deplored" the landing operation. The problem is that it illustrated, in American eyes, the European reluctance, including that of the best allies of the United States, to support Washington in what it considered a necessary police operation; it showed, as Mrs. Kirkpatrick put it, a "lack of concern for United States security." And even if the successful evolution of events in Grenada soon softened the criticism (in Europe as in the United States Congress), the fact remains that no government in Europe approved the Grenada invasion as President Reagan would have liked. Some political leaders did support it, but they were mainly opposition leaders speaking on their own, like Valéry Giscard d'Estaing in France; it is doubtful that the same people would have spoken in the same way had they been in power.

The reasons for this have been discussed above. There is first of all a difference in perception of security interests: European states cannot look at United States security as if they were on the American continent. Then there is the spectacle of the American political scene, particularly of the debates on Capitol Hill: Why would Europeans feel more "American" than a United States congressman? To be sure, some Europeans are concerned by the "Vietnam syndrome" illustrated by congressional reluctance for any military involvement abroad, particularly for deploying ground troops; they look at that reluctance as a bad omen for the protection of Europe. But those views are to be found rather at the right of the political spectrum, and certainly are not aired publicly by governments.

A third reason is the old dependency of Europe on the United States in matters of security. For over thirty-five years now the Atlantic Alliance has offered to Europe an American umbrella behind which European states could, first, forget partially about their security needs by doing only what the American NATO command demanded of them (sometimes less, but never more, in any case); and second, put a good face on the other aspect of their policies, look more "moral" and sometimes more "peaceful" than the American protector, if only because they were partially freed from strategic considerations and other "dirty" duties of the Pentagon's "hawks." Their "lack of concern" for what the United States perceived as its security interests was all the more understandable since there was already a lack of concern on the part of Europeans, at least in many American eyes, for their own security needs. American attitude in the Falkland crisis was not the point: there is in fact no reciprocity there.

A TEST CASE FOR THE FRENCH LEFT: EL SALVADOR AND NICARAGUA

Britain was a test case of the general European attitude toward American concerns in Central America, outside any particular "ideology." France is another test case, since the arrival to power of the Socialist-Communist coalition in 1981, of the attitude of a large component of the European "Left"—mainly an intellectual and "Latin" Left—toward the problem. (To be sure, as Mrs. Kirkpatrick herself admitted after a visit to Paris in April 1984, the French position has "evolved a good deal" since 1981 and has become "more sensitive to the complexities of the region." But there is still a wide gap in perception.)

From the very beginning, François Mitterrand, as the new president of France, made a sharp turn in French policy toward Central America. His predecessor, Valéry Giscard d'Estaing, had joined the Reagan administration in criticizing Soviet involvement in El Salvador. Jean-François Poncet, his foreign minister, had accepted in February 1981 the evidence brought to him by Lawrence Eagleburger which justified the presence of United States military advisers in El Salvador by "massive Soviet weapons delivery" to the insurgency. This very attitude had been heavily criticized by the French Socialist party, still then in the opposition, as "opportunistic." The Socialist party reaffirmed its solidarity with the Democratic Revolutionary Front of Guillermo Ungo. Lionel Jospin, its first secretary, went so far as to compare any support of the Duarte regime with the "collaboration" during Nazi occupation of France. "During the resistance period in France," said Jospin on March 2, 1981, "would anybody have recommended a reconciliation with the Militia forces (pro-German), for example?"

François Mitterrand, who has known Ungo for a long time as a "quiet Social Democrat," whose wife Daniele is an active member of a committee called "Solidarité Salvador et Amerique Centrale," and who has brought to the Elysée Palace Regis Debray, a leftist writer and close associate of Ché Guevara in his Latin American guerrilla days, supports this line. As he put it in *Le Monde* (July 2, 1981), "I have serious reservations, not to say more, about United States policy in Central America. . . . What is happening there is not Communist subversion but resistance to misery and indignity. When [these people] cry for help, I would like Castro not to be the only one to hear them." A month later, France signed with Mexico a common declaration recognizing that the alliance of the Farabundo Martí Front for National Liberation (FMLN) and of the Democratic Revolutionary Front (FDR) constitutes a "representative political force" and demanding that the two "participate in the creation of the mechanisms of rapprochement and negotiation necessary for a political solution of the crisis."

This statement was badly received not only by the Salvadoran and United States governments, but also by many Latin American nations, including countries with democratic regimes such as Colombia and Venezuela. In Europe, only the Netherlands approved. Spain criticized it, arguing that a country like France "is too far away from the area to take a position." This cool reception did not prevent the French government from persisting in its vocal political support of the Salvadoran insurgency, at least until the general elections in Salvador in 1982. Before these elections, Claude Cheysson, the French foreign minister, had gone so far as to deny any significance to the "so-called election, organized and controlled by the army" and to state unequivocally that the insurgency was "supported by the population."

Only when it had to be admitted that the electoral process was fair and that the population looked differently at the situation, did this support recede somewhat. French Socialist leaders who had contacts with the FDR and the FMLN admitted privately that those organizations were highly Marxist-Leninist and of a very dogmatic type, even if the figurehead of the insurgency, Guillermo Ungo, continued to be considered a partner (he was again received by President Mitterrand on April 19, 1984). In any case, the disappointment with this leftist cause never took the form of an open disassociation. There was no official statement in Paris either before or after the election of Napoleón Duarte as president of El Salvador this year.

The disassociation was more open with Nicaragua, though the support to the Sandinista government took a more active form at the beginning of the French Socialist government. On December 21, 1981, France signed with Managua an agreement for the delivery of a $15 million package of weapons, including two small ships, two helicopters and seven thousand air-to-surface rockets. The deal, which was announced in January 1982 as French Defense Minister Charles Hernu was visiting Washington, found Caspar Weinberger "very disappointed," but it was controversial in Paris from the very beginning. Claude Cheysson admitted later (August 4, 1983) that he approved it "with reticence," and criticism was aired in the French diplomatic community at the time. It was soon officially stated that this agreement was the last one and that no further weapons delivery was considered, even though Ortega, the junta coordinator in Managua, was offered financial aid of $20 million for civilian purposes during a visit to Paris in July 1982. But a year later (May 19, 1983), Cheysson admitted publicly that the Sandinista revolution "has not kept all its promises."

To be sure, the mining of the Nicaraguan ports by the CIA, revealed in April 1984, initially triggered a new upsurge of criticism against United States policy and a new reaffirmation of solidarity with Nicaragua's government. This was not the case in France alone, since most governments in Europe condemned or "deplored" this action. But France went further by offering technical help for demining the ports. This step was prudent, however: the letter offering the help was sent to the governments of the Contadora Group, not to Managua, and presented the eventual acceptance of the group as a condition for the move to become effective.

That acceptance never came, and the offer developed no further. France was also isolated in Europe in this cause, since only the Netherlands supported Paris in approving a resolution of protest in the United Nations Security Council. Even "socialist" Spain, which had officially protested the mining to the United States government, abstained in the vote. Furthermore, France itself was not eager to support Nicaragua in its claim to the High Court of Justice in the Hague: in the years before, Paris had regularly refused to admit the authority of the court in the handling of New Zealand's protests against French nuclear tests in the Pacific.

The same progressive and discrete disenchantment with revolutionary causes in Central America was clear during the Grenada invasion. To be sure, François Mitterrand repeatedly condemned this American action as an encroachment on the "rights of people to self-determination," but he admitted there were some mitigating circumstances such as the assassination of Prime Minister Bishop ("whom I knew well") and the presence in Grenada of "some [Cuban] military forces disguised as workers." And there was no mobilization of protesters in Europe as there had been for other affairs of this kind, not even on the part of the French Communist party; the only demonstration organized in Paris lasted one hour and gathered no more than two thousand persons.

The early enthusiasm for the revolutionary cause in Central America and the successive disillusionment illustrate the dilemma in which recent evolution has put the French and European leftist intelligentsia. For many years political "thirdworldism" developed in those circles as a reaction to American "imperialism" and also as a sort of rehabilitation for the colonial past of many European countries. It had focused on the Vietnam war, on the heroic fight of the Vietnamese "peasants" against the best-equipped army in the world. After the end of the Indochina war in 1975 the focus of this "political thirdworldism" shifted quite naturally to Latin and Central America: the enemy was the same "American imperialism"; the area was more familiar with and congenial to the Latin Left for cultural reasons; the leftist part of the Catholic Church found counterparts in local churches; and last but not least, Fidel Castro had maintained in these circles his prestige as an "authentic and national revolutionary leader" at the same time that the appeal of Soviet-style socialism was radically declining (and despite the obvious diplomatic rapprochement between Cuba and the USSR in the 1970s). The "good Castro" could usefully be substituted for the "bad Brezhnev."

Furthermore, the French "new-type Socialists" brought to power by Francois Mitterrand in 1981 were genuinely non-Communist, but nevertheless positioned more to the left than regular European Social Democrats, whom they considered with suspicion. Their ambition in Central America, repeatedly stated by the new French president, was to prevent revolutionary movements in the area from becoming Communist, to offer them an alternative support and model between Soviet-dominated socialism and oligarchic pro-United States regimes. To be sure, the interpretation of this doctrine varied according to the degree of ideological commitment of various wings inside the Left. Some policymakers emphasized this need for a "third way," others did not hesitate to speak of a "complementary policy" with that of the United States, to evoke a "division of labor" between Washington and Europe, each aiming at the prevention of Communist takeovers but with different means. But the result was about the same for the two schools: both pleaded for help to the revolutionary movements, in order to maintain among them a democratic and Western influence.

Unfortunately, this line could not be maintained for long. First, the experience of Southeast Asia had deeply reduced the prestige of pro-Communist revolutionary movements among the Western intelligentsia. The brutal communization of South Vietnam, the tragedy of the boat people, and the horror in Cambodia could only have a negative effect on all true believers in authentic national revolutions, on those who had overestimated, for example, the role of local insurgency in South Vietnam (the NLF) and the potentialities of the "third force" so much talked about in Saigon in the pre-1975 years. Even if the genocide in Cambodia was a more local phenomenon, it brought suspicions on others: from then on, the shadow of Pol Pot hung over the guerrilla movements in the rest of the world. That is why the sympathy for the Salvadoran guerrilla and its extremist "antieconomic" warfare, not to mention the Sendero Luminoso terrorism in Peru, could only be rather weak indeed.

Second, the question of prevention of a Communist domination of these movements had to be looked at more closely. A policy of sympathy and support to revolutionary movements makes sense only as long as those movements have not fallen into the orbit from which one wants to keep them. If they are already in this orbit (notwithstanding the presence at their heads of some non-Communist figures like Ungo), the same policy becomes counterproductive, since it gives a moral caution to totalitarian forces. It not only anticipates support to regimes of this type resulting from the victory of the Revolution, it also would introduce even more into local conflicts the East-West dimension that was not recognized in the first place. Furthermore, this East-West dimension has developed since the 1970s, if only because of the Soviet military buildup and the new capacity of Moscow to get involved in local conflicts, by arms delivery and power projection, at an early stage. Third World revolutionary leaders are no longer pure mass agitators as were Arbenz in Guatemala or Lumumba in the Congo. They emerge quickly as constituted military commanders equipped with Soviet weapons, trained by Soviet or Cuban advisors, sometimes protected by East German policemen. And the country they will dominate after victory is very likely to become a Soviet or Cuban military power base in the future. This is not to say that these new developments have penetrated very deeply in the minds of the leftist—particularly French—intelligentsia and that all illusions have been dispelled. But the fact remains that a more complete and realistic approach has emerged. Guerrilla movements in general in the world have a little bit less appeal now after other precedents, like Vietnam, like Cambodia, which have thrown a shadow on so-called liberation movements and Marxist guerrillas.

To sum up, the Europeans are not enthusiastic supporters of American policy in Central America, and one should not expect that, particularly since there is not too much to be enthusisatic about. Second, Europe is not in fact an obstacle, and not even a nuisance for the United States. No government in Europe has really been an obstacle or created strong difficulty for the Reagan administration in whatever it did in Central America. Even the French Socialist government, which has a very official close connection with the guerrilla movements, and which continues to state rather radical positions in the United States view, even this government is not a real obstacle. The last point is that the reaction to and the criticism of United States policy would have been even stronger a few years ago. The United States can complain about a lack of support from Europe for their security preoccupation in Central America. This should not prevent their noting that this lack of support would have been much greater earlier, say five years ago. Indeed, there would have been a real outcry at that time against their present policy, instead of the timid reservations of today.

Chapter 13

THE CENTRAL AMERICAN CRISIS: IS THERE A ROLE FOR WESTERN EUROPE?

Wolf Grabendorff

The United States obviously cannot grant our European allies a veto over our policy decisions on Central America.[1]

WHAT MAKES CENTRAL AMERICA SO FASCINATING FOR WESTERN EUROPE?

THE SUDDEN INTEREST in Central American issues in Western Europe has a variety of origins.[2] Not all of them are directly related to the developments in Central America since the Nicaraguan revolution in 1979. European self-interest with regard to its position in the world, its trade relations, and concerns about domestic power relations have contributed at least as much as the conditions in Central America and the United States response to them.

The manifold answers to the basic question why Western Europe seems to have become more preoccupied with Central America than with any other region of the Third World reflect the pluralistic way of foreign-affairs thinking in many Western European states. The Left and the Right see the conflict primarily in the context of the United States role: imperialism and intervention versus free-world leadership and fighting Soviet expansionism.

The democratic Left is more worried about Western relations with the Third World in general and the credibility of the Western industrialized nations' commitment to social change in underdeveloped countries than with the credibility of United States power, which the Reagan administration and many conservatives on both sides of the Atlantic seem to believe is the basic issue at stake in Central America.[3]

Many Western Europeans assume that, because of historical relations and cultural as well as political ties, they understand Latin America better than other parts of the Third World. This, combined with a preoccupation with human rights and social justice in that region, has led to the conviction that in

Central America there is a unique opportunity to further Western interests with little political risk and strong moral benefit.

Though the Carter administration seemed to share this attitude, many Western Europeans found themselves in an odd position after the Reagan administration made it perfectly clear that this was a great power conflict that endangered the security of the United States. Suddenly, the European fascination with the "benevolent revolutions" in Central America became an issue of global dimension. The developmental perspective was forced into the background by the heated discussion about the role of the superpowers in a Third World crisis area.

Many Europeans began to see the dangers of a great power conflict over small, relatively unimportant states as a new form of the East-West confrontation they had strived so hard to avoid in Western Europe.[4] A shared consciousness of vulnerability has since developed—a vulnerability interpreted very differently by those on the left and the right of the ideological spectrum in Western Europe. While the Left tends to fear that the East-West conflict could be intensified by the emergence of such new long-lasting Third World crisis areas, the Right sees danger that the United States might have to divert military resources from Western Europe to the Caribbean Basin.

To understand Western European preoccupation with Central America, therefore, means basically to sort out the origins of developmental perspective over security-related perceptions of the crisis, their immediate impact upon domestic political relations, and the resulting strains within the Atlantic Alliance. By lumping all European perceptions and reactions to the Central American crisis together, no role for Western Europe can evolve, much less an intra-Western consensus about the most skillful management of that crisis.

However, by taking certain Western European initiatives seriously, new ways of dealing with the multifaceted crisis could be developed. Such an approach would certainly imply a less rigid insistence of the United States upon its role in the region. The continuous dissatisfaction with United States leadership in that respect, which is felt in many European quarters, seems to result mainly from the fact that European advice—as partial as it may be—has been rejected altogether, while United States policy has become "less clear in its goals, questionable in its methods, and of a double standard in its morals."[5]

PERCEPTIONS OF THE CENTRAL AMERICAN CRISIS IN WESTERN EUROPE

The origins of the Central American crisis have been fiercely debated not only in the United States but also in Western Europe. Advocates of a "regional" solution to the political violence blame the problems on the extreme social injustice, illegitimate political systems, and continuing suppression of popular participation in countries like Guatemala, Nicaragua prior to its revolution, and

El Salvador prior to its recent elections. This group maintains that change in Central America is inevitable and that any attempt by Western powers to preserve the status quo in that area will only lead to more radicalization and violence—and increase the tendency in the area to turn to the Socialist bloc for help.[6] According to this view, the longtime association of the United States and Western countries in general with the "old order" has spurred "anti-imperialism" among people who favor a change in government. Previous United States policies make it very difficult for Western powers to try to mediate these basically socioeconomic and endogenous conflicts in Central America. Because the internal and regional political processes have gone beyond the moderate reformist stages in most cases, any efforts to "modernize" political systems in Central America are believed to be doomed.

The advocates of a global solution do not deny the internal problems but stress the importance of external, radical forces—Communist-inspired if not Communist-directed—in the breakdown of the old order.[7] Since the representatives of the old order were "friendly," non-Communist elites, their weakening has almost automatically led to a decline of United States influence in the region.

This group views the ability of Marxist influence to destabilize Central American societies in the context of the East-West power struggle. Containment of communism and the Soviet and Cuban influences in the Western Hemisphere are of decisive importance for all Western powers; therefore, the dissolution of the old order in Central America has to be stopped and new democracies have to be constructed before the old order crumbles completely. The "globalists" would even prefer authoritarian governments to possibly totalitarian societies, such as the one they see developing in Nicaragua.[8] From this group's perspective, it would be in the best interest of the Central American societies themselves and the West in general if the breakdown of regimes could be stalled and they could be replaced by more legitimate ones, ending external influence. Once the radical left has been cut off from external support, reform could be successful and more democratic systems would evolve. In short, a security-related solution would be necessary before a political or even socioeconomic one could be achieved.[9]

Both groups have influenced Western European perceptions of the Central American crisis. Generally, the regionalist approach seems prominent among the Social Democratic parties and governments, and the globalist approach is more representative of their Christian Democratic counterparts.[10] But this generalization is simplistic. The German Christian Democrats, for example, are well aware of both the importance of the internal origins and of the north-south dimensions of the conflict. The Social and the Christian Democrats differ more over the direction and instruments of change in Central America than over the causes of recent upheaval.

Throughout Western Europe, the regional approach to the Central American crisis has definitely taken priority over the global approach. The general view in Western Europe is that internal socioeconomic and political conditions must be improved before any stabilization of the region will become feasible.

The priorities are therefore clearly different as seen from the globalist view and as increasingly implemented by the Reagan administration. The threat perceptions and threat definitions that have been so much in the forefront of the justification for the Reagan administration's policy are, obviously, almost absent from most Western European views. That has not only to do with geographical distance but also with some difficulty on the European side—which has to a certain degree become accustomed to living with Soviet threats—in seeing the extent of a real threat to United States security evolving from the Central American turmoil. Also, European states are at best medium powers whose security views might indeed be narrower than those of a superpower.

Quite a number of analysts have, therefore, concluded that United States policies toward Central America are really meant, for extraregional reasons, as a show of strength in a traditional area of influence, demonstrating to the Soviet Union as well as to radical Third World states the limits of United States tolerance toward revolutionary change and external meddling. Even though such a policy of reassertionism might indeed reap benefits for the global position of the United States, it is virtually certain that it cannot contribute to the stabilization of the region or to a serious effort to boost internal development and external independence. Since the looking glass of the Reagan administration is inadequate to the region's problems, its solutions are bound to fail.[11] This failure will reflect upon the United States leadership position within the Atlantic Alliance.

For many Western Europeans, the dangers of self-fulfilling prophecies seem to be abundant in Central America. Inasmuch as Nicaragua has been treated since 1979 as Cuba was in the sixties, it becomes almost plausible that its leadership might indeed turn more and more toward the Socialist bloc.[12] Political pressure from the United States—especially in the form of (c)overt war— necessarily creates more internal militarization (and less freedom) and more dependence on help from Soviet and Cuban sources. Even if the Reagan administration should succeed in forcing the Sandinistas to comply with the original goals of their 1979 revolution (free elections, mixed economy, nonalignment), its choice of instruments to achieve United States political demands (mining of harbors, nonacceptance of World Court rulings, arming the contras) might have led to more loss of influence than a highly dubious "positive" outcome might at first suggest.

Given the historical relationship between the United States and Central America, it seems very likely that the stronger United States engagement (directly or indirectly) becomes, the greater will be the problems between the United States and its Latin American and Western European allies.

Here is where the globalist and the regionalist perceptions in Western Europe meet; the United States position will suffer as long as the United States tries alone to impose a solution upon the Central American countries. A regional solution can only be found by actively, and not only rhetorically, supporting the Contadora process and by pressuring for political negotiations between feuding ideological groups and states. A military solution can only result in further anti-Americanism and continuing civil wars in the future.

The global solution becomes impossible as long as democracy is brought to one country by supporting counterrevolution (Nicaragua) and to another country (El Salvador) by allowing the original powerbrokers, the oligarchy and the military, to define the terms of democratization. Since the community of values in the Atlantic Alliance is based not only on achievements but also on the use of law and its accepted instruments, a long-term negative effect could very well develop from the short-term display of United States strength in Central America.

The bottom line of the diversity of Western European perceptions seems to be that the European partners in the Atlantic Alliance view the Central American crisis as:

—a north-south problem in and of the Western Hemisphere;
—a problem deeply rooted in the historical relationship of the United States with its southern neighbors;
—a test case for the United States to come to terms with the solution of its informal empire;
—a test case for the Western powers to deal with revolutionary change and self-determination in the Third World;[14]
—a problem of how to restrain the military engagement of the Soviet Union and/or radical Third World states;
—a problem of how to avoid a superpower confrontation in the region and the resulting spillovers.

Basically, the Western Europeans would like the United States to succeed in finding a way to transform the outmoded political and social structures in the region without isolating some political movements or governments to the point that their anti–United States position will lead them to intensified or even permanent cooperation with the Soviet bloc. At the same time, the Western Europeans would like to have the United States avoid direct military involvement at almost all costs, since such a scenario would not only hurt the United States position vis-à-vis the Third World but would also trigger domestic unrest in many European countries.

Some might call such a position naive. It therefore seems necessary to define the priorities of Western Europe in dealing with the direct or indirect effects of the Central American crisis in more detail. Only when the different interests and conflicting goals of various European national, transnational, and multinational actors become clear will the possibilities and limitations of a Western European role in Central America be less blurred.

Western European Interests in Central America

West European countries are both uneasy and surprised about the "linkage" that has developed between Atlantic Alliance problems and the revolutionary process in Central America since the advent of the Reagan administration. They feel uneasy because some events in Central America have been greeted with some understanding, if not satisfaction, by the rather large constituency for Third World problems in most Western European countries. They feel surprised because even those who generally favor a containment policy against Soviet global expansion do not consider Central America the most urgent place to press such a policy. Obviously the Western Europeans lack adequate understanding of United States sensitivities—in the country at large and among the decision makers of the Reagan administration in particular—regarding this region so close to home.

Since the different perceptions of the origins and remedies for the Central American crisis have become well known on both sides of the Atlantic, the problems of Alliance cohesiveness have been taken very seriously by the Western Europeans. Most parties and governments do not want to risk yet another Alliance problem with the Reagan administration.[15]

The political implications of the Central American crisis for Western Europe have to be seen in three contexts:

—the Atlantic Alliance;
—the East-West conflict;
—Third World relations in the north-south context.

There can be little doubt that in all three areas Western European interests are highly vulnerable. Therefore Western European reactions to developments that touch on all three areas will necessarily appear strong but by no means united.

Most Western European parties and governments believe that any Third World conflict involving one of the superpowers is likely to become an East-West issue. Afghanistan is one such case, and Central America has become another since the United States seems to be convinced that only a winning situation can preserve its national interest. Such a development, if it included military intervention, would seriously strain the Atlantic Alliance, and there is a general fear of dramatic domestic as well as international repercussions of a United States–sponsored intervention in Central America.

Many Western European analysts also question whether every Socialist system established in Central America will necessarily become a Soviet ally and base for offensive sophisticated weapons. Indeed, many Europeans consider the preoccupation of the United States with its perceived security in Central America as inconsistent with its position as a superpower. They do not see the restriction of Communist influence as the most important task for the United States in a region which, for political and strategic reasons, has been of low priority for the Soviet Union.

The argument of the Reagan administration that outside interference in Latin America in general and in the Caribbean Basin in particular is a threat to the United States global position is based on the geopolitical concept of zones of influence. Even though this concept is well understood, it is hardly shared in Western Europe because of the fear that, once criteria based on zones of influence are accepted, the Soviet Union might use them to defend its own aggressive policies in what it considers its zone of influence.

If the United States, many Europeans wonder, views a change of government from a friendly, oligarchic, free-enterprise system to an unfriendly Socialist system with a centrally planned economy as incompatible with her role as superpower, will that United States view infringe the sovereign rights of Third World countries to determine their own forms of government? Would it not be much better instead to leave sufficient space for truly independent and nonaligned states to develop in the former "backyard" of the United States in order to demonstrate to the Third World that it is the West who can offer them self-determination and development?[16]

Some Western European countries find it, therefore, hard to preserve political unity within the Atlantic Alliance with respect to United States policy in Central America.[17] Those who view the conflict in north-south terms are unwilling to back United States policies because they feel that their own economic cooperation with the Third World should not be jeopardized by unreasonable United States opposition to any political change that does not occur in a democratic context. It has also not gone unnoticed in Western Europe that most United States attention to Central American problems has come only after the Nicaraguan revolution succeeded[18]—not unlike the Alliance for Progress, which was conceived after the Cuban revolution twenty years earlier.

One of the principal European interests in the Central American crisis is therefore to find out if the United States response is sufficiently flexible to satisfy Third World demands for autonomy and self-determination, yet sufficiently strong to deter Soviet expansion. Because many Europeans have been aware how formidable such a task must be, there have been many efforts on different levels to signal willingness to share some of the burdens in that region. The United States has not approved of most of those offers unless they demonstrated outright support for the policies of the Reagan administration.[19]

Instead of embracing European offers to deal with specific problems in El Salvador and Nicaragua, which might have given the Central American political forces an intra-Western option between the contending policies of both superpowers, the Reagan administration seemed almost annoyed with "European meddling."[20] All it was willing to concede was European engagement in economic and aid issues.[21]

The concern of many European political leaders goes beyond the immediate effects of the Central American crisis. They see the intra-Western lack of consensus on this "out-of-area" issue as a catalyst for wider-ranging policy differences in the Atlantic Alliance. Four basic questions seem to be involved, in which Atlantic Alliance cohesiveness is obviously lacking:

—a strategy for furthering Third World development;
—a strategy to cope with revolutionary change;
—an understanding of Soviet strategy in the Third World;
—an understanding of Western security interests in the Third World.

For many analysts the Central American crisis presents a unique opportunity to establish a wider consensus in the United States and Western Europe on these problems and to look for a division of labor with regard to the necessary management of such crises in the Third World.[22]

The differences among Western Europeans themselves as well as between them and the Reagan administration lie mainly in the choice of instruments and strategies to achieve common goals (preventing increased Soviet/Cuban influence, establishing democratic systems and furthering social justice and economic development) in Central America and in the establishment of priorities. The United States government—influenced by domestic political factors and its superpower position—seems to favor short-term solutions, whereas the Western Europeans tend to accept some short-term instability in the interest of reaching long-term stability in the region.

Western European Approaches to the Region

The Western European presence in the region is characterized by a multiplicity and diversity of actors and levels of interaction. But most actors are quite limited in their effectiveness because their actions are circumscribed by other Western European actors—at times of different ideological convictions—and by outside influence, especially that of the United States.

Such multiplicity has led to a great deal of speculation and publicity, especially with regard to the party relations between both regions and the role of the Socialist International (SI).[23] But such party activity has only been one expression of the increasing transnationalization of the interregional relationship. The growth of such relations on the substate level has been at least in part a Western European response to Third World instability.

Most Third World societies are, by definition, societies in change; as the old order in these countries crumbles, dealing with their political representatives becomes increasingly difficult. This is especially true in Central America. Maintaining relations only with the ruling forces in these countries has proved inadequate, since such action excludes contacts with the forces that may not only be more responsive to the needs of the majority of the population but also are very likely to be the governments of tomorrow. As a result of the deficiencies in the pattern of bilateral relations and in response to the needs of various political and pressure groups in Central American countries, West European nonstate, transnational activities have dramatically increased during the past decade.

Churches and trade unions have been in the forefront of such activities, but political parties and some professional groups have followed their lead—in contrast to the United States tradition of relying mainly on local businessmen and/or military officers. The Christian and Social Democratic parties of West Germany—largely because of the expertise and efficiency of their respective political foundations (Konrad Adenauer Stiftung and Friedrich Ebert Stiftung)—have become the most active Western European groups in Central America aside from church groups. This has been supplemented lately by the close cooperation of other Western European political leaders in the Christian Democratic World Union and the SI. During the late 1970s, both organizations used their long-term relationships with a number of Latin American parties to advance democracy in the region, building upon their experience during the democratization process in Portugal, Spain, and Greece.

This transnational approach has been used especially by West Germany: this can be partly explained by the strength of the German Social and Christian Democratic parties within their respective international groupings, and partly by the very clear unwillingness of all German governments—given their special relationship with the United States—to escalate the policy differences with the Reagan administration to the official bilateral level.

Nevertheless, these transnational activities have met with a great deal of criticism not only from the United States[24] but also from the Latin American side.[25] Needless to say, the ruling elites in many countries find such relations between their opposition forces and leading European parties "subversive." The principal aim of such policies has been to facilitate international legitimization for opposition groups and to stabilize postrevolutionary regimes. This has been seen by many critics of the Western European transnational involvement as opening the way for revolutionary activities and increasing the internationalization of the conflict, thereby reducing the leverage of the United States.[26]

In contrast to the German approach of focusing upon transnational relations with Central America, France has stressed the national approach and opted for direct bilateral diplomatic initiatives, which have often clashed openly with United States policy toward the region. It has certainly been the most active of the Western European nations in Central America, followed by Spain and West Germany, with Italy, Holland, and Sweden trailing. The Mitterand government has openly advocated that the East-West conflict must be won in the south.[27] France used its search for important allies in the Third World for a lineup with

Mexico on almost all questions of the Central American crisis beginning with their joint declaration in favor of the FDR in El Salvador. France's very friendly relations with Cuba and Nicaragua and its willingness to extend to the Sandinistas not only economic but also military aid has led to a certain credibility of a "second option" in the West for the more radical forces in the region. But it has also strained United States–France relations to the point that the Mitterand government has recently found it suitable to lower its criticism of United States policy and its diplomatic activity in Central America.

Of all Western European actors Spain has probably the largest role to play.[28] But it has so far not acted out its positions very forcefully, trying instead the multilateral approach by looking for concerted efforts to contribute to the reduction of tensions in the region. Felipe Gonzales is, of all the European leaders, by far the most knowledgeable about Central America and the most experienced in dealing with all sides of the conflict, largely because of his previous position as one of the SI leaders. He has given all his weight to strengthen the work of the Contadora Group,[29] and he has even called for a conference on cooperation and security in Central America as a first step to stabilize relations between countries of different ideological orientations in the region.[30] As soon as Spain becomes a member of the European Community it will certainly contribute to an even more active role of the Western European countries in Central America.

In addition to the transnational and national actors from Western Europe, the European Community—the European Commission as well as the European Parliament—has played a very active and independent role in Central America.[31] Its activities have not always gained the approval of the United States government, however. In 1981 the United States even tried to stop the provision of $1.5 million in relief aid for refugees in El Salvador, fearing that aid might end up supporting the guerrillas.[32]

Since 1982, an effort has been made to lay the foundations of a common global policy of the EC vis-à-vis the countries of Central America. After many controversial discussions about the scope and content of such a program, an ASEAN (Association of Southeast Asian Nations) type of agreement has been devised for signing in September 1984. West Germany has suggested such a concept of interregional cooperation to facilitate stronger ties between Central America and Western Europe in the fields of trade and aid, and also to promote regular political consultations. The subregional agreement would be nonexclusionary and, one hopes, will not only foster intraregional relations in Central America but also contribute to a lessening of dependence on the United States and of Nicaragua's propensity to look for stronger ties with the Soviet bloc. In many respects this intensive focus upon the crisis region by the European Community signals its readiness to offer a "second Western option" for Central American development, which might reflect the pluralism of approaches Central America has been accustomed to from Western Europe.

THE FUTURE WESTERN EUROPEAN ROLE IN CENTRAL AMERICA

The crucial question about the Western European role in the region seems to be: Would a European option offer sufficient incentives to be acceptable to a large coalition of regional interests, and, most importantly, would Western Europe be strong enough to pursue such a "new order" internally and regionally in Central America?

The first limitation is obviously security-related. Inasmuch as the Central American crisis is seen mainly in a security context—as by the Kissinger Commission—there seems to be no room for a Western European role.[33] It is therefore no sheer coincidence that practically all European actors stress the socioeconomic and political dimensions of the Central American crisis. For them, the economic and social stabilization of the region is the foremost necessity. Discussion about the internal and external legitimization of the different regimes is very important but can come later.

If a European option were to be constructed for the Central American region it would possibly consist of the following set of objectives:

—Internal—The regimes should be characterized by political pluralism, a mixed economy, and adherence to the principles of nonalignment.

—Regional—A regional international subsystem should be nonexclusionary, accepting ideological pluralism among its members and agreements on a nonaggression and nonintervention pact as well as on mutual arms reduction procedures.

—International—An aid consortium should be formed to avoid economic disaster (consisting of the United States, Canada, Western Europe, and the Latin American regional powers); an agreement on the closing of foreign bases and a limitation on the quantity of military advisors should be reached, and the establishment of a peace zone contemplated to avoid security threats and foreign interventions.[34]

Many of these proposals seem to have a ring of familiarity since they echo in large part the various proposals of the Contadora Group. The similarity of views reflects the moderating position of regional powers on both sides of the Atlantic who have come to prefer negotiations to confrontations since they do not command the instruments of power. A European role will therefore have no chance of being implemented as long as regional power cooperation is not forthcoming. Such cooperation is also preferable to superpower hegemony to Central Americans themselves, if only because it offers a degree of choice and maneuverability for regional actors. Nevertheless, even a strong cooperation between the regional powers of the Contadora Group and Western European states cannot replace United States influence in Central America, partly because they do not speak with one voice and partly because even their combined resources could not rival the United States possibilities once it should make up its mind to make a concerted effort—as suggested by the Kissinger Commission—to pour its resources into Central America. But a Western European role could widen the political options and give the regional states a possibility of diversification that allows them to avoid the unpleasant choice between United States or Soviet dependency—which seems to be characteristic for the entire region up to now.

It cannot, therefore, be the role of Western Europe to act as a broker or mediator between United States security interests and demands for independence by Socialist revolutionary movements in Central America. Its only role can be to contribute to internal and regional conflict reduction by offering a partial partnership, which is less threatening, but also less complete, than any superpower connection. For some—but by no means all—Central American political actors that might be a welcome role indeed.

NOTES

1. *Report of the National Bipartisan Commission on Central America* (Washington: GPO, January 1984), p. 124.

2. For earlier treatments of this question see Wolf Grabendorff, "Western European Perceptions of the Turmoil in Central America," in *Central America: The International Dimensions of the Crisis*, Richard E. Feinberg, ed. (New York: Holmes and Meier, 1982), pp. 201–212; and Wolf Grabendorff, "The Role of Western Europe in the Caribbean Basin," in *Confrontation in the Caribbean Basin*, Alan Adelman and Reid Reading, eds. (Pittsburgh: University of Pittsburgh, Center for Latin American Studies, 1984), pp. 275–293; and Heinrich Krumwiede, "Centroamérica vista desde Europa Occidental," in *Centroamérica más allá de la crisis*, Donals Castillo Rivas, ed. (Mexico: Ediciones SIAP, 1983), pp. 407–423.

3. "It is not the safety of shipping lanes, or the prospects of a flood of refugees to this country, or the danger held out to the stability of Mexico that is ultimately at stake in Central America; it is the credibility of United States power," writes Robert W. Tucker, "Their Wars, Our Choices," the *New Republic* (October 24, 1983), p. 26.

4. See Rolf Linkohr, "Perspektiven parteipolitischer Beziehungen zwischen EG und Lateinamerika," discussion draft presented at the conference on EEC–Latin American relations of the Friedrich-Ebert-Foundation, Bonn, September 22, 1983.

5. See the commentary by Theo Sommer, "Macht und Moral: Reagan und Mittelamerika," *Die Zeit* (May 4, 1984).

6. Addressing the Eleventh German-American Conference in Princeton on March 21, 1981, the deputy chairman of the German Social Democratic Party, Horst Ehmke, drew attention to that fact: "We have for such a long time helped to defend outmoded structures that we should not be surprised that the revolutionary movements seek help wherever they are able to get it—and that the Soviet Union and Cuba are taking advantage of that situation." [Author's translation]

7. *The Department of State Special Report*, no. 80 (February 23, 1981), "Communist Interference in El Salvador," mentions "another case of indirect armed aggression against a small Third World country by Communist powers acting through Cuba" and

"the gravity of actions of Cuba, the Soviet Union, and other Communist states who are carrying out what is clearly shown to be a well-coordinated, covert effort to bring about the overthrow of El Salvador's established government and impose in its place a Communist regime with no popular support," p. 1.

8. President Reagan himself has been very outspoken about it. "The Sandinista rule is a communist reign of terror," and "What the Sandinistas have done to Nicaragua is a tragedy. But we Americans must understand and come to grips with the fact that the Sandinistas are not content to brutalize their own land. They seek to export their terror to every other country in the region." *Department of State Current Policy*, no. 576 (May 9, 1984), "U.S. Interests in Central America," S. 2.

9. This policy has been in effect since November 16, 1981, when U.S. actions in Central America were approved by President Reagan following a National Security Council discussion. For details see "Ultimate Goal of U.S. Policy in Central America Still Unresolved," *Washington Post* (April 29, 1984), p. A15.

10. This has become especially apparent in the German case, when the Christian Democratic leader Kohl took over from the Social Democrat Schmidt. See "West Germany: Hardening the Line," *Latin America Weekly Report* (March 31, 1983), p. 7; and "Opposition: Wende in Bonns Mittelamerikapolitik," *Süddeutsche Zeitung* (January 28–29, 1984).

11. See the excellent critique by William M. LeoGrande, "Through the Looking Glass: The Kissinger Report on Central America," *World Policy Journal*, vol. 1, no. 2 (Winter 1984), pp. 251–284.

12. "In assessing the development of revolutionary Nicaragua one must not forget that the Sandinista regime has faced an external threat to its very existence," observes Heinrich-W. Krumwiede in "Revolution in Central America: A Western European Approach." Draft of a policy proposal prepared for the conference Europa ante la crisis centroamericana, Santander, Spain, July 1984, p. 11.

13. "Every effort has been made to downgrade the proposals of the Contadora Group and strip them of their content—by obstructing their sponsors, by holding up the measures advocated and by cutting the project off from any form of international solidarity or commitment," criticizes the deputy chairman of the Foreign Affairs Committee of the Spanish Chamber of Deputies, Miguel Angel Martinez. See U.S. position in his paper for the Bilderberg meetings, "The Soviet Union, the West and the Third World: A Case Study: Central America," Saltjöbaden, Sweden (May 11–13, 1984).

14. "The attitude of Western industrialized states toward Nicaragua, El Salvador, and Guatemala is an important indicator of the extent to which these industrialized states are willing and capable, either individually or collectively, to seek constructive political solutions for those Third World countries in which, as the result of oligarchic and repressive as well as antireformist and antidemocratic regimes, the political center has been weakened and the social-revolutionary movements have gained mass support." See the introduction to *Political Change in Central America: Internal and External Dimensions*, Wolf Grabendorff, Heinrich-W. Krumwiede, and Jörg Todt, eds. (Boulder, Colorado: Westview, 1984), p. 5.

15. "Needing to collaborate with the Reagan Administration on other, more pressing foreign policy concerns and being ultimately dependent on the American security umbrella, many European parties and governments wish to avoid overly sharp criticisms of

the United States." See Eusebio Mujal-León, "Europe and the Crisis in Central America," in *Report of the National Bipartisan Commission on Central America: Appendix* (Washington: GPO, March 1984), p. 704.

16. "In failing to concede political and economic space for non-alignment, the United States, far from guaranteeing its security, jeopardises it." See *The Hague Declaration: An Alternative Policy for Central America and the Caribbean* (The Hague: Institute of Social Studies, June 1963), p. 7.

17. Specific problems arose from the U.S. decision to mine the Nicaraguan harbors. See "After Initial Anger, W. Europe Eases Up on U.S. in Mining Case," *Washington Post* (April 15, 1984).

18. "It is perhaps unfortunate that such a shift in American policy has occurred at a time when violence and political polarisation in Central America have eroded the forces of the political centre to the point where governments of the extreme left may appear to provide the only alternative to governments of the extreme right." See House of Commons, Fifth Report from the Foreign Affairs Committee, *Caribbean and Central America* (London: HMSO, October 1982), p. XV. "It is clear that the American discovery of the importance of human rights, land reform and democratic elections in Central America follows directly from the success of the Sandinista revolution in Nicaragua." See Stuart Holland and Donald Anderson, *Kissinger's Kingdom?* (Nottingham: Spokesman, 1984), p. 14.

19. Pierre Schori, the former international secretary of the Swedish Social Democratic Party, writes: "We find it curious and unfortunate that instead of querying and counteracting the involvement of European social democracy the U.S. does not make positive use of it. Our purposes are not extremist or even extreme. We believe, like Mexico for example, that it is unrealistic to try to exclude from a solution armed resistance against the regime." See "Central American Dilemma," *Socialist Affairs* (no. 1, 1981), p. 37. But note also "European Christian Democratic parties have been generally more supportive of American policy in Central America," Eusebio Mujal-León, "Europe and Crisis," p. 702.

20. "Although West European involvement can contribute to the region's economic and political development, this general push-pull process is fostering the internationalization of local conflicts and eroding U.S. leverage," writes David Ronfeldt, *Geopolitics, Security and U.S. Strategy in the Caribbean Basin* (Santa Barbara, California: RAND, 1983), p. 30.

21. "We should seek their political and diplomatic support where this is possible, and their restraint where it is not. . . . And we should encourage their economic involvement in the region. . . ." See *Report of the National Bipartisan Commission on Central America*, p. 124.

22. "Central America presents an ideal opportunity to realize the strategy of reconciliation between Western industrialized nations and the social-revolutionary regimes and mass movements of the Third World." See Heinrich-W. Krumwiede, "Revolution in Central America: A Western European Approach," p. 8.

23. For a detailed treatment see the excellent study by Eusebio Mujal-León, "European Socialism and the Crisis in Central America," in *Rift and Revolution: The Central American Imbroglio*, Howard J. Wiarda, ed. (Washington, D.C.: AEI, 1984), pp. 253–302.

24. See Constantin Menges, "Central America and Its Enemies," *Commentary* 72, no. 2 (August 1981), pp. 32–38.

25. For such a critique of the SI from the Right, see Carlos Alberto Montaner, "The Mediation of the Socialist International: Inconsistency, Prejudice and Ignorance," *Caribbean Review* 11, no. 2 (Spring 1982), pp. 42–45, 57.

26. See David Ronfeldt, *Geopolitics*.

27. See Jean-Pierre Cot, "Winning East-West in North-South," *Foreign Policy* 46 (Spring 1982), pp. 3–18.

28. Such a role seems to be even envisioned by the U.S. "Moreover, if negotiations between various groups are begun, some European governments (perhaps the Spanish) might be used either as mediators or as participants in a possible multinational peacekeeping force." See Eusebio Mujal-León, "Europe and the Crisis in Central America," p. 705. "Would there be any value in our sharing leadership with any West European states—e.g., Spain—in creating and managing a political and economic framework for Central America? Would either side be willing to do so?" See Robert E. Hunter, "Long-Range Diplomatic and Political Options Factors External to Central America," in *Report of the National Bipartisan Commission on Central America: Appendix*, p. 294.

29. See *El País* (May 26, 1984).

30. See "Full of Good Intentions," *Latin America Weekly Report* (October 22, 1982).

31. "These surprisingly enterprising policies of the European Community can be partially accounted for by Germany's preference for multilateral rather than bilateral initiatives. But one should also take into account the fact that the European Commission and the European Parliament must distance themselves from American policy if they are to generate recognizable policies of their own." See Erik Jan Hertogs, "Western European Responses to Revolutionary Developments in the Caribbean Basin Region," in *Towards an Alternative for Central America and the Caribbean*, George Irvin and Xabier Gorostiaga, eds. (The Hague: Institute of Social Studies, 1984), p. 84.

32. See "EEC Assures U.S. of Delay in El Salvador Relief Aid," *International Herald Tribune* (February 19, 1981).

33. "To date, other Western powers have left much of the responsibility for the region's security to the United States." See *Western Interests and U.S. Policy Options in the Caribbean Basin* (Washington, D.C.: The Atlantic Council of the United States, October 1983), p. 19.

34. See my own similar assessment about a Western European option for the Caribbean Basin, Wolf Grabendorff, "The Role of Western Europe in the Caribbean Basin," p. 288.

Chapter 14

CENTRAL AMERICA'S IMPACT ON THE INTERNATIONAL SECURITY ORDER

Michael Harrison

ONE THING SOMEONE who knows very little about Central America has learned at this conference is that the American elite opinion is very divided and confused by the Central American crisis. I think West Europeans are also divided and confused, and perhaps even more frustrated than Americans as they try to assess the significance of the Central American crisis for themselves and for the Atlantic relationship. This is frustrating for Europeans because, unlike the case of the United States, there is no clear European interest in the region, but they know that their future relationship with the United States and the Atlantic Alliance is likely to be affected by what happens there and by United States policy and behavior. So Europeans tend to look at the crisis through the prism of American perceptions, reactions, and policies, and it is the way the crisis affects United States behavior in the world, and by implication the Alliance, that is of real importance to the Europeans.

It strikes me that if you look over the past, present, and likely future of European perceptions and reactions, three different perspectives emerge. They are all represented on the panel. One I would label essentially a perspective of the past, namely, the tendency for Europeans to focus on the internal and local Central American dimension of the crisis. This is represented by Wolf Grabendorff's analysis, and obviously it is still of some significance, though I believe it is of waning importance as far as Europeans and the Atlantic Alliance are concerned. The second perspective is currently dominant, and Michel Tatu has discussed it thoroughly in his paper. This is the tendency to assess the situation as a test of American foreign policy and United States crisis-management capabilities. The third and, in the future, most important implication of Central America for the Europeans is its possible political and geostrategic effect on American security commitments and especially on the Atlantic Alliance.

The internal dimension of the Central American crisis has already been discussed at length. The Europeans have tended to focus on this dimension and, until recently, have attempted to influence what went on in Central America and present themselves as interlocutors, or moderating influences with an ability to

affect what happens in the area through their multilateral ties. European Socialist and Christian Democratic parties have tried, and to some extent still try, to
influence the outcome of political processes in countries like El Salvador and
Nicaragua. This was best exemplified by the French (and Spanish) attempts to
play a broker role and posit themselves as a kind of external third force alternative to dependence on either one of the superpowers. This is a very traditional
French approach in the Third World, one that sometimes works and sometimes
doesn't—it hasn't, in this case. I think Wolf Grabendorff has a romantic view of
what the Europeans can accomplish in this domain, and it seems that the
relevance of this approach has waned considerably. This is mainly because the
global, bipolar, superpower dimension of the crisis now takes precedence for
everyone except the unfortunate victims trapped in Central America itself. The
now obvious alignment of Nicaragua with the Soviet Union and Cuba has led
most European leaders to recognize that the crisis in the region can no longer be
contained and insulated from superpower involvement, so that the struggles of
indigenous political forces have instead become hostage to great power conflicts.

More generally, as Michel Tatu points out in his paper, there has been a
European disillusionment with Third World revolutionary processes and even
with the likelihood of successfully managing social change, whether from the
center or the left. There is now a more pragmatic perspective that amounts to a
disenchantment with the Third World and a skepticism about anyone's ability to
handle these problems, either the Europeans or the supposedly less adept
Americans. I don't think even French leaders adhere to their old socialist ideals
in this domain, although the rhetoric is still around because it has a domestic
audience and there is a perceived need to keep alive the notion that France is
still a friend of progressive forces around the world. But it seldom amounts to
more than rhetoric.

If Central America is no longer a very significant test of European political
doctrines and formulas of how to manage social change and interpose oneself
between the superpowers, it has increasingly become a test of United States
crisis-management capabilities. This has clear implications for the Alliance,
since one aspect of the test is to determine whether the United States is a steady
and reliable partner.

For the Reagan administration, the standard apparently should be its ability
to achieve a victory by imposing new domestic and foreign policy priorities on
the Sandinista regime while ensuring the survival of moderate leadership in El
Salvador. For the West Europeans, on the other hand, United States efforts will
be judged mostly by a willingness to pursue a peaceful negotiated settlement
with Nicaragua along the lines of the Contadora proposals.

Although the outcome is uncertain, Central America is probably a test
United States policymakers cannot pass to the satisfaction of Atlantic allies. A
moderate course of compromise may be insufficient to subdue antagonisms in

the region, so that it may not succeed and would even leave Washington open to charges of failing to stem the expansion of Soviet and Cuban-sponsored regimes in its own backyard. Europeans would surely be dismayed at such a demonstration of American inability to protect and foster vital security interests abroad. On the other hand, Western Europe's rampant antimilitarism would force politicians publicly to condemn a decisive armed move against leftist regimes and guerrillas in Central America, even though in private most would be relieved to end this diversion of Washington's energies from more important zones of conflict outside the Western Hemisphere.

There is a sort of standard European hypocrisy arguing that the United States really shouldn't take any military actions, and when it does, even with justification and success as in the case of Grenada, it is condemned because the Europeans have turned into a kind of civilian power that cannot easily contemplate the exercise of force themselves, and they don't want the United States to do it either. This is a situation where the United States is damned if it does and damned if it doesn't and there is really no easy way out of it. Perhaps one just has to ignore the Europeans on this issue, although there is certainly no easy case to be made that militarism is a better guideline for United States policy than Europe's hapless pacifist tendency.

The third and most profound dimension of the Central American crisis for the Europeans and the Atlantic Alliance is its expanding international dimension as it is transformed into a global political and geostrategic problem with ramifications for the worldwide interests of the superpowers and all their allies. Like Afghanistan and Poland for the Soviet Union, like Vietnam in the 1960s and early 1970s for the United States, Central America is a relatively minor issue in its own right, but it is of great importance because it may affect the broader international security order.

For Europeans, there are two dimensions to this problem. One is that the crisis intensifies the bipolar struggle between the United States and the USSR, reducing West European room for maneuver and increasing the prospect for an outbreak of actual conflict somewhere that may have ramifications in Europe itself. Already worried about the revived Cold War between the superpowers and an apparent breakdown of any dialogue until after the United States elections, Europeans naturally fear that tensions emanating from Central America will only reinforce the hostile environment in Europe and elsewhere, increasing the general risks of an actual confrontation. The potential danger will depend on how far the Soviet Union will be willing to assist an incipient Marxist-Leninist regime in Nicaragua and risk further antagonizing the United States in an area as important to it as Poland is to the Soviets.

Afraid of heightened tensions, Europe's Central American headache becomes a potential nightmare as allies begin to contemplate the long-term implications of the crisis for United States–Atlantic security commitments. Europeans have for some time speculated about a shift in American attention from the Atlantic to the Pacific and the Southern Hemisphere. Changing American trade patterns, the new ethnic makeup of the United States, and the strong possibility that today's conflict to the south is only a precursor of a series of conflagrations that may even engulf Mexico all point to a diversion of United States attention and resources away from Europe and the Atlantic Alliance to contiguous regions of more pressing national concern. In this sense, the current Central American problem represents a possible turning point for the Alliance and United States commitments, marking the first stage in a profound reorientation of United States international security responsibilities and presenting the Europeans with an intense dilemma of how to cope with the slow, fragmentary, but increasingly visible United States disengagement from its Atlantic commitments. This prospect is disturbing in its own right, but it is even more alarming that no one on either side of the Atlantic appears capable of understanding, much less managing, the problems such a dramatic development would pose for the entire postwar international security system.

Chapter 15

RAPPORTEUR'S REPORT

Michael Clark

ROBERT O'NEILL INTRODUCED the panel with the suggestion that this discussion be focused on two central concerns. First, O'Neill recommended, the
basis of European concerns about United States policy in Central America ought
to be considered. This issue, he noted, feeds in two directions: Europeans are
concerned that a United States failure in Central America might produce negative repercussions within the Western Alliance and could perhaps further aggravate the East-West situation; Americans, on the other hand, are concerned that
the Europeans don't know anything about the Central American situation, and
are uninclined to take any constructive action. A second concern would be to
consider what the Europeans can or should do in Central America.

Michel Tatu argued that security concerns have to be considered from an
"egoistic" point of view. Leaders of one nation cannot easily shift perspectives;
and Europeans simply do not see Central America in the same way as do
Americans. Nevertheless, Europeans do see Central America as a test for
United States policy. For some, it represents a test of the United States' ability
to handle relations with Third World countries in an area close to the United
States. It is also a test of the United States' ability to manage a very complicated
problem requiring the development of a statecraft designed both to promote
long-term political, economic, and social justice, and to protect national security. At the same time, Central America is seen as a test of the decision-
making process in the United States, and in the longer term, of the capacity of
the United States to conduct military operations—whether covert or overt—at
all. After the recent events in Beirut, Tatu noted, questions have emerged in
some European circles about whether the United States can conduct military
operations on the ground. It is interesting to compare this situation with the
French involvement in Chad, which, despite criticisms by the opposition parties, carries none of the domestic opposition that United States policy must
overcome in Central America.

It is perhaps also true that Central America represents a moral test for United
States policy. Europeans have gotten used to receiving morality lessons from
Americans with regard to foreign policy, and now Central America seems to
provide an opportunity to turn the tables. Nevertheless, European intervention,
even covert intervention in 1974–1975, has a long and continuing history.

France intervened covertly to topple Jean-Bedel Bokassa in the French empire, and the European Socialist parties intervened, not with arms but with large financial resources, to bring about a change not merely in Portugal's ruling party but in its political system. Tatu took issue with those who argue that Europeans see Central America as the United States' backyard simply because the United States says it is. While Europeans are used to living with hostile regimes in their own backyard, or, in the case of Germany, in their own territory, the United States is not. Were the United States to become preoccupied with an East-West problem at its own doorstep, Europeans would have to reevaluate their views not only of the importance of Central America but of the viability of the Atlantic Alliance and of the role of the United States in it. Europeans are thus not disinterested in Central America. And while a successful United States intervention in Central America would doubtless provoke an immediate outcry, the long-term European reaction is likely to be far more supportive.

In sum, Tatu noted, Europeans cannot be expected to be enthusiastic about American policy in the region, especially since there is nothing much to be enthusiastic about anyway. On the other hand, no European government has presented real obstacles to United States policy, not even the French Socialist government of François Mitterand. Finally, Tatu observed, the European response to United States actions in Central America and the Caribbean has not been nearly so strong as it would have been just a few years ago. In large part, this is due to the sharply diminished appeal of Third World revolutionary movements in the wake of events in Vietnam, Kampuchea, and elsewhere.

Wolf Grabendorff voiced no objections to Tatu's general picture of European reactions to United States policy, but proposed instead to examine the underlying issues from the perspective of at least one rather significant European point of view. Placing Central America first in the context of the overall Alliance relationship, Grabendorff noted that there are several other issues which are, and should be, more important to the Alliance. But even if Central America is placed in broader strategic perspective, as the Reagan administration recommends, it does not follow that Central America is a test case merely of the ability of the West to draw a line against Communist aggression in the United States backyard. Instead, he urged, it is more of a test of the ability of the Alliance to face up to social revolutionary movements in the Third World. Drawing upon the lessons of past failures, the Alliance must learn to cope with the continuous and expected instability of the developing nations.

All democratic groups in Europe share a basic commitment to prevent Soviet-bloc adhesion to Third World countries. Division arises then, not with respect to goals, but with respect to an appropriate strategy for achieving those goals. Perhaps because of disagreements over how development should look, or because of differing perceptions of Third World challenges to Western security, or because there is no shared view of Soviet strategy in the developing world, no common allied strategy has emerged. Nevertheless, Grabendorff argued, it is natural, necessary, and should be seen as helpful that there are divisions within the Alliance. The variety of strategies adopted by the European states offer pluralistic opportunities to emerging revolutionary governments, and provide an intra-Western option to Third World countries who claim that the historical character of their relations with the United States and geographic proximity make it impossible to come to grips with United States interests.

France has adopted a "national approach" typified by its joint French-Mexican initiative and by its weapons deliveries to Nicaragua. Germany, on the other hand, has adopted a transnational approach emphasizing party contacts, which in some cases date back as far as eighteen and twenty years. And Spain has advocated still another "multinational" approach—Contadora would today be moribund if not for Spain's timely and decisive support. Together, these efforts hold out the possibility of an emerging triangular relationship between the United States, Latin America, and Europe in which the Europeans might be able to perform certain functions that the United States cannot because of its need to send signals to the other superpower.

Grabendorff closed by noting that he could recall no instance in which the application of military pressure had brought about the reconstitution and moderation of a revolutionary regime. That strategy ignores what revolutionaries are all about. They are not pragmatists who calculate, in the style of Americans, costs and benefits. Rather, they see the option of conceding to force as presenting a marvelous choice between political suicide and being shot.

Michael Harrison observed that Europeans' views of Central America have evolved considerably and are likely to continue to change. In the past, Europeans have focused on the local dimensions of a crisis and attempted to present themselves as interlocutors, or moderating influences, with an ability to affect what happens through multilateral—party, trade union, and other—ties.

In the present, by contrast, the superpower dimension of the crisis takes precedence for both Americans and Europeans. Central America is no longer a simple test of political doctrine and ideological formulas; rather, it is seen as a test of United States crisis-management capabilities as well as a test of whether the United States is a steady and reliable partner.

In the future, Europeans are most likely to be concerned about the expanding geopolitical significance of the Central American crisis. Much as Afghanistan and Poland recently, or Vietnam in the 1960s and early 1970s, represented relatively minor issues in their own right but became genuine international crises capable of affecting all aspects of international relations, Central America is emerging as the focus of considerable international attention and tension.

More importantly, the Central American crisis provides the first significant confirmation of escalating European fears that the United States is gradually turning away from the Atlantic and starting to focus on the East and South. Shifting American economic interests, combined with social, political, and security developments, encourage a growing preoccupation with problems in these regions and a diminishing attention and commitment to Europe and the Atlantic Alliance.

In the discussion that followed, considerable attention was devoted to the nature of allied obligations with respect to United States policy in Central America. Belize was raised as a special case of European involvement which has received surprisingly little attention; European claims of greater sympathy to Third World revolutionary movements were challenged; and the long-term shift in United States commitments and interests was further explored. Finally, the different roles that Europeans might play in Central America were reviewed.

ALLIED CONCERNS

Michael Palliser attempted to dismiss the notion that the Atlantic Alliance obliges Europeans and Americans to look at the problems of the world in the same way. What has kept the Alliance together, he suggested, has been a shared interest—in particular, a common interest in the defense of Europe and a common posture toward the Soviet Union—but also a recognition that there will be differences outside the Atlantic area and that these should not be allowed to upset the underlying relationship. If the Europeans, including the French, had allowed the Algerian crisis to become a really divisive element, the damage done to the overall relationship might have been severe, for Algeria posed a major problem for France. Thus it is important that the Alliance manage to avoid allowing issues like Central America, or like some of the Southern African problems, from becoming critical tests of loyalty.

Andrew Pierre agreed, but added that one cannot expect to isolate areas like Central America from debate. Perhaps it is true that if Americans wish for European cooperation in the Persian Gulf today, they must be prepared for European advice and comments with respect to Central America. In time it will become important for the United States and Europe to work more closely together on the "out of area" problem, Pierre noted, and it is already apparent that more transatlantic discussion is taking place with respect to Central America than was evident a year ago. Moreover, the moderate tone of the European participants in the conference is striking, and may reflect European fatigue after the debate on arms control, or European vulnerability in the Persian Gulf, or perhaps even a growing awareness of the complexity of the United States' problem in Central America. Even so, it will be difficult to avoid European criticism of United States policy in Central America. If the United States intervenes in Nicaragua, it will be open to sharp rebuke; on the other hand, if the situation is allowed to drag on without solution, then the credibility of the United States will be challenged by its failure to resolve a small problem in the American backyard.

Wolf Grabendorff agreed that whatever the United States does will be criticized in Europe, but added that the criticism will come from different groups in each case and that the Reagan administration can choose which group to please. Perhaps, in the absence of unanimity among the allies, Grabendorff suggested, it would be better to establish a minimum consensus permitting free and continuing discussion of the issues. *Michael Harrison* questioned the wisdom of adopting an approach based upon a minimum common denominator and allowing for a diversity of Allied responses. If such an approach were to prove efficacious, fine; but the more likely result would be that the European approaches would cancel one another out.

Joseph Cirincione doubted whether it is in the power of Alliance leaders to keep Central America from being an issue. Extensive polling of European public opinion by the United States Information Agency in 1983 indicated, surprisingly, that the United States policy with the highest negative saliency among European publics was the United States involvement in Central America. Concern over American policy in the Caribbean Basin scored higher than Pershing II and Cruise missile deployments, and even seemed to have shaped European views of the missiles.

Robert Leiken expanded on Michael Harrison's comments by noting that the American elite seems to be divided between Atlanticists, who support the postwar alignments in United States foreign policy, and "hemisphericists," who advocate a "fortress America." With a significant base in the sunbelt, the hemisphericist "cowboys" in the Reagan administration have a vested interest in the most dynamic sectors of United States trade, particularly in the Far East and in Central and South America. Echoing the concern of an Atlanticist in the Reagan administration, Leiken wondered if it was possible that Central America could prove such a distraction to American policy that the United States might lose interest in Europe. In reply, *Michael Harrison* observed that Europeans are concerned about the long-term shift in United States elite intentions. Last year, for instance, United States trade flows across the Pacific were greater than those across the Atlantic for the first time in United States history, but the most likely result would be the continuation of an ongoing process, never leading to complete rupture or isolationism, but the gradual fragmentation and diversion of United States interest. Europeans see that it is not Central America, but Mexico, that looms largest in the future crisis, and so expect American involvement to continue and perhaps deepen over time.

Finally, *Susan Kaufman Purcell* suggested that Reagan administration expectations of European support in Central America arose in part from hopes of reciprocity for United States support of Britain in the Falklands war. *Michael*

Palliser replied that the Falklands issue illustrates the problem of differing perceptions across the Atlantic. Most British did *not* see the Americans coming down firmly on the British side, even if this is the way that most Americans, North and South, did. A more important consideration, in any case, is the fact that Central America is not an Alliance issue. Even so, the fact that Europeans feel that Central America ought not be made into an Alliance issue doesn't mean the allies shouldn't get involved. One should not underestimate the importance that the United States attaches to European involvements in areas of common concern—not as an Alliance effort, but as a shared effort.

A GUARANTEE FOR BELIZE

Jonathan Alford raised the question of Belize. A genuine democracy, not Latin, but certainly in Central America, and without a real defense force of its own, Belize contained the largest external force in Central America until the United States began its massive buildup in Honduras. There is no doubt that Britain would like to get out of its very expensive commitment in Belize, but despite several attempts it has not proved possible to withdraw without exposing Belize to the vastly superior Guatemalan forces. In the 1970s, the United States was not sympathetic to the British position, but, given recent events, there may have been a change of heart, and a clarification of the United States position now seems in order. *Michael Palliser* added that the case of Belize illustrates a further aspect of European, and especially British, views of the Central America crisis—namely, that these views are shaped not only by participation in the European community and in NATO, but also by the Commonwealth, which includes several industrialized nations, Canada most notably, whose views of the Third World are quite different from those of the United States. With respect to the British commitment in Belize, *Susan Kaufman Purcell* expressed the view of the previous United States administration that Britain should remain. The United States doesn't need to take on any additional commitments, and the British presence is likely to provide greater stability.

A EUROPEAN ROLE IN CENTRAL AMERICA

Do Europeans enjoy special advantages in dealing with social upheaval in the developing world? If so, what are the limits of interallied cooperation in Central America? *Alan Berger* doubted that Europeans have, in fact, greater sympathy for revolutionary movements in the Third World. Where European interests are at stake or where there are gains to be made as in Chad, Central Africa, Iraq, and even Turkey and Argentina, the position adopted seems to be: "Lord, give me the strength to be chaste—but not just yet." In reply, *Wolf Grabendorff* argued that Europeans enjoy easier relations with Latin Americans because Europeans, unlike North Americans, are more familiar with the ideological spectrum—from far left to far right—of Latin American nations. Moreover, Europeans, who must deal with strong and threatening neighbors, have learned to be more flexible and pragmatic.

With respect to European involvements in Central America, *Michel Tatu* then observed that it is easier to identify what Europeans do not wish to see than it is to specify what they would wish for as an outcome. What Europeans clearly do not want is an intervention by the United States, Vietnamization of that conflict, or Sovietization of the revolutionary movements. Were the United States to intervene, it is certain that there would be strong criticism from Europe, but even then it is doubtful that this would provoke a major crisis. Still, Europeans feel that the only way they can exert an influence upon events in Central America is through indirect means, that is, by providing diplomatic support and economic aid. Yet, as the conflict is militarized, these avenues are closed, and, in the event of war, the most the Europeans can do as good allies is to stay out of the way.

Europeans might provide an ideological alternative to revolutionary governments in Central America, Tatu added, and in fact some European governments have experience in dealing with regimes that were initially hostile to them. When Algeria demonstrated that it intended to remain nonaligned, for instance, it created the conditions for rapprochement with France. In Central America, however, the French Socialist government was disappointed to discover that the hard core of the FMLN leadership—Social Democrats like Guillermo Ungo aside—was not only Marxist-Leninist, but of the very dogmatic type. This accounts for the French withdrawal from high-level involvement over the past two years. *Christopher Makins* suggested that multilateral European and United States support for Central American development, perhaps along the lines suggested by the report of the Kissinger Commission, had been too easily dispensed with as a realistic policy option. Such aid is often more effective than other, more politicized, forms of assistance. *Thomas Hughes* concluded by noting that nonofficial European involvements in Central America deserved greater attention. Long-term connections with Central American leaders enable European political parties, for example, to provide not only an alternative to policy, but also, at times, an effective complement. Salvadoran President Napoleón Duarte's recent and highly successful pre-inaugural visit to Washington, for instance, took place under the auspices of the West German (CDU) Konrad Adenauer Foundation.

Soviet Strategy and Central America

Chapter 16

THE USSR AND CENTRAL AMERICA: GREAT EXPECTATIONS DAMPENED?

Robert S. Leiken

THE 1979 SANDINISTA Revolution seemed to mark a dramatic departure in Soviet relations with Latin America. It received unprecedented attention in Soviet press and academic circles. Sergei Mikoyan, editor in chief of the Soviet journal *Latinskaya Amerika,* declared that the revolution was of "colossal international importance."[1] Unlike the Cuban revolution, the Nicaraguan generated a major revision of Moscow's political line for the region: "peaceful transition to socialism" gave way to support for armed struggle. While Moscow waited sixteen months to extend diplomatic recognition to Castro's Cuba, to Sandinista Nicaragua it did so the next day. Within a few weeks, five Soviet generals paid a secret visit to Nicaragua. By March 1980 the Soviet Communist party had signed a mutual support agreement with the Sandinista National Liberation Front (FSLN), a measure normally reserved for Communist parties in countries of "socialist orientation." Expectations abounded of a dramatic Soviet involvement in Central America.

Sandinista hopes and Reaganite fears were reinforced by Soviet-bloc involvement in the Salvador guerrillas' "final offensive" in January 1981. Moscow, Havana, and Managua kept up a steady triumphalist drumbeat. In Washington, within the incoming Reagan administration, there was panic; in Managua, hubris.

Yet after the failure of the final offensive, El Salvador seemed virtually to disappear from the Soviet press. Havana and, subsequently, Moscow began to urge Salvadoran and regional negotiations. Soviet propaganda and analysis switched from talk of a regional "revolutionary upsurge" to defense against American interventionism. Russia continued to supply arms, but for purposes of Sandinista consolidation and defense, not expansion. It provided neither MiG aircraft to compensate for Honduran air superiority nor desperately needed foreign exchange. Military and economic support for Nicaragua in 1982–1983 hardly compared with that for Cuba in 1961–1962 in a similar crisis. Kremlin reaction to the American hailing of Soviet ships last summer and to the mining of Nicaraguan ports this spring was notably restrained.

Why did Moscow fail to meet the expectations it had aroused?

STRATEGIC PARAMETERS

Moscow's overall strategic objective in Latin America is to convert the region from a "strategic reserve" of the United States into an area of instability and superpower contention. Soviet publicists have pointed out that American "freedom of action" depends on "stability in the Caribbean basin."[2] Instability and conflict in the Caribbean can at the very least, they believe, divert United States resources and attention from other areas of the world of higher priority to Moscow.[3]

However, Soviet activities in Latin America historically have been subject to severe constraints. Lenin is reported to have stated that Latin America would be the last area of the Third World to achieve liberation because it was in the sphere of influence of the rising American empire.[4] This geopolitical fatalism prevailed up to and well after the Cuban revolution. Cuban attempts to ignite revolutionary struggle in Latin America during the 1960s encountered stiff opposition from Moscow. It was only in the late 1970s, on the heels of a major Soviet buildup and a string of successes in the Third World, that Moscow began to extend material support to revolutionary movements in Central America. Yet Moscow is well aware that the geopolitical factors that historically have constrained Soviet efforts in Latin America have not all disappeared.

Precisely because of the United States' historical domination of Latin America, the region offers special opportunities for the Soviet Union. Repeated American interventions on behalf of corrupt, tyrannical regimes in Latin America have created a legacy of anti-Yankeeism. Revolutionaries in the so-called American backyard inevitably target United States hegemony and often tend to assume that the Soviet Union is their "natural ally." Nonetheless, even here, Moscow must tread with caution. Nationalist revolutionary movements like the Chinese and, for a time, the Cuban have tended to harbor suspicions of "the other superpower." The Nicaraguan and Salvadoran revolutions today represent, respectively, examples of these two tendencies—attraction and revulsion.[5] Efforts to convince revolutionaries that Moscow is their "natural ally" risk alienating major Latin American governments—like Argentina, Brazil, Colombia, Mexico, and Venezuela—which the USSR has been courting for two decades. Overt Soviet intervention can arouse against Moscow the very anti-hegemonist sentiment it seeks to direct against the United States. However, Moscow's recent strong ties with Cuba have enabled it to identify with revolutionary movements while evading the blame for their activities.

These factors form the parameters of the complex triangular relationship between the Soviet Union, the United States, and Latin America. American hegemonism has "protected" Latin America from Soviet influence. On the other hand, United States domination invites the identification of national liberation and independence movements with Moscow, thereby providing Moscow with easy opportunities in Latin America. Yet these opportunities are limited by geopolitical factors. Thus Moscow proceeds with extreme caution.

Tactical flexibility does not signify inattention to strategy. As Seweryn Bialer and Joan Afferica note, "While the general tendency of Soviet foreign policy makes it dynamic, assertive and ambitious in the long run, . . . its tactics in the short run oscillate between expansion and retrenchment."[6] Soviet tactics are subordinate to global and regional strategy. Soviet probes in Latin America in the late 1970s, merited concern not as an independent threat to United States security but as a component of the Kremlin's global strategy.[7] Moscow's abandonment of geopolitical fatalism toward Latin America resulted, as we shall see, from its view that the "global correlation of forces" had shifted in its favor. "But the correlation of forces is characterized by dynamism," as the chief of the Cuban Communist party's Department of the Americas recently stressed.[8] The correlation of forces can move in one's favor but can also be reversed. The shifting correlation of forces constitutes another basic parameter of Soviet strategy in Central America.

1975–1979: THE HEYDAY OF SOVIET EXPANSIONISM IN THE THIRD WORLD

1979, the year of the Nicaraguan Revolution, but also of the invasion of Afghanistan, was indeed a turning point in Soviet foreign policy—but in an unexpected direction. This year marked the beginning of the end (for the time being) of Moscow's Third World adventurism.

From 1965 through 1979 a major shift had occurred in the "global correlation of forces." The Soviet Union overtook the United States in most nuclear categories and eroded the technological advantages long enjoyed by NATO forces in Europe. Its dramatic naval buildup and air transport programs gave it, by the mid-1970s, the capacity to air- and sea-lift troops and equipment over great distances. The repudiation of United States intervention in the Third World enabled the Soviet Union to forge a more effective strategic "natural alliance" with many Third World national liberation movements.

Early in the Brezhnev period Moscow abandoned the Khrushchevian doctrine of "peaceful transition to socialism" in the "national liberation zone," which, by the 1970s, was extended to include Southern Africa. From 1975 to 1979 Moscow enjoyed a string of successes in the Third World. It won a preeminent position first in Vietnam and then, via its military assistance to Vietnam, through out Indochina. Cuba, highly dependent on the Soviet Union after 1968, became Moscow's cat's-paw and the model for pro-Soviet regimes in Africa. Soviet and Cuban military assistance swung Angola, Ethiopia, and (to a lesser degree) Mozambique toward Moscow. Soviet-backed coups failed in the

Sudan and North Yemen but succeeded in South Yemen. A pro-Soviet regime was installed in Afghanistan. Soviet tactics during this period of expansion into the Third World exhibited major innovations:

1. Moscow dropped its past insistence on vanguard Marxist-Leninist parties and acknowledged that "political-military fronts" modeled on the Cuban July 26 Movement could substitute for them.[9]

2. Whereas previously Soviet economic ties were considered the main factor for "noncapitalist" development, in the mid-1970s Moscow began to assert that "material aid on the part of the socialist states has ceased to be a factor directly promoting the transition to a noncapitalist path." The fundamental factor was now "the political, military-strategic and moral influence of the states of the socialist community."[10]

    The shift from economic to military factors reflected both the growing weakness of the Soviet economic system—its failure in Khrushchev's vaunted "peaceful competition" with the West—and growing Soviet military strength. Accordingly, Moscow recommended to countries like Angola and Ethiopia, and later Nicaragua, the preservation of commercial ties with the West, "multinational corporations" (such as Gulf Oil in Angola), and a mixed economy. While the Russians' economic weakness obligated them to resign themselves to Western dominance in the economic realm, they sought decisive influence in the military, security, and intelligence apparati where Soviet-bloc arms and advisers could be significant.

3. To pursue this policy Moscow enlisted the comparative advantages of its allies. Typically, the USSR and Czechoslovakia provided material military equipment; Cuba, troops and, along with the East Germans, military advisors; East Germany, assistance in internal security; Bulgaria, economic advisors; and so forth. Russian personnel generally stayed in the background.

4. New pro-Soviet Third World regimes were sometimes granted "friendship treaties" (as in Vietnam, South Yemen, Syria, Ethiopia, Angola, Mozambique, and the Congo) but never defense guarantees. As Seth Singleton notes, "flexible Soviet commitments are designed to allow action but to avoid forcing Soviet credibility into a corner over any place not essential to Soviet security."[11] The host country frequently furnished facilities or bases for Soviet naval and air forces (as in Vietnam, Kampuchea, Afghanistan, Angola, and Ethiopia) as well as sanctuaries for certain approved liberation movements (Libya for Chad; South Yemen for Oman; Angola for Namibia and South Africa; and Nicaragua for El Salvador).

5. Moscow frequently claimed that Soviet military might had become indispensable to Third World liberation and sovereignty.[12] Soviet gains in the Third World were explicitly regarded as a reflection of the "changed correlation of forces on a world scale." Karen Brutents, the leading Soviet Communist Party Central Committee specialist on the Third World, explained in 1977 that in the past Moscow's strategic posture had been

largely a matter of defense of the first socialist revolution against imperialism, whereas today it is a question of carrying on the offensive against imperialism and world capitalism as a whole in order to do away with them.[13]

It was easy to find a similar pattern in the Nicaraguan Revolution. In 1977, Havana, perceiving that the long struggle of the Nicaraguan people against the United States–backed Somoza tyranny was entering a new phase, activated support for the FSLN, presumably with Soviet approval. The traditional Moscow-backed Nicaraguan Socialist party formed an armed wing in 1978. The Cubans furnished contacts with international arms dealers and some weapons directly, often in concert with neighboring countries who joined the broad Latin American anti-Somoza coalition. In the summer of 1978 Havana mediated differences among the Sandinista factions, helping to achieve by March 1979 a reunification that gave hegemony to pro-Cuban elements. As the 1979 uprising approached, Havana increased direct arms deliveries, organized and armed an "internationalist brigade" to fight alongside the FSLN guerrillas, and dispatched military specialists to the field. During the spring of 1979, Cuban military advisers from the Department of Special Operations accompanied FSLN forces into battle while maintaining radio communications with Havana. These advisors, led by Julian López Diaz, a covert action expert who later became ambassador to Nicaragua, remained in the country after the Sandinistas took power. Within a week they were joined by several dozen additional Cuban military, security, and intelligence personnel. Key military advisory and intelligence positions were awarded to Cubans. That practice finally led Panama's nationalist General Torrijos to withdraw Panamanian advisors in 1980 and to offer "friendly warnings" against overreliance on Cuba.[14]

The Sandinista victory occasioned a general revision of Soviet tactics for Latin America.[15] Khrushchev's policy of "peaceful transition to socialism" had been pursued with singular dedication in Latin America. The line was not repudiated despite the crushing defeat of that policy in Chile in 1973. But in the wake of the Sandinista Revolution Soviet Latin American experts declared that "the armed road . . . is most promising in the specific conditions of most Latin American countries" and that "only the armed road has led to victory in Latin America."[16] Moscow now urged local Communist coordination or integration with organizations pursuing armed struggle, previously scorned as "petty bourgeois adventurist" and "ultra left." Ché Guevara, the *bête noire* of Moscow and local Communist parties of the 1960s, was rehabilitated along with his main tactical principles. Guevara's then "subjectivist" assertion that "it is not always necessary to wait until all the conditions are ripe for revolution, the *foco* can create them," was now lauded as "a fundamental contribution to Latin American revolutionary movements."[17]

Moscow wasted no time in recognizing the new Nicaraguan government and

in declaring its interest in "multifaceted ties."[18] In the first year of the Sandinista regime exchanges of visits between Soviet and Sandinista officials became commonplace. Four days after Nicaragua's refusal to condemn the Soviet
invasion of Afghanistan in a United Nations vote, five Soviet trade and planning
officials arrived in Managua to advise the regime on its 1980 economic plan and
to initiate bilateral trade.[19] In March 1980, high-level Sandinistas officials
visited Moscow and signed party-to-party and state-to-state accords. In January
1981, a scientific and cultural program based on the 1980 accord was announced. That announcement also revealed that "immediately" after the July
1979 victory, Soviet specialists in "hydropower engineering, agriculture, geol-
ogy, metallurgy, forestry, fisheries, education," and other fields had gone to
Nicaragua to draw up recommendations to assist in economic and social development planning. The announcement also indicated that "delegations of
Nicaraguan specialists" had visited the Soviet Union and that "large groups of
Nicaraguans are studying" in Nicaragua to serve as "future cadres."[20] By July
1980, the Sandinista regime had signed economic, scientific, and cultural
accords with East Germany, Bulgaria, and Czechoslovakia, as well as with
Cuba and the Soviet Union.

Thus, before President Reagan took office in January 1981, the familiar
Soviet-bloc division of labor in the Third World had begun to operate in Nicaragua. Though evidence is typically partisan and partial, former Sandinista leaders, defectors, diplomats in Managua, and official United States sources draw a
general picture. The Cubans provide doctors, teachers, construction workers,
military specialists, intelligence operatives, and advisors to the Sandinista party
and to various governmental ministries; the Soviets concentrate on state security
along with numerous Cubans, East Germans, and Bulgarians; the East Germans
also assist in intelligence and communications; the Bulgarians handle finance,
economic planning, and construction; and the Czechoslovakians provide some
military advisors.[21]

Soviet-Sandinista military relations also predated the Reagan administration.
As mentioned, five Soviet generals covertly visited Nicaragua in August of
1979. Defense Minister Humberto Ortega was among the four Sandinista
officials to visit Moscow in March 1980. Moscow equipped the Nicaraguan army
with boots, packs, and rifles during 1980. A portion of the Soviet-bloc military
shipments forwarded to the Salvadoran guerrillas equipped the Nicaraguan
armed forces.[22]

If the Soviet problem in Nicaragua was not created by the Reagan administration, the pro-Soviet inclinations of much of the Sandinista leadership must be
understood in the first instance as a reaction to Washington's repeated interventions and its creation and long backing of Somoza's National Guard. Fidel
Castro's defiance of the United States inspired young Nicaraguans. Many Sandinistas who fled Nicaragua in the 1960s lived in Cuba; some lived in the Soviet
Union.[23] Anti-Americanism and Fidelismo created a receptivity for Soviet-brand

Marxism nurtured in the universities by the pro-Soviet Nicaraguan Socialist party. A number of *comandantes* readily embraced Moscow's view that the shift in "the global correlation of forces" toward Moscow had prevented United States intervention.[24] Convinced that Moscow was their "natural ally," they harbored enormous expectations of Soviet economic and military support. Needed to assure such support, in this view, were concrete signs of fidelity.[25] Thus, in August 1979, the Sandinista delegation supported the Soviet-Cuban-Vietnamese position in the Nonaligned Meeting in Havana in August 1979. Later, in the face of overwhelming Third World condemnation in the United Nations of the invasion of Afghanistan, the Nicaraguan delegation abstained. Havana sought to broker the developing Nicaragua-Russian relationship, but Sandinista leaders (arguing that while Fidel had "preferences," Moscow was "decisive") soon began to compete among themselves (and with Havana) for Moscow's favor.

ANOTHER SHIFT IN THE CORRELATION OF FORCES

Soviet-bloc support for the "final offensive" in El Salvador and its early and "multifaceted" involvement in Nicaragua seemed to confirm the expectations of some Sandinista leaders and some members of the incoming Reagan administration that Moscow would make a major commitment in the region. However, the 1979–1980 period saw an accumulation of internal and external difficulties for the Soviet Union. These, along with adverse shifts in the regional situation (including the failure of the "final offensive" itself) would lead in 1981 to another shift in Soviet tactics in Central America.

Moscow's strategic offensive in the Third World unfolded in the "resistant medium" (Clausewitz) of Third World nationalism, Western alarm, and sharpening internal contradictions. "Everything is very simple in War, but the simplest thing is difficult. These difficulties accumulate and produce a friction."[26] It was just such "friction" that forced Moscow into a "holding pattern" even as Sandinista expectations mounted.[27]

By 1980 the guerrilla struggles against the occupations of Kampuchea and Afghanistan and in Eritrea, Tigre, the Ogaden, and Angola; the challenge of Solidarity; the economic difficulties of Cuba and Vietnam; political friction with Third World allies such as Ethiopia and Angola; the distancing of significant nonaligned countries like India, Iraq, and Algeria; NATO's resolve to deploy Pershing and Cruise missiles, and the American rejection of SALT II—all were darkening Moscow's international panorama. Moslems and other Arabs were alienated by the invasion of Afghanistan, the abandonment of Somalia, and the betrayal of Eritrean Moslems. The Shah fell, but Khomeni evolved toward "open anti-Sovietism."[28] Mugabe's Zimbabwe kept Moscow at a distance and frustrated its hopes of a Soviet-oriented southern African bloc. Increasing United States–

Chinese–NATO–Japanese contacts and cooperation and the Chinese call for "parallel actions against Soviet hegemonism" raised the spectre of a worldwide "antihegemonist united front."

Detente and the centrifugal force of European unity fueled discontent in Eastern Europe. Tensions among Soviet Asiatic national minorities were aggravated by the invasion of Afghanistan. Moscow's capacity to aid the mendicant Vietnamese and Cuban economies flagged as the Soviet economy faced severe problems of factor productivity, management, export competitiveness, financial dislocation, and a succession of poor harvests. The performance of Soviet weaponry in the Iran-Iraq war and in Syria's defense against the Israeli invasion of Lebanon led many to question the value of Soviet military aid and training. Soviet economic hardships reflected a general malaise also manifested in increasing alcoholism and racism, absenteeism, a succession crisis that would prove to be chronic, and low morale in the armed forces. Moscow would face difficulties in mobilizing its population for a prolonged strategic offensive.

An article in the important Soviet journal *Problems of Philosophy* in 1982 stated bluntly that the Soviet economy no longer was a source of inspiration for the Third World.[29] Recently liberated Third World countries and others like India, Iraq, and Algeria with long histories of economic relations with the Soviet Union now looked to the West for trade and aid. On many sides the putative "natural alliance" between Moscow and the Third World was fraying. Third World "united action" against United States imperialism was overcome by fierce factional, religious, and regional strife. Guerrilla insurgencies were now targeting Moscow's friends Ethiopia, Afghanistan, Kampuchea, Angola, and, eventually, Mozambique and Nicaragua. The Vietnamese and Cuban economies hardly inspired enthusiasm for "socialist orientation." Soviet economic relations with the Third World, put on a "commercial footing" by Khrushchev, were now routinely denounced as "typically Northern" in Third World fora.

In 1981 the military buildup and fierce anticommunism of the Reagan administration enforced discretion. "Clearly, the time had come to consolidate and defend gains while restoring a benign reputation." Entrenchment had become "imperative."[30]

The stridency of the Reagan administration facilitated a rapid shift to defensive tactics. Taking a cue from Stalin's United Front against Fascism, which targeted Nazi Germany as the main enemy, Moscow sought to organize a "United Front against [United States] Imperialism." Soviet propaganda focused on Reagan's belligerence as the main danger to the peace and Third World independence. Forgoing their recent emphasis on armed revolutionary struggle, the Soviets called for broad alliances—domestically against United States–supported regimes and internationally against United States "hegemonism." They sought to break up United States–NATO–China coordination by trying to mend fences with the Chinese and to woo the European peace movement.

In the 1980s Moscow has evaded new Third World commitments. It has sought to consolidate and defend "the gains of socialism" in Ethiopia, Angola, Mozambique, Syria, Vietnam, Kampuchea, Laos, Cuba, and Nicaragua but not new military facilities or clients. Soviet arms transfers to the Third World declined slowly after 1979 and sharply in 1983.[31] In integrating its closest Third World clients into an extended Soviet economic empire, Moscow has ceased urging the Third World to imitate Soviet-style rapid industrialization and advocates preservation of agrarian economies—à la Cuba—as part of a "socialist international division of labor" that resembles remarkably the traditional North-South system Moscow routinely denounces in other contexts.[32]

SOVIET RETRENCHMENT IN CENTRAL AMERICA[33]

In retrospect the failure of the Salvadoran "final offensive," in the context of a general shift to defensive tactics, appears to have occasioned a reassessment of Moscow's Central American policy during 1981. Soviet-bloc involvement in arms procurement for the offensive had been accompanied by an international propaganda campaign. The Soviet Communist party provided Salvadoran Communist Shafik Handal space in the November 1980 issue of its party organ *Kommunist*. *Pravda* greeted the final offensive with triumphant battlefield reports, adding that "it is to these forces that the future belongs."[34] Tass announced the establishment of "bodies of peoples' power . . . in the liberated towns and villages."[35]

After the defeat of the final offensive, optimism vanished from the Soviet-bloc media and a curtain descended on El Salvador. Secretary Brezhnev omitted El Salvador and Central America from his assessment of the world situation at the Twenty-sixth Congress of the Soviet Communist party. Concerned with Reagan administration threats, the Kremlin dispatched its deputy defense minister to Havana in a highly publicized February 1981 visit. This was followed by Moscow's largest shipment of arms to Cuba since 1962.

By early 1982 Moscow and Havana were anxious to appear as peacemakers in the Caribbean basin. The heady optimism of the 1979–1980 period, which once "marked the beginning of a qualitatively new stage in the development of a Latin American people's struggle," gave way to a more guarded view of revolutionary possibilities in Central America. Soviet analysis no longer referred to a regional upsurge but stressed the "ebb and flow" of specific national situations. Moscow pictured the revolutionary movements as now reacting defensively to a revanchist American foreign policy, characterized as a return to the "big-stick diplomacy" of the pre-Vietnam era. "The aggressive United States counteroffensive" in Central America was portrayed as one aspect of a resurgent United States "militarism" counterposed to the Soviet "peace offensive."[36]

Moscow remained on the sidelines in the Falklands/Malvinas conflict while it blasted American support for Great Britain as "neocolonial" and as another aspect of a global counteroffensive:

> The present masters of the White House apparently hope to . . . obtain political successes precisely under the conditions of conflicts, tensions, military clashes and confrontation. This is how they are acting in the Middle East and this is how they are trying to act in the South Atlantic.[37]

Soviet passivity in the Falklands/Malvinas crisis and its abandonment of the PLO appeared to cause consternation in Managua in the summer of 1982. This was reinforced by a secret letter from the Central Committee of the Soviet Communist party to the Sandinistas and to the Salvadoran FMLN suggesting Soviet limitations and focusing attention on the Soviet peace offensive.[38] Soviet advice to other revolutionaries in the region grew circumspect. In Honduras, "the main objective for progressive forces" became the frustration of plans to turn that country into "the stronghold of the crusade against democracy in Central America." For Costa Rica the principal task was to prevent that country from becoming a "bridgehead for attack on neighboring Nicaragua."[39]

Soviet-bloc arms transfers to El Salvador fell off sharply after the final offensive and never recovered their late 1980 level. The guerrillas procured an increasing portion of their arms from those purchased or captured from the Salvadoran armed forces. Nicaragua continued deliveries of ammunition, medicine, and occasionally arms. Salvadoran revolutionaries have voiced off-the-record concern at lack of Soviet support. This was apparently echoed by Shafik Handal's reference on Radio Moscow to the "great danger to the Salvadoran people" and his plea for "solidarity from the people of the world, and above all, from people in the USSR."[40]

With regard to Nicaragua, Moscow has adopted a policy of cautious but steady consolidation. Since 1981 the Soviet-bloc presence in Nicaragua has deepened, but it has undergone no qualitative change. For its part, Reagan policy has vindicated the expectations of the more dogmatic and pro-Soviet Sandinistas. Paradoxically, Soviet "penetration" of Nicaragua has been promoted more eagerly by the Sandinista National Directorate than by the Kremlin.

Soviet cautiousness and Sandinista eagerness were on display during Nicaraguan head of state Daniel Ortega's visit to Moscow in May 1982. Ortega offered "full support" for Soviet positions on the arms race, detente, the Soviet "unilateral" moratorium on the deployment of nuclear weapons in the European part of the USSR, and the aggressiveness of the United States.[41] Brezhnev responded with a speech emphasizing the "vast oceanic expanses" separating Nicaragua from the Soviet Union. Nonetheless, Brezhnev was careful to note that today "the peoples and countries of the world are drawn nearer not so much by geography as by politics," and to warn that in a general confrontation the Western Hemisphere would no longer, as in the past, be exempt from "the flames of war."[42] Between May 1982 and mid-1983 there were eight visits to

Moscow by five different *comandantes*, and Managua, pronouncing the death of Yuri Andropov a "loss . . . to mankind," declared a three-day national mourning period, and sent a high-level delegation led by Daniel Ortega to his funeral.[43]

In the United Nations and other international fora the Sandinistas echoed Moscow's efforts to set both the Falklands/Malvinas and Central American crises against the context of Soviet "peace" efforts. Managua has even participated directly in the Soviet peace offensive in Europe. In an April 1983 West German peace-movement action conference, Sandinista youth-leader Evelin Pinto set off "an outstanding five minutes of wildly enthusiastic applause by announcing that Nicaraguans would demonstrate against the Pershing II and Cruise missiles in October."[44]

By going to such lengths to please Moscow (and to vex Washington) the Sandinistas sometimes have embarrassed the Soviets and themselves. Thus, apparently, without ever having been asked by Moscow, Defense Minister Humberto Ortega told a *New York Times* reporter (Oct. 4, 1983) that Nicaraguan national security justified his seriously examining any proposal for installing Russian SS-20s in Nicaragua. After the Soviet ambassador appeared on American television to deny that Moscow had made such a proposal, Daniel Ortega at length denied that Nicaragua had ever entertained the notion.[45]

For all the Sandinista efforts to elicit a major Soviet economic and military commitment to Nicaragua, Moscow has proceeded judiciously. Soviet economic aid doubled between 1981 and 1982 from about $75 million to over $150 million,[46] but in 1983 it declined to about $100 million. Total Soviet-bloc aid rose from about $280 million in 1981 to $300 million in 1982 and then fell to somewhere between $200 and $250 million in 1983.[47] Most experts regard this as a remarkably low level of assistance especially in the light of the continuing deterioration of the Nicaraguan economy. Moreover, despite repeated Sandinista requests for foreign exchange to compensate for their grave trade imbalance, Moscow has been unforthcoming.[48]

Moscow has granted emergency assistance when propaganda dividends were evident. In late April 1981 it made a highly publicized shipment of twenty thousand tons of (probably re-exported United States) wheat after the United States cut Nicaragua's credit line for such purchases. After Mexico reduced its concessionary sales in December 1983 Moscow began oil shipments to Nicaragua, and now supplies 25 percent of Nicaragua's petroleum needs. After insurgents' speedboat attacks on Puerto Sandino damaged oil-storage tanks earlier this year, Moscow supplied credit for replacement purchases. However, Moscow did not come to the rescue after the United States cut the Nicaraguan sugar quota in the spring of 1983.[49]

Most of the Soviet bloc's assistance has been in the form of long-term development aid such as medical and laboratory equipment, farm machinery, prefabricated houses, and the construction of a hydroelectric power plant, a technical training center, a hospital (staffed entirely by Russians), and a yarn factory. There are now twenty bilateral projects underway in telecommunications, hydropower, geological prospecting, and technical training, along with technical assistance for the textile industry, microwave system, and metal industry.

The Soviet bloc has become a major trading partner of Nicaragua to the extent of somewhat over 10 percent of total Nicaragua imports and exports.[50] However, it still trails the United States, EEC countries, Central America, and the rest of Latin America. The Soviet bloc purchases moderate amounts of Nicaraguan coffee, cotton, and raw sugar but has not become a crucial market for traditional Nicaraguan exports as in Argentina and Cuba.

In September of 1983 Nicaragua was admitted as an observer to the Council for Mutual Economic Assistance. In February a CMEA delegation to Nicaragua met with government officials, instructed local personnel assigned to various agro-industrial and energy projects, and drafted plans through a joint CMEA-Nicaraguan working commission for cooperation in economic planning, agriculture, cadres, training, forestry, textiles, and mining.[51] Nonetheless, Tass excluded Nicaragua from a list of "developing states of socialist orientation" with whom cooperation through the CMEA "is most intensively developing."[52] Previously Nicaragua had joined Inter-Sputnik, the Soviet-bloc telecommunications organization.[53] Reportedly Moscow is constructing a ground station to provide Nicaragua with television links to Warsaw-pact countries.[54] Nicaraguan bookstores and newsstands now conspicuously feature Soviet-bloc literature. Soviet manuals and texts predominate in schools and the universities, and one thousand Nicaraguan students are now studying in the Soviet Union.[55]

From 1981 through January 1984 the Soviet bloc provided approximately 17,500 tons of military equipment.[56] While deliveries have increased substantially, compensating for the escalation of insurgency activity, the totals in no way compare to those provided to Cuba in the comparable period of the early 1960s.

Moscow was slower to establish military contacts with Cuba but by early 1961 Cuban troops were openly equipped with Soviet and Czech-made weapons. In 1962 the USSR delivered 250,000 metric tons of arms to Cuba; in 1963, 40,000; 1964, 20,000. This contrasts dramatically with the Nicaraguan figures. Despite the greater and more protracted threat to the Sandinista regime and the major buildup of Soviet strategic power, Moscow's military aid to Nicaragua is far more limited than to Cuba in a comparable period.

Warsaw-pact countries have supplied the following military hardware: over 90 T-55 tanks and an unspecified number of amphibious tanks; over 150 howitzers, antitank guns, mortars, and rocket-propelled grenade launches; 8 AN-26 transport planes; up to 18 helicopters (including troop-transport helicopters); 120 air-defense artillery guns; 30 surface-to-air missiles; amphibious ferries and field kitchens; over 1,000 transport trucks; and thousands of infantry weapons. With the exception of the T-55 tanks, most heavy weaponry was delivered after 1981, when the insurgents began to represent a threat. There are approximately one hundred Soviet advisory personnel and roughly two thousand Cuban military advisors presently in Nicaragua.[57]

Moscow has been extremely circumspect in its military involvement. For example, it has preferred to utilize intermediaries such as Bulgaria, East Germany, Cuba, and even Algeria for the delivery of arms.[58]

Moscow has not publicly acknowledged weapons transfers to Nicaragua, though it has emphasized Sandinista statements that Nicaragua has the right to seek arms from any source it wishes.[59] It has also failed to acknowledge Nicaraguan public requests for fighter planes.[60] Since 1981 there have been reports that Nicaragua is expanding airfields to receive sophisticated jet aircraft.[61] It has also been widely reported that seventy Nicaraguans have been trained in Bulgaria to pilot and repair MiG aircraft.[62] There is evidence that Soviet planes earmarked for Nicaragua remain in Cuba because of United States warnings.[63] Unlike Moscow, Havana has reported Nicaraguan appeals for fighter airplanes. However, one observer believes that Moscow may disagree with Managua and Havana on the need for MiGs and believes that antiaircraft missiles might better deter the insurgents' light-aircraft attacks.[64]

Total Soviet arms transfers to Nicaragua have been valued at approximately $300 million.[65] This puts Nicaragua in roughly the same category as Peru, Cape Verde, Guinea, Mali, Nigeria, the Congo, Zambia, Mozambique, Tanzania, Madagascar, Iran, Laos, North Korea, and South Yemen. It is well below the amounts transferred to Cuba, Algeria, Ethiopia, Iraq, Syria, India, Vietnam, and Angola. With Nicaragua the USSR has signed no treaty of friendship, unlike the Congo, Mozambique, Ethiopia, Syria, South Yemen, Iraq, Afghanistan, India, Laos, and Angola. Unlike Cuba, Libya, Mozambique, the Seychelles, South Yemen, Ethiopia, Vietnam, and Angola, Nicaragua provides Moscow no naval facilities. And unlike in Cuba, Libya, Ethiopia, Angola, South Yemen, and Vietnam, it has no access to Nicaraguan airfields.

Despite frequent statements by Sandinista leaders that Nicaragua is in a period of "transition to socialism," Moscow appears reluctant to award Nicaragua symbolic "socialist" status with its implied commitments. In November 1980 and January 1981 a leading Soviet ideologist, Boris Ponomarev, announced that states of "socialist orientation" were emerging in Asia, Africa, and Central America."[66] However, Nicaragua was specifically designated only as a "people's democracy" around this time. In June 1983 *Pravda* did include Nicaragua in a list of countries of "socialist orientation." However, this reference has not been repeated even though Nicaragua is usually treated in protocol and depicted as are other "socialist-oriented" regimes.[67] Moscow has not publicized Sandinista declarations of fidelity to Marxism-Leninism. Soviet diplomats in Managua have reportedly stated that Nicaragua is not ready for Soviet-style socialism.[68] The explanation for Soviet reticence in conferring this status would seem to lie in the realm of economics and security, not ideology.

Disappointment with Soviet economic and security commitment may have widened the breach inside the Sandinista leadership between self-styled "realists" and "revolutionaries."[69] Some Sandinista leaders may now regret their expectations of Soviet support that helped convert Nicaragua into a pawn in the superpower contention. Yuri Andropov appears to have been excessively frank when in an April 1983 interview with the German magazine *Der Spiegel* he explicitly compared Nicaragua and Afghanistan:

> We have a long common border and it does make a difference what kind of Afghanistan it will be. To make this better understood, let us put it this way, for example: as if it would not make any difference to the United States what kind of government Nicaragua would have.[70]

Afghanistan, he went on to explain, was in "our corner of the world." In the Tass version the term "our corner of the world" was suppressed, presumably for its blatant contradiction with national liberation and independence.[71]

Soviet authorities have frequently intimated to United States diplomats that the "Nicaraguan problem" could only be resolved in the context of "United States–Soviet relations." Sandinista eagerness for close ties with Moscow has permitted the Soviets to pursue a virtually cost-free policy. Nicaragua could represent a "bargaining chip" in Moscow's preferred "political settlement" in Afghanistan. On the other hand, should the United States intervene directly in Nicaragua, attention would be distracted from Afghanistan and Moscow could exploit the intervention for propaganda purposes and reap future gains. If despite United States pressure the Sandinistas survive, a pro-Soviet regime could gradually be consolidated.

Moscow appears to be pursuing a wait-and-see, long-term strategy in Nicaragua. It has made minimal economic investments and encourages the Sandinistas to diversify their trading partners and aid-donors.[72] Meanwhile, Moscow directs its efforts to the training of a new pro-Soviet technological, cultural, and political elite. Soviet-bloc presence in the intelligence, security, communications, and military fields has deepened, but Moscow provides only enough military aid to make United States military intervention costly and save the Soviet "revolutionary" reputation, but not enough to guarantee survival or risk confrontation.

In early 1983 Moscow reportedly donated a dry dock for the port city of San Juan del Sur, along with numerous Soviet technicians for its construction and maintenance.[73] The port is now being deepened and expanded. At the same time, the Bulgarians agreed to provide $140 million in credit over three years for the development of a deep-water port at El Bluff on Nicaragua's Atlantic coast (capable of handling 28,000 metric-ton oceangoing ships).[74] Such activities have traditionally been a harbinger of future Soviet access to facilities for naval surveillance and other military purposes.

However, Washington has been especially prone to confuse potential long-term dangers—often manageable through diplomatic and other peaceful instruments—with immediate short-term threats requiring military action. For example, during February and March of 1983 administration spokesmen and the President himself claimed that Grenada was being converted into a Soviet strategic base in the Caribbean. They pointed not only to a Grenadian arms buildup and Cuban construction of an international airport but also to Soviet construction of a naval base with facilities for receiving Soviet submarines.[75] However, after United States troops had occupied Grenada and captured state and party documents, State and Defense Department reports made no mention of submarine facilities—only of a possible Soviet study of the "feasibility of a Grenadian port to service large deep-draft ships."[76] While large quantities of weapons and agreements for further supplies from the Soviet bloc were discovered, the amount and type of these weapons do not seem incompatible with perceived defense needs of a country fearing invasion. At most these weapons suggested a capability for arming small bands of guerrillas for insurgencies on other small islands, though inventories included no transport capabilities. Moreover, one source of the rift in the Grenadan leadership was the visit of late Prime Minister Maurice Bishop to the United States in late June of 1983. Bishop apparently offered to resolve United States concerns through political and diplomatic channels.[77]

Both before and after the invasion of Grenada there have been numerous reports of differences between Moscow and Havana over Grenada and the Caribbean as a whole. There is some evidence that the Cubans had been interested in promoting a Social Democratic tendency in the Caribbean via former Jamaican Prime Minister Michael Manley and Bishop. Bishop's opponent in the New Jewel Movement, Bernard Coard, was linked with Manley's extreme leftist pro-Soviet opponents, Trevor Monroe and the Jamaican Workers' party. According to the State Department's director of Cuban affairs the Grenada events produced "frictions" between the USSR and Cuba because the latter thought "Moscow should have done something to prevent the political chaos that engulfed Grenada" after Bishop's ouster.[78]

In the aftermath of the invasion Castro acknowledged that in the case of the United States intervention in Nicaragua "we would face the same problems as in Grenada: we lack the naval and air means to send direct assistance to Grenada."[79]

This statement is consistent with Cuba's new defensive posture. In July 1983 Fidel Castro indicated he would withdraw Cuban advisors from Nicaragua and refrain from sending any weapons to Central America in the context of a settlement arranged by Contadora.[80] At the same time the Sandinistas began to signal their willingness to make serious concessions to Contadora's agenda for a regional settlement. They appear more willing to compromise externally than with their internal opposition. The Sandinistas apparently would prefer to sacrifice the FMLN and reduce the Soviet military presence in exchange for United States abandonment of the contras and withdrawal from Honduras. No meaningful internal settlement seems to be contemplated. Such a policy would not be inconsistent with Moscow's new orientation in the Third World—consolidation of "the gains of socialism." There is reason to believe that many in the current Sandinista leadership expect the fortunes of what they call "the socialist camp" eventually to revive.[81]

THE REAGAN ADMINISTRATION AND THE SOVIET THREAT

A curious contradiction has arisen. While Moscow has shifted from expansion to consolidation and as the immediate Soviet-Cuban danger threat recedes and the United States threat to the Sandinista regime mounts, Washington's warnings about an urgent Soviet peril grow louder, not softer. In a speech on April 17, 1984, President Reagan stated:

> Today a far-away totalitarian power is committing enormous resources to change the strategic balance of the world by turning Central America into a string of anti-American, Soviet-style dictatorships. . . . It is [toward] all of America that this assault is aimed.[82]

United Nations Ambassador Jeane Kirkpatrick recently claimed that the greatest threat in Central America "is in fact nuclear missiles, it's chemical weapons, which are another really important threat moving on the horizon."[83] According to the President's May 10 speech on Central American policy, the Soviets' adventurism in the Third World is "intensifying."[84] Yet that very week a Soviet specialist from the President's National Security Council wrote that Soviet policymakers feel "overcommitted" internationally, and the specialist sees "signs" of reduced Soviet commitments to Third World clients.[85] Even CIA Director William Casey allegedly "accepts the basic CIA analysis that the Soviets proceed with caution in the Western Hemisphere," and that their short-term activities are mainly intended to divert United States attention. Reportedly Casey has said that "the real battleground is the Middle East and its strategic position and those oil fields."[86]

White House exaggerations of the immediate Soviet danger were evidently directed to securing the passage of the recommendations of the administration and the National Bipartisan Commission on Central America (the Kissinger Commission). The latter's report warns of an "advance of Soviet-Cuban power on the American mainland" and the prospect of "a major strategic coup" affecting the global military balance.[87] Both administration statements and the commission's report ignore the shifting global correlation of forces and the altered regional balance of power.

The President's speeches and the Kissinger report regard all Central American revolutionaries as "tied to Cuba and the Soviet bloc."[88] They overlook the diversity and even collision of views among Central American revolutionary groups in general. For example, two of the three most important Salvadoran guerrilla groups have been critical of the Cuban presence and influence in Managua. They have anti-Soviet origins and their documents have referred to the Soviet Union as "social imperialists" ("socialist in name, imperialist in deed").[89]

Many in Latin America, the United States, and Western Europe worry that behind a rhetoric of anti-Sovietism Washington seeks to restore United States hegemony over Central America.[90] Administration policy toward the Nicaraguan insurgency illustrates the muddling of the objectives of opposing Soviet influence and restoring United States hegemonism. The administration has consistently sought to subordinate the anti-Soviet, but not pro-American, movement of Edén Pastora (the Revolutionary Democratic Alliance, ARDE) to the Democratic National Front (FDN), trained by the CIA. The administration is suspicious of Pastora's avowed aim of negotiating with rather than overthrowing the Sandinista leadership. As a result, the democratic opposition to the Sandinista National Directorate has been weakened and Nicaraguans have been forced to align with one superpower or the other. The option of a nonaligned "third way," which most Nicaraguans and most Central Americans desire, is thereby foreclosed.[91]

Such a policy is not in the long-term national security interest.[92] Indeed, a restoration of United States hegemony may well augment Moscow's long-range opportunities, not only in Central America but in Latin America as a whole. As one expert on Soviet–Latin American relations has observed,

> Moscow believes that U.S. involvement in Central America will inevitably run into the long-term trend of Latin American assertiveness, independence, and anti-Americanism. Thus, the United States may win in Central America but jeopardize important positions elsewhere on the continent. The main area of struggle in the hemisphere will not be in Central America or in the Caribbean but in the major Latin American countries. . . . As in other areas, Moscow foresees "ebbs and flows," successes and temporary defeats in Central America, an approach which makes it possible for Moscow to accept leftist setbacks, if not with equanimity, then at least with a belief in ultimate reversal.[93]

Current administration policy toward Central America may create new opportunities for Moscow. Washington has revived the specter of "United States imperialism" in the Third World, created grave doubts among our NATO allies, undermined Contadora, weakened the Inter-American system, and done little to relieve Latin America's widening financial crisis—a graver threat to United States security than events in Central America. There is a danger that American policy may once again help to set the stage for another shift in the correlation of forces, this time in Moscow's favor.

ACKNOWLEDGMENTS

I would like to thank Scott B. Martin for his excellent research assistance.

NOTES

1. Sergei Mikoyan, "Las particularidades de la revolucion en Nicaragua y sus tareas desde el punto de vista de la teoría y la práctica del movimiento libertador," *America Latina* 3 (1980), p. 37.

2. See Robert S. Leiken, "Eastern Winds in Latin America," *Foreign Policy*, Spring 1981, p. 95.

3. Furthermore, NATO analysts have become concerned that an expanded Soviet-Cuban naval presence in the Caribbean could eventually threaten NATO contingency plans to relieve Western Europe from United States Gulf ports. Such an offensive interdiction capability could bolster Soviet efforts to demonstrate to Western European countries that the United States is both unwilling and unable to offer effective assistance in a crisis. In addition the Caribbean, the Panama Canal, the Atlantic narrows, and the sea-lanes around the southern tip of South America are potential choke points where Soviet navy and submarine forces could disrupt the flow of raw materials and oil to the United States. For a discussion of Soviet strategic objectives, see Robert S. Leiken, *Soviet Strategy in Latin America*, The Washington Papers, No. 93 (New York: Praeger, 1982), pp. 11–14, 42–43, 61–65.

4. This is the account given by M. N. Roy, who attended the second Congress of the Communist International, in *M. N. Roy's Memoirs* (Bombay: Allied, 1964), p. 346.

5. See Robert S. Leiken, "The Salvadoran Left," in Robert S. Leiken, ed., *Central America: Anatomy of Conflict* (New York: Pergamon, 1984), pp. 111–114.

6. Seweryn Bialer and Joan Afferica, "Reagan and Russia," *Foreign Affairs*, Winter 1982–1983.

7. See Leiken, "Eastern Winds in Latin America," pp. 94–113.

8. Manuel Pineiro Losada, "La crisis actual del imperialismo y los procesos revolucionarios en América Latina y el Caribe," *Cuba Socialista*, September–November 1982, p. 40.

9. Karen N. Brutents, *National Liberation Revolutions Today*, vol. 2, (Mowcow: Progress, 1977), p. 217; Morris Rothenberg, *The U.S.S.R. and Africa: New Dimensions of Soviet Global Power* (Coral Gables, Florida: AISI, 1980), p. 257.

10. N. I. Gavtilov and G. B. Starushenko, eds., *Africa: Problems of Socialist Orientation* (Moscow: Mauka, 1976), pp. 10–11.

11. Seth Singleton, "Defense of the Gains of Socialism: Soviet Third World Policy in the Mid-Eighties," *Washington Quarterly*, Winter 1984, p. 104.

12. Leiken, *Soviet Strategy*, p. 27.

13. Karen N. Brutents, *National Liberation Revolutions Today*, vol. 1 (Moscow: Progress, 1977), p. 16. See also Rothenberg, *The U.S.S.R. and Africa*, p. 257.

14. United States House of Representatives, Subcommittee on Western Hemisphere Affairs, "Impact of Cuban-Soviet Ties in the Western Hemisphere," Hearings, 96th Congress, 1st and 2nd sessions, April 25–26, 1979, p. 29; March 26–27, April 16–17,

May 14, 1980, p. 17; Gilbert Lewthuaite, *Baltimore Sun*, June 19, 1979; *Diario Las Américas*, March 28, 1981, p. 10; Central Intelligence Agency, "National Intelligence Estimate," May 2, 1979; "A Revolutionary Friendship Turns Sour," *Latin America Weekly Report*, WR-79-08 (December 21, 1979), p. 2; *Washington Post*, September 30, 1981; *New York Times*, September 9, 1981, p. A3.

15. For further discussion, see Leiken, *Soviet Strategy*.

16. Nikolai Leonov, "Nicaragua: Experiencia de una revolución victoriosa," *América Latina*, 3 (Moscow, 1980), p. 37; Mikoyan, "Particularidades de la revolución," pp. 102–103.

17. Boris Koval, "La revolución: Largo proceso histórico," *América Latina*, 3 (Moscow, 1980), pp. 76–79; Sergei Mikoyan, "La creatividad abre el camino hacía la victória," *América Latina*, 2 (Moscow, 1980), p. 5.

18. Leonid Brezhnev, as cited in Morris Rothenberg, "The Soviets and Central America," in *Central America: Anatomy of Conflict*, pp. 131–149.

19. Nina Serafino, "Soviet Interests and Opportunities in Central America," discussion draft presented at the 1984 Pacific Symposium," "The U.S.S.R. as a Pacific Power: Opportunities and Problems, February 9, 1984, p. 11.

20. See "Soviet Aid to Nicaragua Spurts," *Soviet World Outlook*, 9 (September 1981), p. 3.

21. Don Oberdorfer and Joanne Omang, *Washington Post*, June 19, 1983, pp. A1, A4; Gerald F. Seib and Walter S. Mossberg, *Wall Street Journal*, August 17, 1983, p. 1; Richard Halloran, *New York Times*, August 2, 1983; also, interviews by author, Leiken, with former Sandinistas, diplomats, etc.

22. United States Department of State, Bureau of Public Affairs, "Communist Interference in El Salvador," Special Report No. 80, February 23, 1981, pp. 5, 7.

23. Arturo Cruz, Jr., "The Origins of Sandinista Foreign Policy," in *Central America: Anatomy of Conflict*, p. 100.

24. Ibid., p. 102.

25. Ibid., p. 103.

26. Karl von Clausewitz, *On War*, book I, chapter 7.

27. Bialer and Afferica, "Reagan and Russia."

28. Karen Dawisha, "The U.S.S.R. in the Middle East: Superpower in Eclipse?," *Foreign Affairs*, Winter 1982–1983.

29. Y. Novopashin, *Problems of Philosophy* (Moscow), no. 8 (August 1982), as quoted in *Soviet World Outlook* (Coral Gables, Florida: AISI), pp. 5–6.

30. Singleton, "Defense of Gains of Socialism," p. 107.

31. Congressional Research Service, "Trends in Conventional Arms Transfers to the Third World by Major Suppliers," May 1984, p. 23.

32. L. N. Lebedinskaia, "Peoples of the Former Colonial World and Real Socialism," *The Working Class and the Contemporary World*, no. 4 (July–August 1982).

33. For a discussion of recent Soviet policies in the Caribbean basin, see Robert S. Leiken, "Soviet and Cuban Policy in the Caribbean Basin," in Douglas Graham and Donald Schulz, eds., *Revolution and Counterrevolution in Central America and the Caribbean*, (forthcoming from Westview Press).

34. *Pravda*, December 30, 1980, as cited in Peter Clement, unpublished discussion draft on Soviet policy toward El Salvador, Fall 1983, p. 4.

35. *TASS*, January 11, 1981, as cited in Clement, unpublished discussion, p. 4.

36. M. F. Gornov, "Latin America: More Intense Struggle against Imperialism and Oligarchy and for Democracy and Social Progress," *Latinskaya Amerika*, (July 1982), JPRS Translation No. 81859, p. 39. See also M. L. Mishina, "Central American Democratic Community," *Latinskaya Amerika*, 7 (July 1982), JPRS Translation No. 81859, p. 47. A. V. Kuz'mischev, "Political Situation in Honduras," *Latinskaya Amerika*, 7 (July 1982), JPRS Translation No. 81859, p. 47. N. S. Leonev, "Guatemala's Worries and Hopes," *Latinskaya Amerika*, 7 (July 1982), JPRS Translation No. 81859, pp. 30, 32.

37. Ibid., p. 12.

38. Letter from the Central Committee of the Communist Party of the Soviet Union, June 1982.

39. A. V. Kuz'mischev, "Political Situation in Honduras," *Latinskaya Amerika*, 7 (July 1982), JPRS Translation. No. 81859, p. 47; Alexander Trushin, "There Should Not Be More Policemen Than Teachers," *New Times*, 23 (June 1982), pp. 24–25.

40. Radio Moscow, March 8, 1982, as cited in Clement, unpublished discussion, p. 6.

41. *Foreign Broadcast Information Service* (hereafter cited as "FBIS"), *Soviet Union*, May 5, 1982, pp. K2–K4, May 10, 1982, pp. K3–K4.

42. *TASS*, May 4, 1982, as cited in Peter Clement, "The Soviets in Nicaragua; Cultivating a New Client," paper prepared for conference of the American Association of Slavic Studies, October 21–25, 1983, p. 4.

43. Rothenberg, "The Soviets and Central America," p. 134.

44. Diane Johnstone, "Peace Movement Adds Third World Groups to Its Cause," *In These Times*, September 28–October 4, 1983, p. 7.

45. *New York Times*, April 10, 1983.

46. Serafino, "Soviet Interests," pp. 14–15; Rothenberg, "The Soviets and Central America," p. 135; *FBIS, Latin America*, May 11, 1982, p. P18.

47. Serafino, "Soviet Interests," pp. 13, 15; Rothenberg, "The Soviets and Central America," p. 135; Jiri and Virginia Valenta, "Soviet Strategy and Policies in the Caribbean Basin," in Howard J. Wiarda, ed., *Rift and Revolution: The Central American Imbroglio* (Washington, D.C.: American Enterprise Institute, 1984), p. 217.

48. As recently as February 1984 the planning minister appealed to the Council of Mutual Economic Assistance for help in alleviating Nicaragua's severe "cash shortage." *FBIS, Latin America*, February 14, 1984.

49. "Soviet Aid to Nicaragua Spurts," *Soviet World Outlook* 9 (September 1981), p. 3; Peter Clement, "The Soviets in Nicaragua," p. 3; Kinzer, *New York Times*, March 28, 1984, p. A4; *FBIS, Latin America*, March 30, 1984, p. P14.

50. *Pravda*, August 1983, as cited in Rothenberg, "The Soviets and Central America," p. 141.

51. *FBIS, Latin America*, February 15, 1984, p. Q5.

52. *FBIS, Latin America*, April 4, 1984, p. BB3.

53. Rothenberg, "The Soviets and Central America," pp. 135–136.

54. *Miami Herald*, November 28, 1982.

55. Stephen Kinzer, *New York Times*, March 28, 1984, p. A4.

56. United States Department of Defense, *Soviet Military Power 1984*, third ed. (Washington, D.C.: U.S. Government Printing Office, April 1984), p. 122.

57. Ibid., pp. 121–123; Gerald F. Seib and Walter S. Mossberg, *Wall Street Journal*, August 17, 1983, p. 15; Clement, "The Soviets in Nicaragua," p. 4.

58. Clement, "The Soviets in Nicaragua," p. 9. For a very recent example of such deliveries through third parties (in this case, Bulgaria), see Jay Mallin, Sr., *Washington Times*, March 12, 1984, p. 1.

59. Rothenberg, p. 140, in *Central America: Anatomy of Conflict*.

60. Clement, "The Soviets in Nicaragua," p. 15.

61. Seib and Mossberg, *Wall Street Journal*, p. 15.

62. Ibid., p. 15; statement of Thomas O. Enders before the Senate Foreign Relations Committee, Apr. 12, 1983, p. 1.

63. *Washington Post*, July 29, 1982 and June 19, 1983.

64. Clement, "The Soviets in Nicaragua," p. 15.

65. Bernard Gwertzman, *New York Times*, April 15, 1984, p. A12.

66. Boris Ponomarev, "The Cause of Freedom and Socialism is Invincible," *World Marxist Review*, January 1981, p. 13.

67. Rothenberg, "The Soviets and Central America," p. 136.

68. Kinzer, *New York Times*, p. A1.

69. "Gloom But Not Yet Doom," *Time*, May 14, 1984, pp. 31–32.

70. *Der Spiegel*, April 1983, as cited in *FBIS, Soviet Union*, April 25, 1984, pp. AA1–10, April 27, 1984, pp. AA3–10.

71. *FBIS, Soviet Union*, April 25, 1983, p. AA3.

72. Rothenberg, "The Soviets and Central America," p. 141.

73. *FBIS, Latin America*, March 16, 1983, p. I-8.

74. *Financial Times* (London), March 17, 1983.

75. President Ronald Reagan, speech before the annual meeting of the National Association of Manufacturers, March 10, 1983, in *Weekly Compilation of Presidential Documents*, March 14, 1983, pp. 377–378; address to the nation, March 23, 1983, *Weekly Compilation of Presidential Documents*, March 28, 1983, p. 445; "High Anxiety and A Fear of Runways," *Newsweek*, April 11, 1983.

76. Department of Defense, *Soviet Military Power*, p. 128. See also the Departments of State and Defense, *Grenada: A Preliminary Report* (Washington, D.C.: U.S. Government Printing Office, November 1983).

77. Patrick E. Tyler, *Washington Post*, October 10, 1983, p. A14.

78. Alfonso Chardy, *Miami Herald*, February 10, 1984, p. 4A. Apparently speaking of Coard and his associates, Juan Marrero, chief of *Granma*'s International Department, asserted that the "appearance of veritable hyenas in the ranks of the New Jewel Movement paved the way for U.S. intervention." In "A Better Lot Is the Dream of Latin American Peoples," *International Affairs*, February 1984, pp. 73–74. Moreover, Fidel Castro commiserated with the Cubans in Grenada just prior to the U.S. invasion:

> I understand how bitter it is for you, as well as for us here, to risk compatriots in Grenada, after the gross mistakes the Grenadian party has made and the tragic developments to which they gave rise. . . . It is not the new Grenadian government we must think of now, but of Cuba, its honor, its people, its fighting morale. . . . If the United States intervenes, we must

vigorously defend ourselves as if we were in Cuba. . . . We would thus be defending ourselves, not the government or its deeds. (*Statements by Cuba on the events in Grenada: October 1983* (Havana: Editora Politica, 1983), p. 7.

79. Ibid., p. 27.

80. Fidel Castro, "Talks with U.S. and French Journalists," July–August 1983, pp. 7, 10.

81. Speech to military specialists by Humberto Ortega Saavedra, Commander of the Revolution, August 25, 1981.

82. As quoted in *Washington Post*, April 18, 1984, p. A22.

83. Charles R. Babcock and Bob Woodward, *Washington Post*, April 16, 1984, p. A19.

84. As quoted in *New York Times*, May 10, 1984, p. A16.

85. Stephen Sestanovich, "Do the Soviets Feel Pinched by Third World Adventures?," *Washington Post*, May 20, 1984, p. B1.

86. As quoted in *Washington Post*, April 16, 1984, p. A19.

87. Report of the *National Bipartisan Commission on Central America*, January 1984 (mimeographed), p. 92.

88. Ibid., pp. 84, 88–91.

89. See Leiken, "The Salvadoran Left," in *Central America*.

90. See Viron Vaky, "Reagan's Central American Policy: An Isthmus Restored," in Robert S. Leiken, ed., *Central America: Anatomy of Conflict* (New York: Pergamon, 1984), pp. 233–257.

91. For a discussion of a "third way" in Central America, see Leiken, "Can the Cycle Be Broken?," in *Central America*, pp. 11–14, 18–23.

92. For an examination of U.S. policy options, see Ibid., pp. 14–27.

93. Rothenberg, "The Soviets and Central America," pp. 146–147.

Chapter 17

SOVIET VIEWS ON CENTRAL AMERICA

Jiri Valenta and Fred Shaheen

ROBERT LEIKEN HAS provided us with a very good analysis of Soviet precep-tions and motivations concerning Central America. It is both concise and fac-tual and provides the Latin Americanist and the Sovietologist with increased food for thought. We find ourselves in general agreement on the contents of the chapter; however, we also feel the need to dissent on several specific issues raised.

The Leiken chapter has successfully avoided any extremist interpretations, which appear to be a common pitfall of much of the current writing about the Soviet Union and Central America. A good example of this is Cole Blasier's premature analysis of the relationship between the Soviets and client states in the region.[1] Leiken correctly suggests that the Soviet Union is a unique super-power acutely aware of military, political, and ideological payoffs in Central America. Additionally, he is quick to recognize the importance the region holds in the superpower balance: "Moscow's overall strategic objective in Latin America is to convert the region from a 'strategic reserve' of the United States into an area of instability and superpower contention. . . . Instability and conflict in the Caribbean, they believe, diverts United States resources and attention from other areas of the world of higher priority to Moscow."[2] The implications for United States security by having United States forces tied up in the Caribbean when they could prove critical in a NATO conflict elsewhere is of key importance and a point not overlooked in Robert Leiken's essay.

A point at which we must part ways concerns the contention that 1980 saw the Soviets shifting into a sort of "holding pattern" in Central America. Follow-ing the coup in Grenada and the Nicaraguan revolution in 1979, Soviet policy-makers, their advisors, and Soviet analysts began to exercise a much greater degree of optimism about revolutionary trends in the Caribbean Basin. Both events proved that "Socialist-oriented" revolutions are possible in the im-mediate geographic proximity of the United States and that the United States may be forced to tolerate them. Furthermore, these successes led the Soviets to take a more positive look at the revolutionary situation in El Salvador and in other countries of the region.

The Soviets' new optimistic line about the Caribbean Basin must have received approval at the highest level of the Soviet leadership. This is suggested by the much-changing tone discernable in the writing of candidate Politburo member and Secretary of the Central Committee of the CPSU Ponomarev. Whereas in 1976 he was rather guarded about the revolutionary process in Latin America and the Caribbean Basin, by January 1980 Ponomarev could hardly conceal the Soviets' joy over the successful revolution in Nicaragua. In a rather sophisticated analysis of the worldwide liberation struggle, published in *Kommunist*, Ponomarev deals in heretofore unusual detail with Nicaragua and the Caribbean Basin, equating the Sandinista government with the "progressive" regimes of Angola, Mozambique, and Guinea Bissau, and the Nicaraguan revolution with the "anti-imperialist," popular revolutions of Ethiopia, Afghanistan, and Iran.[3] This assessment of these movements by Ponomarev differs considerably from *Kommunist*'s assessment of several months before, which placed Nicaragua and Grenada in the same category as Bolivia, Iran, Palestina, Surinam, and Zimbabwe.[4]

Ponomarev takes a long historical view in describing the revolution in Nicaragua:

> The Nicaraguan nation for many years led the struggle against fascist dictatorship; however, for a long time there had not been sufficient force to deal with it. There was not a sufficient degree of unity and organization within the ranks of the patriotic avant-garde. When all the necessary conditions for the success of insurrection became ripe, there was nobody who could restrain the national anger; even the guards of Somoza, with their American weapons, were not able to preserve the rule of the doomed clique of a despot."[5]

Another important aspect of this piece is the implicit argument that Latin American countries are able to embark on the path of "Socialist orientation." As late as 1981, a number of leading Central Committee consultants seemed to want to reserve this special status for African and Asian nations. However, Ponomarev's article represents the official Soviet position.

Soviet views and policies toward Central America and the Caribbean in general and El Salvador in particular were changed in 1980, but not as Leiken's article suggests. Not only do we have Ponomarev's extensive analysis discussed above but also Shafik Jorge Handal's contributions to *Kommunist* in November 1980, suggesting his close ties to Soviet leadership. Handal's PCES has already begun to make an abrupt about-face in the spring of 1979, which corresponded to incipient changes in official Soviet thinking. At the Seventh Congress of the PCES in April of 1979, Handal declared that armed revolution was necessary and that it was heresy to disagree. About a year and a half later (November 1980), this turnabout was being sold to Soviet readers on the pages of *Kommun-*

ist, where, with what had to have been the highest Soviet blessing, Handal argued that new conditions in El Salvador—"open fascist tyranny" and the "ultrareactionary" orientation of the ruling elites—made it "impossible at the present time to solve the national crisis on a reformist basis."[6]

Robert Leiken is correct in concluding that an about-face was taking place during this time frame, but the new attitude in Moscow was one of *increased optimism*, and not a felt need to slow down or pull back on commitments.

Soviet optimism about the revolutionary potential of the Caribbean Basin after the successes of Nicaragua and Grenada in 1979 are best reflected in the editorial policies of *Latinskaia Amerika* and *World Marxist Review*. A review of *LA* in the last four years (1980–83) shows that for the most part Soviet Latin Americanists focused their attention on the successes of Grenada and Nicaragua and possibility of a repetition of these successes elsewhere in the Caribbean Basin. The dean of Soviet Latin American specialists, Professor Shul'govskii, and his Latin Americanist colleagues no longer needed to apologize for the revolutionary failures in Chile and Peru in the late 1970s or debate critics like Mirskii who implied that the former had exaggerated the revolutionary potential in these countries.

Shul'govskii remains optimistic about revolutionary trends in Central America and repeats Zagladin's earlier and now famous dictum of April 1983 about Central America and the Caribbean region being the "weakest link in imperialist domination."[7]

Shul'govskii also argued that the Soviets, while focusing on Central America, should not "pass over" the Caribbean islands, particularly Grenada, where recent developments demonstrated "many of the important changes in the countries of the region, specifically changes related to the development of a state structure, by revolutionary-democratic forces, which would be an alternative to the neo-colonialist political system based on the Westminister model." Another Soviet writer, A. I. Stroganov, goes so far as to suggest, while reviewing Shul'govskii's new book on the subject of recent trends in Latin America, that in both Nicaragua and Grenada revolution had led "to the establishment of a *'new revolutionary, popular democratic state order'*"[8] an expression that was used by the Soviets in the late 1940s to refer to the Eastern European countries that eventually developed into proper Leninist states. This is obviously a higher ideological plane than suggested by the Leiken article.

The second major point we would like to make concerns Soviet payoffs to be reaped for supporting revolutionary forces in the Caribbean Basin and Central America in general. Ogarkov specified the conditions favoring a combat-readiness of progressive forces in the region: "Over two decades ago there was only Cuba in Latin America; today there are Nicaragua and Grenada and a serious battle is being waged in El Salvador."[9]

In strictly economic terms, the Caribbean Basin is not important to the

Soviets, whose trade is conducted primarily with Cuba and Nicaragua, and to a lesser degree with Mexico and Panama. However, economic ties with these countries are growing. Between January and June 1983 Soviet trade with Nicaragua represented a turnover of almost thirty million rubles, making Nicaragua the Soviets' second trading partner in the Caribbean after Cuba (with Mexico coming in third).[10] Moreover, the Soviets acknowledge that the Caribbean region is "a potentially large source of raw materials," primarily in terms of fuel but also manpower. This runs counter to Robert Leiken's economic analysis of the region.

The benefits to be accrued, in all likelihood, were seen by the Soviets to be increasing in the late seventies due in part to their perception of the Carter administration. Although Soviet analysts conceded that the Carter administration had taken some steps "to reduce confrontations with its southern neighbors regarding issues on which there was a high degree of regional unity,"[11] this being most prominently exemplified by the Panama Canal agreement, in their view this was only a new tactic, not a new strategy. As Soviet analysts agree:

> U.S. attempts to adjust to the charged situation and formulate a "new approach" in relations with Latin America are not aimed at a drastic structural change in inter-American relations, but merely at modifying them in its own interests in order to slow down the erosion of U.S. positions in the region.[12]

In the Soviet view Carter's new approach was unproductive: "The [Carter] campaign . . . boomeranged at the United States in Latin America."[13] As the Soviets stress, however, essentially this policy did not alter in the least the United States' Latin American policy, which continued to be staked on right-wing forces. A careful reading of the Soviets' analysis of Carter's policies, however, suggests the Soviet belief that Carter, with his new emphasis on human rights, was less able to use "traditional methods of 'power politics'" to deal with the revolutionary wave (or its supporters in Cuba and the USSR, for that matter) which had materialized during the final two years of his tenure, 1979–80. The Soviets seem to suggest, at least indirectly, that their support for new revolutionary movements in the Caribbean Basin and Central America was *less costly* under Carter than under his successor. This perception further argues against any "backing down" or dampening of the Soviet attitude toward Central America in the early days of this decade.

Even a more confrontational United States president could not quell Moscow's expectations. The Reagan administration had shifted the thrust of United States foreign policy to the Caribbean Basin, making it the central object of concern, something the Carter administration had sought to avoid.

The main objective of the Reagan policy, in the Soviet view, was "to try and accomplish what the preceding administration had failed to do, namely, to bring a halt to or at least discredit the liberation movement in the region and get even for the triumphant revolutions in Cuba, Grenada, and Nicaragua." Moreover, the Reagan administration aimed "for the edification of the world (the developing nations in the first place), to teach a lesson to all who do not accept the imperialist interpretation of problems."[13]

In spite of Reagan's strategy, United States policymakers, in the Soviets' opinion, were unable to prevent further radicalization of the Caribbean Basin. This generally was the Soviet view prior to the Grenada operation of October 1983. According to Soviet analysts, there were two important factors that hampered the realization of Reagan's policies: (1) high international costs, and (2) the lack of a national consensus. Soviet periodicals argued (before October 1983) that there were great international obstacles pursuant to Reagan's policy of escalation of the conflict in Central America. United States policymakers would have to cope with what *World Marxist Review* called "favorable opportunities for the struggle and victory of the peoples." These consisted of

> the wide dissemination of progressive thought; the strong impact of the revolutions in Cuba, Nicaragua and Grenada; the long-standing traditions of guerrilla warfare; the existence of militant revolutionary organizations; and the growing solidarity of the peoples of the world.[14]

To be sure, the Soviets and their proxies, the Central American Communist leaders and regional allies—the leaders of the Communist parties in Central America—did not rule out entirely a United States or OAS (Organization of American States) intervention in Nicaragua or El Salvador. However, they let the United States know, via the same proxies, that the international costs of such a policy would be extremely high, particularly in the region itself. As Manuél Mora Valverde, general secretary of the People's Vanguard party of Costa Rica, elaborated in *World Marxist Review:*

> Indeed . . . there is every reason to ask: Will the USA send troops to Central America? Technically, it can. However, it should ponder whether it is in its interest to kindle a major conflict that would have only one result—the emergence of another Vietnam in the very heart of Latin America.[15]

The nightmare of Vietnam is often evoked in Soviet-controlled periodicals to highlight the domestic and international dilemma of United States policymakers when coping with the problem of Central America and the political costs of further involvement. The policy implication of this argument seems to be that because of these constraints on United States policymakers, the revolutionary wave in Central America may be kept alive for years to come with Cuban and Soviet support. In spite of the Reagan administration's policy shift to the region, the United States, prior to October 1983, has not been able to contain the revolutionary situation, mainly because the ultimate means of containment—military force—seems to have been excluded as a real policy option. At least in part because of this, the Soviets often referred to their support (though unspecified in terms of the nature of the support) for the revolutionary forces in the region in 1980–83. Thus in 1981, according to *International Affairs*, the Soviet Union had a "clear-cut position on developments in El Salvador," that of "siding with the heroic struggle of the people of that Central American country for their liberation."[16]

The above conclusion coupled with the Soviets' awareness of the lack of consensus in the ongoing and heated public policy debate in the United States were clear signals to proceed at best speed in fomenting revolution in Central America and the Caribbean Basin.

Our last point is ironically very similar to Robert Leiken's original thesis that a certain turning point has been reached by the Soviets in support of revolution in the region. Our contention is that the turning point, if indeed it has occurred, took place after the October 1983 invasion of Grenada, and not any sooner.

The Soviets saw United States pressure and "gunboat diplomacy" in Nicaragua, their primary area of concern, as doomed to fail in the long run. When Soviet officials discussed a hypothetical United States intervention in Nicaragua, the Soviet response was always placed in relatively ambiguous terms.

With their attention focused on Nicaragua, the Soviets did not expect a United States intervention in Grenada. The October 1983 United States–East Caribbean security forces invasion basically came as a shock to the Soviets. The swift United States response to the crisis in the ruling NJM party and to the killing of Premier Maurice Bishop and, most important, the lack of a significant United States internal opposition to that event greatly surprised the Soviets. Subsequently, the invasion appears to be precipitating some noticeable change in Soviet perceptions regarding the United States propensity toward the use of military force in the Caribbean Basin. Up to October 1983 the Soviets believed that because of United States domestic constraints the Reagan administration could ill afford to pursue a "gunboat diplomacy"; after Grenada, Reagan was seen to bypass gunboat diplomacy for "direct armed interference . . . the armed invasion of the sovereign state of Grenada being a case in point."[17]

Indeed, Grenada might well become a turning point in the Soviet assessment of American intentions and of the cost-benefit ratio of the United States' direct use of force. "Grenada showed," as pointed out by a leading Soviet observer, Aleksander Bovin, that a military intervention in Nicaragua and El Salvador "is possible in principle." Or, as he argued, "Grenada was a signal, a signal that America has recovered from the 'Vietnam syndrome' and that America is once more ready, as in past times, to pursue military adventures and to use military might to defend its vital interests."[18] This is a new line not seen in the Soviet press since the end of the Vietnam war in 1975.

Is a pessimistic new Soviet line evolving, which, as Robert Leiken suggests, will lead to a reassessment of Soviet perceptions of the cost-benefit ratio of their policies in Central America and the Caribbean Basin? It is too early to say, but there is no doubt that Grenada was a watershed in the Soviet's previously optimistic outlook of 1980–83.

In conclusion, we feel it safe to say that between 1980 and 1983 the Soviet approach toward the region changed across the board, altering the perspective of policymakers, advisor-generalists, and Latin Americanists. Instead of the pervasive pessimism of the 1970s, Soviet writing of this period is characterized by a prevailing optimism on all levels of analysis. This unbridled optimism in Soviet writing and outlook from 1980 to 1983 has, on occasion, been punctuated with pessimism. In their net assessment, however, the Soviets appear still to be relying on powerful internal and external constraints to curb the scope of United States coercive policies in the region. Judging from Soviet commentary, the Grenada operation is causing an important reassessment of the costs and benefits of promoting revolution in Central America and the Caribbean Basin.

NOTES

1. The captured Grenada documents thus refute the view that Moscow was providing mainly moral support to Grenada. For an example of this view, see Cole Blasier, "Comment," in Alan Adelman and Reid Reading, eds., *Confrontation in the Caribbean Basin: International Perspectives on Security Sovereignty, and Survival* (Pittsburgh, Pennsylvania: University of Pittsburgh Press, 1984), pp. 268–274.

2. See above Robert S. Leiken, "The USSR and Central America: Great Expectations Dampened?", p. 156.

3. B. Ponomarev, "Neodolimost' osvogoditel'novo dvizheniia" (Invincibility of the Liberation Movement), *Kommunist*, no. 1 (January 1980), pp. 11–27.

4. See a short essay by the not too well known analyst R. Tuzmulshamedov, "Vliiatel'nti Faktor mirovoi politiky" (An Influential Factor of World Politics), *Kommunist*, no. 14 (September 1979), pp. 119–125.

5. Ponomarev, *Kommunist*, pp. 21–22.

6. Shafik Jorge Handal, "Na puti k svobode" (Along the Road to Freedom), *Kommunist*, no. 17 (November 1980), pp. 94–103.

7. A. F. Shul'govskii, "Gosudorstva i barba for demokritiiu" (The State and the Struggle for Democracy), *Latinskiia Amerika* no. 4 (April 1983), pp. 5–21.

8. A. I. Stroganov's review of Shul'govskii's edited book, *Politicheskaia sistema obshestva v Latinskoi Amerike* (The Political System of the Soviets in Latin America) (Moscow: Wanka, 1982), *LA* no. 5 (May 1983), pp. 183–185.

9. Memorandum of conversation between Chief of the General Staff of the Soviet Armed Forces Marshal N. V. Ogarkov and Chief of Staff of the People's Revolutionary Armed Forces of Grenada, Grenada Documents, Log no. 100008.

10. *Foreign Trade* (Moscow), no. 9, September 1983, p. 4.

11. "Washington's Latin American Policy," *International Affairs*, vol. 3 (1979), p. 27.

12. Ibid., p. 25.

13. "Latin America: Decade with a Hard Beginning," *World Marxist Review*, vol. 25, no. 3 (March 1982), pp. 19–25.

14. Ibid., p. 21.

15. Ibid., p. 22.

16. Y. Korolyov, "El Salvador: The 'Hot Spot' in Latin America," *International Affairs*, no. 6 (1981), p. 66.

17. *World Marxist Review*, vol. 27 no. 1 (January 1982), pp. 65–68.

18. A. Bovin, "World through the Eyes of a Publicist," *Nedelia* (Moscow), January 1, 1984, pp. 6–7.

Chapter 18

THE FAILURE OF STATECRAFT

Wayne Smith

I THINK I find myself more in agreement with Jiri Valenta than with Bob Leiken with respect to the continuity of Soviet policy. It seems to me that Soviet optimism does fluctuate; it may be somewhat more bearish or more bullish depending upon circumstances, and there is some fluctuation, but in fact that fluctuation has been within very stable parameters since 1962, since the missile crisis at which it was brought home again to the Soviets that geographic determinism in fact was a theory that still held—or was an imperative that was still operative.

Within those essentially stable parameters I do not see the sort of aggressiveness, the sort of adventurism, which is referred to elsewhere. Viron Vaky said yesterday that it is precisely the Soviet-Cuban factor in the equation that brings us here to the conference; otherwise there wouldn't be much interest in what is happening in Central America. That is true, but at the same time the Soviet-Cuban factor in the equation is perhaps in many ways the simplest to address. There is some degree of East-West factor here. Inevitably there is. The two superpowers confront each other on a global basis everywhere. One tries to thrust out, and the other parries it. That is in the nature of our world. But if we wish to parry, if we wish to exclude the possibility of Soviet and Cuban bases in Central America, making certain that no Central American country becomes a military platform for our adversary, we can certainly do it.

Edward Luttwak believes that it is not so much a matter of bases, it is a matter of access. Yes, it is both, but you can exclude both. We have done so in Cuba very effectively. There hasn't been a Soviet missile or nuclear submarine in a Cuban port since 1974. There have not been any Soviet bombers flying out of Cuban airfields since 1962. The Cubans do have MiG-23s—the United States could take out Cuban airfields and every MiG-23 on them within two hours if any international conflict occurred. The Cubans don't have a navy that could threaten our sea-lanes in any serious way. They have two diesel-powered submarines, perhaps they'll acquire more. The idea that the problem we have in

Central America is a threat to our sea-lanes is simply absurd. It is a threat that could be so simply dealt with as not to be worth the discussion.

We could also bring about the withdrawal—or at least the drastic reduction—of Soviet-Cuban military personnel in Nicaragua. There is more Soviet and Cuban presence and influence in Nicaragua than we, as the other superpower, can be comfortable with. I think the Soviets, and even the Cubans, understand that, and that effective United States diplomacy could bring about a withdrawal, and verification. You do not, as the administration suggests, have to make certain that the opposition in Nicaragua has one-third of the seats so that you can be certain the policies won't change. As William LeoGrande was saying yesterday, no one ever should trust anyone else in international politics; you enter into treaties or agreements on the basis of something that can be verified. There have to be some means, obviously.

As to Soviet intentions, I think Robert Leiken in his paper hit it closely on the head in saying that probably its principal objective is to promote instability in our backyard. Our military strategy is built on the assumption that this is a secure area. To the extent that the Soviets can change that, to the extent that we cannot consider it a secure area, they have gained. And they are perfectly willing to do that, perfectly willing to make trouble in our backyard, to provide some weapons, to provide a certain amount, a very limited amount, of funds in order to do that. What they are not willing to do, and so this remains within the very stable parameters I mentioned earlier, is to run any real risk, or bear any very serious cost.

There is no evidence at all that I see to support the administration's contention that the Soviets are determined to thrust aggressively into the hemisphere, turning country after country into Marxist-Leninist states. The Soviets do not accept Nicaragua as a Marxist-Leninist state just as they did not accept Cuba in the early days. The Cubans kept saying they were Marxist-Leninist and the Soviets would dance around the issue (and would not include them in the annual list.) One reason is that once you do accept them as a Marxist-Leninist state, you have a responsibility for them. Soviet ideology may not determine much, just as the Bible may not determine much in how certain churches conduct themselves (everyone says they believe in it, but they operate otherwise). But there is one principle that is sacrosanct, and that is the irreversibility of the process, that once you become Marxist-Leninist, once you are accepted, there is no turning back. That being the case, if the Soviets accepted a country like Nicaragua, which is in a very vulnerable position, as Marxist-Leninist, that would imply new and perhaps dangerous responsibilities that the Soviets simply are not willing to accept. If the Soviets were so intent on thrusting aggressively, turning all these countries into Marxist-Leninist states, one wonders why they don't come to Nicaragua's economic assistance as the Nicaraguans asked, or why they didn't come to Salvador Allende's when he was on the verge of collapse in Chile and asked them to bail him out. They blithely watched him go down the chute.

I think the idea of creating instability is central to Soviet intentions, but I would agree with Cole Blasier who, in his recent book, compared Soviet tactics in Latin America to those of the Asian martial arts, where you use the opponent's weight against him. The United States is certainly dominant in this area, but the United States does have a tendency to charge in like a water buffalo at full charge—that is, to overreact. The Soviets count on that, they count on us to fall into the trap. They use our weight against us.

American overreaction, in fact, is a greater danger than the Soviet thrust itself. It has been suggested that if Moscow's real blueprint, or objective, is to suck us into another Vietnam, see us bog ourselves down in a morass that will divert our attention from the real problems we face in the world, then we are obliging them; we are walking right into Moscow's trap, if it is that.

I sympathize with Edward Luttwak's frustration that our policies are neither the one nor the other. We neither enter into effective negotiations nor do we take decisive and effective military actions. Ed Luttwak, of course, would have us do the latter: that we take effective military actions, that we behave like a superpower and occupy Nicaragua and El Salvador again, or something along those lines. We have done that, over and over again. If I thought that would be the solution to the problem I would say fine, but it won't be. We could, on the other hand, begin serious negotiations. After all, great powers have all sorts of instruments through which they can achieve their objectives, and any policy is an effective mix of sanctions, pressures, and certain military pressures and inducements. Effective diplomacy could accomplish American objectives in Central America. We could certainly address our legitimate security concerns in the area.

I think the basic point is we can certainly sift out East-West aspects, and address those effectively, without falling into the trap of opposing all revolutionary movements or movements for change. That places us in an impossible, no-win situation in Central America. Again, what bothers me the most is that we do it over and over again. When we sent the marines to Nicaragua in 1927, Undersecretary of State Olds said that we had to send them because this was a test of American will; that Bolshevik Mexico, Moscow's surrogate in the area, was supporting those guerrillas, and this represented such a test that we had no choice but to respond to it. American marines in Nicaragua in 1927 didn't solve the problem; and they won't now. I think United States credibility suffers from the fact that we do not intelligently address the problem in the area. Our statecraft is failing. It is not a matter of lack of will, it is a matter of the failure of intelligence, the failure of statecraft.

Chapter 19
RAPPORTEUR'S REPORT
Michael Clark

LESLIE HUNTER MODERATED the panel debate, which centered on *Robert Leiken's* thesis that a Soviet thrust in Central America has been blunted by global and regional developments. When the Reagan administration came to power, Leiken argued, it faced in the Caribbean Basin, a genuine Soviet threat, not one of its own invention. The years prior to the Sandinista victory in Nicaragua marked the heyday of Soviet global expansion, and the coincidence of the Central American revolutionary crisis in 1979 seemed to persuade the Soviets to abandon their "geographic fatalism" in an area close to the United States. Since 1980, however, because of a change on the global correlation of forces, Soviet capacities have been strained, global opportunities have lessened and in Central America the Soviet threat has greatly diminished. But just as Reagan did not create the Soviet danger in Central America, his policies have not been the main factor in alleviating it. Indeed, Reagan rhetoric, and Reagan's policies, have helped Moscow consolidate previous gains.

During the years 1975–1979, the Soviet Union capitalized on the massive buildup of its military power, the subordination of Cuba, and the United States retreat after Vietnam to score dramatic successes in Asia and Africa. Soviet policy toward the Third World in this period exhibited several novel tactical features, including an emphasis on the expansion of Soviet military might as indispensable to the success of national liberation movements; a concordant down-playing of Soviet economic cooperation as an essential feature of the noncapitalist road to development; an emphasis on Soviet-bloc nations' assistance in the communications, security, intelligence, and military apparati of Third World nations; and specialization and a division of labor among Eastern-bloc nations in these fields.

By 1981, a similar pattern of Soviet involvement seemed to be developing in Central America. In 1977 and 1978 the Cubans, and later the Soviets, activated support for the Sandinista insurgency. The Soviet line in Latin America was revised and the traditional advocacy of "peaceful transition to socialism" was abandoned.

Soviet support for the Sandinista revolution, however, has not lived up to the expectations of some of the *comandantes* in Managua or some conservatives in Washington. This fact is due, Leiken argued, not to the efficacy of Reagan policies, but to a fundamental shift in the global correlation of forces. By 1979, the year of Sandinista victory in Nicaragua, the Soviet international panorama began to darken. Guerrilla resistance began to emerge in Afghanistan, Kampuchea, Eritrea, Angola, and other nations; nonaligned countries like India, Iran, and Iraq distanced themselves from the Soviet Union, and in general, Third World nations became more receptive to the West because of Soviet economic failings. Confronted by United States–Chinese and NATO cooperation and beset by internal economic and political difficulties, the Soviets, by the end of 1980, were forced to reformulate their tactics. The ascendancy of the Reagan administration in Washington added to the pressure for change, but as just one among many factors in the shifting global correlation of forces.

The result was Soviet retrenchment. In the Third World generally, the basic aim became to "consolidate the gains of socialism" rather than to take on new military and economic commitments. In Nicaragua, the Soviets adopted a policy of "cautious consolidation." While Soviet ideological penetration proceeds apace—translations of Soviet monographs and articles are readily available and printed in Sandinista organs—and though visits to Moscow by Sandinista leaders are frequent and Managua's support for Soviet foreign policy continues to be vigorous, Soviet economic and military aid has been at most "judicious." Soviet-bloc economic assistance to Nicaragua totals between $200 and $250 million per year (of which $100 to $150 million came from the Soviet Union), and the Soviet share of Nicaraguan trade amounts to just 10 percent. The Soviet military commitment has also been prudent. According to the State Department, Soviet arms transfers to Nicaragua, through January 1984, amount to a value of $17.5 million—a total that simply does not compare to the military support given to Cuba in similar circumstances in the early 1960s.

In substance, Leiken argued, the Soviet idea in Nicaragua is to get the best of both worlds. On the one hand, the Soviet Union may view Nicaragua as a bargaining chip in its relationship with Washington. Otherwise, United States intervention in Central America would not make the Soviet Union unhappy: it would necessitate a significant diversion of United States military and political resources, and would distract world attention from Soviet intervention in Afghanistan.

In conclusion, Leiken warned that Reagan administration policies, which have so far enjoyed the benefits of a favorable correlation of forces, may be laying the groundwork for another, unfavorable shift. In general, those policies have been marked by an excessive emphasis on long-term threats (which are serious but manageable) and by a failure to explore diplomatic solutions. Current policy creates an image of the United States in Latin America, the Third World, and Europe that could damage the United States foreign posture.

Jiri Valenta declared himself essentially in agreement with the foregoing assessment of the Soviet strategy in Central America, but emphasized continuity rather than change in Soviet tactics. With respect to military deployments in the region, Valenta argued, Soviet expectations were not so high as Leiken suggested. The Soviet leadership drew an important lesson from the missile crisis of 1962, and does not wish to repeat Khrushchev's blunder—as Mikoyan put it, Khrushchev played the Western game of poker and not the Russian game of chess. The Soviets do recognize the strategic importance of the region for the United States—in recent years Soviet writers have noted that American logistical support for allies in Western Europe and elsewhere might be delayed by interference in the Caribbean Basin region—but until 1979, Soviet observers remained cautious; in the late 1970s, in a debate about the revolutionary potential of the area, some experts were criticized for having earlier exaggerated prospects in Chile and Peru. Throughout the expansionary period in Soviet foreign policy, Moscow did not encourage but rather discouraged violent revolutionary struggles against the established regimes of Central America and the Caribbean. It was only in 1979 that Moscow was heartened by the emergence of revolutionary movements in Grenada, Nicaragua, and even Guatemala, and abruptly changed its line.

In Central America Soviet commitments have remained limited, it is true, but Moscow's efforts to expand its influence in the region continue on several fronts and are more threatening than has often been supposed. As documents captured in the United States intervention in Grenada reveal, Soviet military deliveries to Nicaragua and Grenada have not been modest but exceed the reasonable defense needs of both countries. Soviet tanks in Nicaragua, which now total between ninety and one hundred, threaten to destabilize the region. Soviet economic aid to Nicaragua also reflects a destabilizing level of Soviet presence. Moreover, while the Soviet press has not included Nicaragua among those nations with a "socialist orientation," it would be wrong to underestimate the degree of Soviet ideological commitment. In fact, the documents captured in Grenada show that the Soviets already regarded the Grenadans and Nicaraguans as Leninists, and actually referred to them as Communists.

If there has been a retrenchment in the Soviet view—and the evidence for this is ambiguous since journals like *Latinskaya Amerika* and *World Marxist Review* still portray Central America as the weakest link in the chain of "imperial domination"—then it has taken place after the United States intervention in Grenada. The Soviets were apparently very impressed and began hinting about a new mood in the United States. They regarded the United States action as a tough one, reminiscent of the pre-Vietnam era. Indeed, Valenta concluded, it is unfortunate that the United States did not seek to exploit these gains from its action in Grenada. Having reinstated the credibility of United States military might, it might have successfully pursued a two-track policy—one combining both military and diplomatic means to put the Sandinistas, and revolutionary movements elsewhere, even in Angola and Ethiopia, on the defensive.

Wayne Smith sided with Jiri Valenta in perceiving more continuity than change in Soviet policy in the Caribbean Basin. Although there have been periodic fluctuations in the level of Soviet activity and interest in the area, these have been contained within the limits of very stable parameters. The limits of United States tolerance were first defined in 1962 when it was brought home to the Soviets that geographic determinism is still a strategic imperative. Since then, Smith continued, the Soviets have not exhibited the sort of aggressiveness that was referred to in the presentation.

Soviet and Cuban involvement in the Caribbean Basin certainly lies at the bottom of United States concern, but in a sense, the military threat is the easiest to contend with. Even if our interest is to deny not only bases but access, we can easily exclude both. The Cubans still do not have a navy that can threaten United States sea-lanes, and what Cuba does have can be so simply dealt with as not to be worthy of discussion. Moreover, if we wish to secure a reduction of the Cuban and Soviet presence in Central America, this can also be brought about since both the Cubans and the Soviets recognize that their presence in Nicaragua is greater than we can be comfortable with and are willing to negotiate a *modus vivendi* acceptable to all.

Smith agreed with the other panelists that the basic Soviet aim is to further instability in the region, thus to erode the local security upon which American military strategy is built. To achieve this, he observed, the Soviets would be willing to supply limited arms and funds to revolutionary movements and governments in the region, but not to run any real risk or bear any serious costs.

In the discussions that followed, conference participants examined Soviet military objectives in Central America; considered the Soviet role in supporting the consolidation of revolutionary regimes; and discussed Soviet involvements in Grenada and Nicaragua.

THE SOVIET MILITARY THREAT

Helmut Sonnenfeldt cautioned that some of the panelists might have taken the direct Soviet military threat too lightly. On paper, United States naval and military might appears preponderant in the region, but in reality, given the overall structure of American commitments, it is difficult to enforce any unwritten understandings with the Soviet Union about the size and nature of its presence in Cuba and elsewhere. Even the relatively small intervention in Grenada required a significant portion of United States forces. Moreover, the sizable military infrastructure that the Soviets established in Cuba in the aftermath of the missile crisis should not be discounted as insignificant. *Jonathan Alford* added that the Cuban threat to United States sea-lanes is also more serious than Smith had suggested. Recalling the extreme difficulties of the British navy in dealing with just two Argentine subs in the recent Falklands war, Alford warned that many naval commanders would have to be gravely concerned about not only Cuban submarines but also the fifty-odd Cuban missile-equipped patrol craft.

Jiri Valenta noted that Soviet strategists do refer to Cuba as an aircraft carrier and would, as Soviet documents captured in Grenada reveal, like to repeat similar deployments elsewhere. Nevertheless, the more immediate threat is the planting of Leninist regimes ideologically hostile to the United States. Valenta took issue with the observation made in an earlier panel that Nicaragua is *becoming* hostile to the United States. There, a central committee is already at work where the Soviet-supported leader, Tomás Borge, is talking about building a revolutionary (or Leninist) party. In El Salvador also, the Soviet press has been suggesting that Shafik Handal's Communist party is becoming the leading force within the revolutionary bloc.

In reply, *Robert Leiken* argued that it is a mistake to confuse the evolution to a Leninist structure in Nicaragua with Soviet commitments. The Soviet-style Marxism-Leninism of the Sandinistas is the product of their own ideological predisposition toward the United States. And although the change in Soviet tactics allows for the "consolidation of the gains of socialism," the Soviets have been reluctant to make a commitment in Nicaragua. Boris Ponomarev, the Soviet expert on the Third World, has talked about the "emerging socialist orientation" of revolutionary movements in Central America, but since 1981 with only a single exception there has been no such reference to Nicaragua.

On the subject of Grenada, *Robert Leiken* observed that it is difficult to assess what the "reasonable defense needs" of a country are. Perhaps it is possible for American observers to agree in retrospect that the arms captured in Grenada were more than were needed to outfit the Grenadan militia, but the perception of the Grenadans may have been quite different, and history may have proven their fears of an intervention well justified.

Joseph Cirincione then asked Jiri Valenta how it was that Grenada posed a threat to neighboring islands. Having examined the Grenadan Central Committee's captured documents, Cirincione observed that he had found evidence of doctrinaire and sectarian infighting among Grenadan leadership as well as evidence of Soviet arms transfers, but little military intervention capability. Since the Grenadans lacked even minimal sea transport and since the airport allegedly being extended to receive Soviet aircraft was now being completed by the United States, was there not good reason to conclude that the military threat had been exaggerated?

Valenta responded by observing, first, that the airport in the hands of a Leninist regime might have served both terrorist and Soviet aircraft. The diary of one Grenadan Central Committee member explicitly refers to possible Cuban and Soviet military use. Moreover, Valenta noted, although the weapons provided to Cuba were old, the total amount was sufficient to equip more than six battalions—in a country of between ninety and one hundred thousand people. Nevertheless, the main value of Grenada in Soviet thinking was not as an overt threat to neighboring islands, but as a base for the promotion of revolution and subversion in the region. According to some witnesses, at the time of the United States intervention, Grenada had already been involved in training and coordinating activities with other movements in the Eastern Caribbean.

SOVIET OBJECTIVES

Albert Wohlstetter further observed that the fact that the Soviet Union had not "sprinkled holy water," or otherwise applied its seal of approval to movements in Central America is irrelevant to whether or not they perceive an opportunity for gain. In countries like Iran and Turkey (where they played both Left and Right against each other) and in the Persian Gulf today, the Soviets have shown a willingness to exploit instability without regard to ideological affinity. It's enough that it weakens Western Europe and the United States, their main adversaries. Moreover, to argue that Reagan administration rhetoric has created the conditions for a shift in the correlation of forces is to underestimate the rather consistent earlier record of the Soviet Union in fomenting instability or enhancing spontaneous dissidence in areas of concern to the United States. Al Haig spoke loudly and carried a big Carrot. Wohlstetter said he was not fond of the loud talk, but the Soviets are not greatly affected by either loud talk or sweet talk.

Robert Leiken replied that, for the purposes of American policy, an important distinction must be made between instability that the Soviets attempt to foment or exploit and Soviet subjugation of revolutionary movements. It is true that instability in itself creates problems for United States policy, but the real danger arises when revolutionary movements are captured by the Soviet Union. The Mexican revolution took place in an area contiguous to the United States, and yet the regime that emerged has never provided bases for the Soviet Union nor promoted instability elsewhere. Similarly, Marxist regimes that are nonaligned do not constitute a security threat to the United States. Leiken estimated that today in El Salvador, three-fifths of the revolutionary movement is independent—some of it outright anti-Soviet. By responding to that movement as if it were a Soviet proxy, we foreclose a "third option" of establishing nonaligned progressive regimes, and force them to choose between unviable pro–United States and also unviable pro-Soviet regimes. Over the long term, Leiken averred, it is the reimposition of United States hegemony, rather than the emergence of leftist but independent regimes in the region that can create Soviet opportunities in Latin America.

Wayne Smith added that, while the Soviet Union may have become somewhat more bullish about opportunities in Central America after the Sandinista victory, it has remained unwilling to take risks in an area so exposed to United States influence. The Soviets may have been reluctant to supply MiGs to Nicara-

gua, for example, because we had warned them indirectly—through the Nicaraguans—that the jets would be destroyed on the ground within hours of their
arrival. In a different vein, *Helmut Sonnenfeldt* observed that in order to prevent
the Soviets from taking risks in Central America, we must raise the stakes; that
without United States opposition to expanding Soviet involvements—even in the
most remote outposts—there are no risks for the Soviet Union.

CENTRAL AMERICAN PERSPECTIVES

Alberto Arene, speaking as a representative of the FMLN/FDR, offered still
another view of the Soviet role in Central America and its relationship to United
States security. After a long period, the Salvadoran opposition, Arene noted,
had come to revise its understanding of United States interests in Central
America. Though it had been widely supposed that United States opposition to
revolution in Central America related to the security of American investments,
it is now recognized that the more fundamental United States concerns relate to
national security. The real issue then, is not the choice between socialism and
capitalism, but between alignment and nonalignment; and in principle it should
be possible for the Salvadoran revolutionary movement to pursue a path in its
domestic and international affairs that would leave room for a long-term transition to a socialist society. Unfortunately, Reagan administration officials have
been unwilling to meet with Salvadoran opposition leaders.

Democrats, however, must also accept blame for the failure to achieve even a
minimal understanding. For when it comes to negotiations, the record of the
United States under both Democratic and Republican administrations is one of
arrogance backed by violence—and this is true of the United States dealings not
only with revolutionaries, but even with "boring democrats." Thus the historical
attitude of the United States has not left room for discussion on the basis of
different strategic premises, and the conclusion to be drawn is that the United
States only respects nonalignment when nonalignment is already a *fait accompli*. Perhaps Cuba's bargaining position was enhanced by the outcome of the
missile crisis. If so, it may be—"and I am no fan of the Soviet Union," Arene
said—that more Soviet interference is required.

Arturo Cruz, Jr., an associate of Edén Pastora's Democratic Revolutionary
Alliance (ARDE), took exception to Arene's proposition that you need to bring
in the Soviet Union to establish independent, progressive regimes. Instead, he
argued, what is needed is economic viability, a united leadership, and a
societal consensus. In Nicaragua, divisions among the Sandinista leadership
and an eagerness to win Soviet favor have allowed the Soviet Union to play the
role of "power broker." And since many, though not all, of the Sandinista
comandantes have been pro-Soviet from the beginning, Soviet influence has
been bought cheaply—the Soviets simply have had no incentive to pay more

dearly. Asked about Cuban influence with the Sandinista leadership, Cruz observed that Cuba enjoyed a certain "relative autonomy" in Nicaragua as long as it was needed as a mediator with the Soviet Union. The Sandinista *comandantes* resented the Cuban role, however, and traveled to Moscow to establish more direct ties. As a result, the real proxy of the Soviet Union today is not Cuba but Bulgaria, whose influence in the economy is decisive.

Judging from the Soviet failure as power broker in Grenada, *Roy Gutman* wondered if the United States might not be more effective in Nicaragua by relaxing pressure on the Sandinista leadership. *Jiri Valenta* answered that in fact the Soviets had been quite successful in Grenada and only United States intervention reversed the consolidation of a wholly pro-Moscow, Leninist regime. In Nicaragua, Valenta added, the Soviets had already come down on the side of Interior Minister Tomás Borge, far and away the Sandinista figure most frequently cited in the Soviet press. *Arturo Cruz, Jr.*, attributed Borge's ideological predispositions not to Soviet favor, but to his own formative experiences of the 1940s and 1950s when pro-Sovietism was simply the reverse side of anti-Americanism. Ironically, though, Borge is among those leaders most willing to come to terms with the United States on El Salvador—thus to buy political space and consolidate the revolution.

But even if a number of Sandinista leaders were pro-Soviet to begin with, Cruz added, current United States policy makes it impossible for Nicaragua to gain autonomy from the Soviet Union. Even leaders like Defense Minister Humberto Ortega who were not pro-Soviet five years ago are forced to cultivate a relationship with Moscow, first to compete in the internal struggle, and second because Nicaragua needs military power in order to survive. As long as they are the "only game in town," the Soviets will continue to exert a decisive influence over Nicaragua's internal politics.

Ricardo Zuniga, a Honduran officer, added a final perspective on the role of the superpowers in Central America. Because Humberto Ortega's decision to have or not to have Soviet MiG aircraft was apparently preempted by Moscow, Honduras has managed to maintain air superiority in the region. Nevertheless, air superiority is not enough. If the Nicaraguans are allowed to have Soviet tanks, then Honduras will find itself "naked" because it "must rely upon Capitol Hill for support." As a result, Honduras and Nicaragua are now engaged in a difficult and deadly struggle. At the same time, a guerrilla victory in El Salvador "threatens to inflict a strategic defeat on the Honduran army." Thus, while the stakes in Central America are far more immediate for the Central Americans than for the superpowers, the most important decisions are being made in Washington and Moscow. The lesson to be drawn, Zuniga concluded, is a familiar one: "When the elephants fight, it's the grass which suffers."

Latin American
Perspectives

Chapter 20

THE NARROW PATH: DEMOCRACY IN CENTRAL AMERICA

*Horacio Crespo and Ricardo Nudelman**

THE CENTRAL AMERICAN crisis has widened and deepened. It presents, as much in its complexity as in its possible courses of resolution, a challenge to the strategic objectives and political creativity of all those directly involved. Moreover, it is a new and difficult test for the already strained ties between the hemisphere's "North" and "South." The current upheaval also figures as an additional element of concern—of which this conference is a good reflection— in the complex relations between the United States and her partners in the Atlantic Alliance. And—although many, especially in Latin America, refuse to admit it—Central America has become another theater in the crowded field of global superpower competition. Seen from a vantage point that takes into account the long and medium term, the crisis is a confrontation between possible future paths of regional development. Its resolution will have profound consequences that will resonate through the whole of Latin America.

A number of developments have brought United States–Latin American relations to a critical point. These include the unfortunate Malvinas (Falkland Islands) War, the aggravation of the Central American crisis, and the Latin American perception of the consequences of Reagan administration policies for the Third World. Serving as the context for and exacerbating negative trends in United States–Latin American relations has been the gigantic economic crisis dating from 1981, with its dramatic social consequences. Anti–North American sentiments and the policies that they encourage are no longer exclusively expressed by leftist groups traditionally alienated from the United States. Such attitudes have become more prevalent among wide sectors of Latin American society including workers, the urban middle class, businessmen, and elite politicians. If not corrected, this situation will result in a long-term intensification of the problems confronting the United States in the region. The Central American crisis is a test, but not in the sense established by the Reagan administration. Wide and influential segments of Latin American opinion view

---

*Translated by Stephen Beede.

this as a decisive moment for United States relations with the region; if the crisis is resolved in the classical style, by the violent reassertion of United States hegemony, the abyss of misunderstanding and resentment will grow to critical proportions.

THE DEMOCRATIC PRESUMPTION

Anyone considering the prospects for, in the words of José Martí, "our America" during the next fifteen years must grapple with this most decisive of questions: Is democracy a viable alternative for the countries of Central America and a means of solving and transcending the current exasperating crisis? Further, one must determine whether or not existing factors inevitably push the Central American and Caribbean states toward paths of resolution that present the choice of either right-wing authoritarian or leftist totalitarian governments, both of which promise nothing but stagnation and dependence. In order to understand all the dimensions of the current crisis, external actors and observers must be aware of the dramatic, at times anguished, emotional burden that this issue bears for us Latin Americans.

Naturally, there exist different interpretations of the crisis. Observers disagree over its origins, the motivations of the participants, the probable development of events, and the proposed solutions. Every point of view is conditioned by a preference for a particular long-term resolution of the crisis. Whether or not this preference is made explicit, it always expresses particular and specific interests. We prefer, for the sake of clarity, to make our biases clear: The elaboration of our analysis of the crisis in Central America is conditioned by a Latin American perspective that emphasizes the necessity and viability of democracy for all the countries of the region. The only hope for extricating ourselves from the present acute crisis and building a stable future lies in a bold turn toward truly representative government.

This perspective demands a prefatory discussion of commonly accepted opinions on the subject of democracy and development. The most influential analysis holds that democracy cannot take root until its material foundations have been secured by a long-term economic development. This thesis was first formulated by nineteenth-century Latin American thinkers. Although this concept owes its origin to aristocratic positivism, it has, paradoxically, won wide acceptance among intellectuals very different from those who engendered it. Indeed, its influence has expanded beyond the borders of Latin America.

This thesis can be summarized by one short phrase: first wealthy, and then democratic. Put another way, it argues the impossibility of establishing democratic regimes in countries that are characterized by terms such as "immature," "insufficiently developed," "underdeveloped," and "dependent," euphemisms frequently applied to the Central American states. There are certain vulgar variants of this analysis, which are more insidiously influential than is usually admitted, that decree our countries to be culturally and even ethnically "unfit" for the exercise and benefits of democracy. Those who indulge in such speculation flirt with racist concepts. Taking note of their Latin, Indian, and black ethnicity, they characterize the people of Central America as essentially unadaptable to democracy, a political system completely alien to their natural inclinations.

This paper, of course, will leave aside this last line of argument and consider only the first, the idea, often uncritically accepted as an objective fact, that Central America is not mature enough for democracy. It is due to this point of view that some justify the sacrifice of democracy for "social conquests" for the dispossessed. This implies that apologists for self-styled regimes of "national liberation" do not consider democracy to be among the essential priorities of the people, an opinion which clearly reveals the ideological poverty and extreme opportunism of those who uncritically defend repressive leftist governments. Such a perspective turns democracy into a "desirable horizon" that always will recede until "conditions" make it possible, a political deception that demonstrates the servility of so-called democrats to the totalitarianism practiced by the "progressive" dictators of the Third World.

In ideological terms, democracy is challenged by both the authoritarian Right and the totalitarian Left. Although adherents of both currents of thought deny the legitimacy of democracy, they do not hesitate to incorporate democratic tactics in their calculated schemes for achieving and exercising power.

Contrary to the perspectives discussed above, we believe that democracy is neither a "luxury of development" nor a "tactical instrument." Democracy is a theory of government and a political practice. It is established only by practice, however imperfect. On this theory and practice it is possible to found a pluralistic political system. Such a democratic system is tolerant of dissent and permits the free expression of unpopular opinions. It allows for the transformation of political minorities into political majorities by the expression of the popular will, and, by the same route, it permits such new majorities to be entrusted with public authority. Another desirable characteristic of this political arrangement is the prohibition of the monopolization of power by any one group. Factors such as these ensure the long-term consensual legitimacy of democratic governments.

Of course, democracy should not be limited strictly to the framework of governance, although that is one of the essential arenas. Democracy should be both the means of continuously widening popular participation in great national decisions and an effective instrument for implementing policies that struggle for a better distribution of the social surplus. Democracy should allow for a national consensus based on a progressively broadening availability of the fruits of economic growth.

Democracy is modernization: the fruit of modernity and, simultaneously, the active agent of it. For this reason, its systematic establishment should adjust itself to each national reality and the particulars of each country's social, economic, and political development. However, particular national situations aside, it should be reaffirmed that democracy is not merely desirable for the future of Latin America. The histories of these countries demonstrate that they are ready for democracy and, further, that democracy is the only system that can provide for equitable and harmonious development tied to political pluralism. It even offers a guarantee of the very viability of national sovereignty, whose maintenance has in some cases been called into question by the present crisis. All the above is as true of countries ruled by right-wing authoritarian regimes and traditional defenders of the status quo as it is of those controlled by leftist totalitarian governments, of which Cuba is the exemplary case.

THE CURRENT CRISIS AND U.S. INVOLVEMENT

Within the framework of the establishment of stable democracy throughout the region, it is necessary to emphasize and reaffirm the right of the peoples of Central America to choose their own road into the future and their own agenda for development.

Today the isthmus presents a panorama of economic, social, and political frustration. In almost all Central America, economic indices reveal the fact that the majority of the population lacks the basic necessities of life. In addition, most of these countries are burdened with tremendously oppressive political institutions. Finally, to this desolate vista have been added the misery of war and state terror, a response to insurgency that virtually precludes the exercise of the most elemental human rights.

Clearly, this dismal situation is aggravated by social and political realities strongly conditioned by low levels of national, not to mention regional, integration. In some countries, profound cultural and ethnic heterogeneity further complicates the picture. These factors constitute a burdensome historical legacy that has been made still more crippling by the execution of inappropriate development projects which have accentuated local tensions and contradictions by ignoring traditional social structures.

Faced with growing instability, the elite rulers of these countries have demonstrated a marked tendency to oppose bitterly and to reverse violently both democratic change and fundamental economic modernization. This trend toward confrontation has accelerated since the Second World War as the democratic and developmental processes have intensified, resulting in an improvement of general social conditions. The Guatemala of Arbenz is a prime example of this dynamic of political reaction, while the Costa Rican experience, with all its problems and limitations, demonstrates the potential for and the viability of democracy in the region, given the political will.

These social and economic conditions fundamentally shape and motivate the emergence of popular movements in the region. In many cases, these movements have taken up arms because of the complete closure of any other road that might lead to progressive political, economic, and social reforms. It should be pointed out that among the important motivations for armed rebellion is the resort to extreme and indiscriminate repression by government agents and right-wing terrorist groups. Armed movements of radical orientation have been constant fixtures of Central American history; their emergence strictly stems from the institutional and structural realities of the countries of the region. This concept is central to a correct diagnosis of the present crisis and to an accurate evaluation of what the future will hold if today's insurgent movements are frustrated by a military strategy that does not alter the conditions that motivated their emergence.

Within the framework of the historical development of the Central American countries, it is necessary to consider the role played by the United States in the region. The North American interest there has been long standing and has always been fraught with strategic implications. Beginning in the middle of the past century, the United States and Great Britain engaged in a protracted struggle for domination of the isthmus, through which passed a good deal of interoceanic trade, which exacerbated all regional conflicts. This competition took place during the long United States–Mexican dispute over Texas, which was resolved by the annexation of half of Mexico's territory by the United States. The price of this North American victory was long-term Mexican resentment, which remains tense and latent.

Admiral Alfred Mahan, the father of United States strategic thought, defined the Caribbean as "the American Mediterranean." This concept continues to be highly influential in the United States, and it informs a particular North American perception of the current conflict in the isthmus.

The Spanish-American War of 1898 marked the full-fledged birth of an "imperial republic" (the fortunate expression of Raymond Aron) with control of the North Pacific and the Caribbean basin via domination of the Philippines, Cuba, and Puerto Rico. The overseas expansion of 1898 was the first significant maneuver of a long-term strategic operation that reached fruition with the secession of Panama and the construction of the Canal. This strategy successfully bound together both coasts of the North American continent and gave the United States a commanding presence in Central America. In the judgment of Washington strategists, this region would constitute the area of "natural influence" of "fortress America." Recently, President Reagan has restored to official language a phrase describing the strategic importance of Central America that is particularly offensive to the Latin American sensibility: the region, he claims, is the "backyard" of the United States. The purchase of the Virgin Islands from Denmark in 1917 further consolidated the North American presence in the Caribbean.

Naturally, to strategic interests were joined economic interests. United States companies seeking to procure tropical products on a grand scale for the North American market extended their activities throughout the countries of the region, giving them the characteristics of colonial-style enclave economies. The marked political and social instability of the region menaced the extensive investments of North American business interests and supposedly called into question United States national security. During the period bracketed by the Spanish-American War and the Second World War, Central American unrest motivated some thirty *direct* United States interventions according to a list prepared for the Senate by the Department of State. The most recent prolongations of this policy have been the landing of the Marines in Santo Domingo in 1965, the invasion of Grenada in 1983, the increasingly menacing presence of United States troops in Honduras, and the participation of North American advisors in the Salvadoran civil war. In addition to direct interventions, it is necessary to mention the effect of diplomatic and economic pressures and covert action operations that have created an enormous abyss of incomprehension and misunderstanding between the United States and the peoples of the region. One point should be made clear: this comportment does not affect merely relations between the United States and those countries that North Americans have disrespectfully labeled the "banana republics." Wide circles of Latin American opinion have come to view United States Central American policy as a paradigm for United States relations with the whole of Latin America.

For decades, United States policy in the region has been characterized by its support of notoriously corrupt and repressive regimes that are incapable of making even minimal contributions to the resolution of the huge problems confronting the countries of the region. The United States has become completely identified with the maintenance of the status quo. This accounts for the inability of United States policymakers to foresee crises that stem from the very structure of Central American societies. It also determines the typically inadequate, brutal, and ill-timed United States response to such problems. An excellent example of this policy and its enormously negative results can be seen in United States treatment of the Cuban revolution during its first stage, before Havana's open alignment with the Soviet Union and declaration of Marxist-Leninist faith. This approach also is observable in the policy of the current administration toward Central America, which for the most part appears to ignore the profound motivations, anchored in reality, for the emergence, consolidation, and development of the insurgent movements.

This North American policy is a consequence of two factors present in the analysis that underlies it. The first is a profound ignorance of the histories and complexities of the countries involved. This fact prevents Washington from recognizing the causes of the current political and social dynamic. The second, conditioned by the first, is a projection of superpower competition on local conflicts.

Nevertheless, there have been two postwar presidents who conceded that local factors deserved a preeminent place in their analysis of regional problems. President Kennedy's Alliance for Progress was a serious attempt to cooperate with the countries of the region to promote democratic modernization. The Alliance was frustrated for multiple reasons whose analysis would constitute an excellent point of departure for a profound redirection of United States policy toward the hemisphere. The overall approach of President Carter also deserves praise. Carter's detractors are in error when they insist that his policies were based on ingenuous and impractical idealism. The human-rights initiative of the Carter administration posed the first serious ideological challenge to the Soviet Union since the end of the Cold War, and it had a strong impact on Central America. Equally as impressive were President Carter's decision to negotiate an end to United States sovereignty over the Panama Canal Zone, his refusal to stand by the regime of Anastasio Somoza to the bitter end, and his tense relations with the military rulers of the Southern Cone. Taken together, these policies held out hope for a new direction in United States-Latin American relations. Had they been pursued, Carter's policies doubtlessly would have borne fruit by now. It can be argued that Carter's approach was of limited scope and that it never came to constitute a clearly defined long-term strategy, but it should also be affirmed that initiatives such as those undertaken by his administration are needed to begin the task of surmounting a long history of controntation, mistrust, and misunderstanding.

THE SOVIET PRESENCE

There exists in important Latin American circles a strong resistance to admitting the Soviet role in the Central American crisis. There are many reasons for this attitude; they run the gamut from the most elemental ingenuousness to hidden self-interest; from strategic calculation in the function of national objectives to the deliberate deceit of Kremlin meddling. In many cases it stems from a desire to defend the correct diagnosis of the causes of the current conflict: the expansionism of the Communist superpower is not the origin of the Central American crisis; it is the structural reality of those countries that motivates the insurgent movements. As it is most commonly put, this thesis asserts that the Central American problem is of a "North-South," not "East-West" nature. This wording is meant both to emphasize the fact that the insurgent movements are profoundly rooted in the social, economic, and political conditions affecting the countries in which they act and to affirm the justice of their cause and the legitimacy of their course of action. This perspective also points to the "imperial" North American presence in the region as an obstacle in the road leading to autonomous development freely decided by the people of Central America. In the context of growing anti-North American sentiments any allusion to the role played by the other superpower is seen by many as a "diversionist" maneuver with respect to the principle objective: overthrowing United States domination. The prestige of the Cuban revolution, albeit in retrocession, also serves the end of concealing the ultimate objective, and even the very presence, of the Soviets in the hemisphere.

As with all reductionism, this attitude is erroneous. Calling attention to the basic nature of the conflict does not require ignoring the complexity of factors that act upon it. This type of reasoning presents two problems. First, it ignores the fact that the Soviet presence—manifested by material and propagandistic aid provided both directly and indirectly through Cuba—is a substantive element in the development of the crisis. This is viewed by Washington as a sensitive issue and, therefore, it must be taken into account in any attempt to achieve a negotiated resolution of the crisis. Second, it ignores, minimizes, or openly disqualifies the anti-Soviet positions taken by groups that have played an important role in the struggle for democratic change in Central America. Therefore, this attitude privileges those who favor alignment with Cuba and the Soviet Union and a social arrangement that is neither pluralistic nor democratic. In this sense, the ambiguous attitude of important leaders of the European social democratic movement, of North American liberals, and of "progressive" circles in Latin America contributes more to the confusion than to the encouragement of the truly democratic actors involved in the crisis.

What interests do the Soviets pursue in Latin America? In its most general aspects the answer should be related to the strategy of the USSR in its struggle for global hegemony. Latin America is not a priority for the Kremlin; Soviet policy is focused on Western Europe, the Persian Gulf, the Indian Ocean, and the maritime passes whose domination could be used to strangle supply lines for the shipment of oil and other strategic raw materials to the United States and Western Europe. The fundamental Soviet objective in Latin America, beyond maintaining its control over Cuba, is not the creation of new satellites in the region but the destabilization of the traditional hegemony exercised by the United States. Therefore, Soviet forces will be directed toward the intensification of any conflict that prejudices or endangers United States dominion, toward "bogging down" Washington's foreign policy in a Central American swamp.

It is out of the question for the Soviets to consider subsidizing friendly Latin American regimes as they do for Cuba. Also evident is the Kremlin's intention to avoid a direct military engagement in the region unless the sovereignty of Cuba is menaced. Nevertheless, the Soviets have transferred and will continue to try to win strategic advantage in the sensitive waters of the Caribbean by increasing their own and Cuba's naval presence, selling arms to "progressive" governments, and augmenting their diplomatic maneuvers. The case of the airport of Grenada and its potential military utility is a good example of this policy. The Soviets will continue to follow the well-worn path of providing

material and propagandistic aid to insurgent movements and aiding the forma-
tion of political and military fronts, a policy that has in general returned good
dividends on their Third World investments. By taking advantage of conditions
created by the convulsive political dynamic of the region, the Soviet Union can
achieve at practically no cost and with little risk a good deal of its limited
objective of destabilizing North American hegemony. Episodes like the Malvinas War, the Central American crisis, and disputes with the United States
over the availability of items that important Latin American countries consider
vital to their development are examples of situations in which the Soviet policy
described above has excellent opportunities for success.

The United States has shown itself to be very sensitive to the possibility of
Soviet advances in Latin America. The triumph of the Cuban revolution and the
course it has adopted since 1961 revived and intensified Washington's worries
with respect to its economic and strategic interests in the Caribbean and Central
America. The missile crisis of October 1962 resulted in a relatively stable
status quo that legalized the Soviet presence in the hemisphere. During the
seventies this situation was slowly transformed as the Soviets augmented their
commercial and diplomatic activity in South America and strengthened their
military presence in Cuba. These developments did not completely unravel the
pact agreed to in 1962, but there were evident increments of Soviet power.

Leftist activity in Jamaica, Grenada, and Suriname, the triumph of the
Sandinista revolution, and the increasing effectiveness of the guerrillas in El
Salvador and, to some extent, in Guatemala combined to convince important
circles of decision in Washington that United States strategic interests and the
very "national security" of the country was being called into question in the
region. The policies of the Sandinista regime encouraged the fear that Nicaragua was following the Cuban path toward total subjugation to Soviet domination.
Finally, the Reagan administration's decision to make the Salvadoran crisis a
test of the effectiveness of its policy of contention with communism ensured that
tensions would run extremely high in the area.

The United States has precisely determined the strategic interests that it
believes are menaced by the expanded presence and heightened power of the
Soviets in the region:

—The Caribbean Basin, of which Central America is a part, is the frontier of
the United States;

—Half of United States maritime commerce circulates through the Caribbean basin;

—Half of crude oil imported by the United States also is shipped on Caribbean sea-lanes;

—Washington is closer to San Jose, Costa Rica, than to San Francisco,
California;

—Central America is the major source of immigration (legal and illegal) to
the United States.[1]

To this list should be added the location of the Caribbean of large refineries that process African and Middle Eastern crude oil and the existence of huge supplies of bauxite in the region. Also, the administration is aware of the political pressure that would be applied by large North American private economic interests if United States investments were adversely affected by a turn toward radical nationalism on the part of important countries of the region.

Rhetorically denying the legitimacy of United States interests does not contribute to the possibility of reaching a resolution of the crisis. In the same vein, denying that the Soviet Union would view with pleasure and, if possible, contribute to the destabilization of North American domination of such a sensitive area is not constructive. Any refutation of the proposition that superpower confrontation is an element of the complex tangle of the Central American conflict must be ingenuous or self-interested. The challenge for Latin Americans who wish to promote the development and the independence of these countries is to avoid a situation in which superpower competition escalates to a dangerous and irreversible stage. The people of other regions of the world that have been converted into fields of battle between the superpowers can testify to the gravity of the consequences of such a development for their vital interests. If the point of view that considers wide zones of Latin America "reserved" for North American necessity can be justified in terms of legitimate United States strategic concerns, it also should be admitted that the defense of this territory and its strategic products is vital for Latin Americans menaced by the East-West conflict. And it is legitimate, in consequence, to demand from the United States an adequate guarantee of respect of our sovereignty and security.

If the United States were to abandon its current self-defeating policy for a program of aid for the development of democratic forces, the security of the United States as well as that of the Latin American countries could be strengthened. Only such a policy could effectively alleviate convulsive social conditions that can be exploited by Soviet destabilization tactics. Collective security cannot be imposed by the superpowers through interventionist and aggressive policies; it must be the result of harmonious political, economic, and social development founded on genuine national forces and mutually beneficial relations.

DEMOCRACY AND SECURITY

The chances for democratic development in Latin America depend, in essence, on the strengthening of the social forces that support it in each country. Also, the growth of the democratic process at the regional level can create strong incentives for success in individual countries to the extent that democratic states establish mutual-aid arrangements, privilege their ties with each other, and limit the benefits of cooperation available to the undemocratic regimes of the regional system. Also, and this should be emphasized, the aid provided by the great democracies of Western Europe, Japan, and, especially, the United States could play a crucial role in encouraging democratization.

We have already analyzed the historical role of the United States as supporter of the status quo, of oppressive and antidemocratic regimes, and of unjust and backward social structures. This policy, which contradicts the basic postulates of the United States system and the political values on which the country was founded, too often has been justified by high North American leaders as necessary to the defense of United States strategic interests menaced by the "expansion of communism" and the possible emergence of totalitarian Marxist-Leninist regimes of the region. The results are plain to see: the United States has become the protector, often despite its wishes and public declarations, of the forces that most recalcitrantly oppose democratic change and progress in Latin America, especially in the Central American region. Thus, the United States leaves the door wide open for the emergence of destabilizing forces engendered by explosive social and political contradictions, conditions that allow Cuba and the Soviet Union to exercise what is at times preponderant influence over indigenous insurgencies.

The foundation of a new United States–Latin American dialog—of which the Caribbean Basin crisis could be a basic test—cannot be built solely on declarations of principle that tend to degenerate into a purely rhetorical discourse. A new departure for hemispheric relations must be sustained by a pragmatic convergence of interests. The basic point of departure for a firm mutual consensus must be the recognition that a program for establishing strong and stable democracies is the only road by which all the countries involved can achieve appreciable and sustained advances toward their fundamental objectives. For the countries of Latin America, democratization will consolidate a path of development that will permit the resolution of their most acute problems. For the United States, the same strengthening of the democratic system in Central America and the Caribbean will bolster its security and "strategic interests."

A principally military resolution of the current isthmian conflict—if it is possible—will only accumulate problems, conserving old ones and creating new ones. Such a policy will give rise to new cycles of radical insurgency until channels of development and political participation are created. Washington must recognize the gravity of the crisis that is convulsing the entire subcontinent; for a problem of this type there exists no definitive military solution.

The current situation in Latin America offers an opportunity to strengthen the relevant groups, sectors, and social classes and to foster an understanding that can provide a framework for real economic development and an effective democratic model. Issues such as the following must be faced: the effects of the foreign debt on the productivity of debtor nations, the need for an open market and favorable terms of trade in the United States market, and fostering of capital flows toward a region drastically drained of capital from servicing the foreign debt. Aid should be channeled not so much through the state apparati, but to the strengthening of the entrepreneurial sector, to the promoting of a transfer of inexpensive technology and the development of cultural and scientific exchanges. These are challenges that Latin America and the United States must resolve in order to reinforce collective security.

The people of Latin America would be receptive to a well-planned cooperative strategy for promoting democracy and development. Such an approach should be marked by adequate mutual consultation and complemented by efforts in the same direction on the part of Western Europe and Japan. The true threats to the strategic interests of the United States in Central America, in all of Latin America, and, by extension, throughout the Third World are hunger, misery, backwardness, and the closure of the paths of development. The challenge of the Soviet Union should be confronted in the economic area, as opposed to the military sphere, where its impotence and the failure of its system cannot be denied or resolved. The United States should eradicate the conditions that invite Soviet destabilization initiatives and which offer the Kremlin the opportunity to implant the seeds of its hegemony within insurgent movements arising from economic, social, and political conditions endemic to the Third World.

To the extent that the obstacles to democratic development increase and are identified by leading Latin Americans as arising from United States policies or interests, new opportunities for Soviet adventurism will occur. For the sake of democracy in Latin America, it is urgent and vital that a vast concerted effort to promote development be undertaken. Without any doubt, a negotiated settlement of the Salvadoran (and indeed of the entire Central American) conflict, development of a strong democratic option in Nicaragua (with guarantees for all from the Sandinista authorities), isolation and condemnation of right-wing terrorist groups, and civilian control over the military (not excluding last-resort military action against opponents of the new democratic order) are points of departure for this ambitious, concerted, long-term project. The discussions of the Contadora Group plus new direct instances of open negotiations could be the operative forums for the development of this means of transcending the conflict.

The resolution of a critical situation demands force, audacity, and imagination. A concerted effort to promote democracy in Central America and the subcontinent as a whole would test the true intentions of each actor in that drama. The sincerity of the motivations of the participants must mirror that of the people of the region; the two successive elections held in El Salvador have permanently demonstrated the enormous support for the democratic option. Such signs are a clear lesson for those who claim to be the representatives of the people yet lack the power to prove their legitimacy.

It is necessary to avoid the frustration that opens the road to totalitarian temptations and reactionary adventures. This is the problem of the hour. As the Mexican writer Octavio Paz says:

Latin American democracy arrived late and has been disfigured and betrayed time and time again. It has been weak, indecisive, unruly, its own enemy, easy victim of the demagogue's flattery, corrupted by money, corroded by favoritism and nepotism. Nevertheless, almost all the good that has been done in Latin America since a century and a half ago has been done under the regimen of democracy or, as in Mexico, on the way to democracy. Much remains to be done. Our countries need changes and reforms, at one and the same time radical and in accord with the tradition and genius of each people. There where they have tried to change the social and economic structure dismantling at the same time democratic institutions, injustice, oppression and inequality have been fortified. The cause of the workers requires, above all, liberty of association and the right to strike: this is the first thing that their liberators snatch away from them. Without democracy changes are counterproductive; better put: they are not changes. In this, intransigence must be strict and the point must be repeated: changes are inseparable from democracy. To defend it is to defend the possibility of change; in their time, only changes will be able to strengthen democracy and insure that it is embodied in the social life. It is a dual and immense task. Not only for the Latin Americans: it is a duty for everyone. The struggle is global. Moreover, it is uncertain, doubtful. No matter: it must be fought.[2]

NOTES

1. See *Report of the National Bipartisan Commission on Central America* (Washington, D.C.: Department of State, January 1984), pp. 92–93.

2. Octavio Paz, *Tiempo Nublado* (Mexico: Seixbarral, 1983), p. 188.

Chapter 21

NO SUBSTITUTE FOR REVOLUTION? DEMOCRACY AND THE MILITARY IN CENTRAL AMERICA

Anibal Romero

HORACIO CRESPO AND Ricardo Nudelman have presented us with a stimulating contribution to the debate on the origins, implications, and likely course of the current Central American crisis. In their paper they make a number of significant points, and the following seem to me particularly relevant:

1. Analyses of the Central American crisis must include an explicit formulation of the nature of the political project that is proposed as an alternative to the status quo.
2. Any viable political alternative in the region should above all be based on the principle of the inalienable right of Central Americans to choose and implement their own solutions.
3. Democracy is both a political theory and a political practice, and its effective exercise in Central America should not be sacrificed to abstractions or "postponed" to an indefinite future.
4. The turmoil in the isthmus has deep local causes, derived from persistent poverty, resource competition, and political repression that lie at the heart of the present revolutionary outbreak; but the crisis also has an international dimension that affects, and is in turn influenced by, United States security perceptions, the antagonisms between the superpowers, and the participation of regional medium powers such as Cuba, Mexico, and Venezuela.
5. United States policies in the area have traditionally been characterized by the contradiction between a declaratory commitment to democracy and an actual preference for "stability" in alliance with dictatorial regimes. The crucial question now is whether United States decision makers are prepared to reorientate their approach to the region, or whether they will succumb once again to the strong temptation to preserve the basic features of the status quo—though this may require the promotion of some limited reforms to the existing order.

Crespo and Nudelman are convinced that a democratic alternative to the area's crisis is feasible, and they implicitly adopt the by-now fashionable distinction—as applied to Central America—between "authoritarian" and "totalitarian" political systems, by denying that the intensity of the contemporary struggle will inevitably force Central Americans to choose between these undesirable options. In their view, there can be no definitive military solution to the crisis, and they urge the development of a "vast plan of action" for democratic change in the region, and for a negotiated settlement of the present conflicts. To my mind, the most valuable aspect of their paper lies in its emphatic plea in favor of democratic rights for the peoples of Central America, and in its principled defense of freedom against political oppression of any sort. They rightly attack the view that democracy is a "luxury" that can only be enjoyed by certain economically "mature" countries, and the tendency to subordinate democratic reforms to the "satisfaction of the (economic and social) needs of the people." They fail however to point out that the notion that "stability" should precede freedom is not only a legacy of nineteenth-century Latin American political thought, of the authoritarian ideology of our contemporary military regimes, or of Marxist dogma, but can also be found in some United States ideologists' approach to the problem of "political development" in our societies—an approach that has been highly influential in determining United States policies toward the Latin Western hemisphere. According to this view, which is basically an elaboration of the Hobbesian concept of "order" as the fundamental political good, "the most important political distinction among countries concerns not their *form* of government but their *degree* of government."[1] As Ambassador Jeane Kirkpatrick has put it, the problem confronting Central America (she refers here specifically to El Salvador) is "Thomas Hobbes's problem: How to establish order and authority in a society where there is none."[2] This theory holds that the challenges of "political development" are directly related to the improvement of the ruling elite's "crisis-management capabilities," and this in turn may require in certain cases the adoption of more participatory political mechanisms.[3] Thus the concern for "stability" and "authority" as the "prerequisites of liberty" and the use of elections as a short-term device to legitimize the rule of what are essentially bankrupt regimes are not only characteristic of a certain tradition in Latin American political practice, but also play a part in the formulation and implementation of United States policies toward the region, particularly in the persistent United States efforts to strengthen the military as the ultimate guarantors of "order."

While I share the Crespo-Nudelman rejection of the Marxist-inspired notions of "bourgeois" freedoms as "unreal" or "false" freedoms, and also their dissatisfaction with the tendency of some "progressive" movements to rate democratic reforms at the lowest end of their priorities, I think that these views should be sharply distinguished from the notion—common among Latin American social democrats—that "democracy" should be defined in relation to three crucial aspects:

—First, the existence of pluralism and of mechanisms for changing the incumbent government by the exercise of the popular will, through free elections;

—Second, the existence of a situation in which the government actually rules, and in which civilian control of the military is effectively exercised;

—Finally, the inclusion of social and economic factors in the definition of "democratic reform" by the implementation of policies that respond to the "logic of the majority," and the creation of a society in which most of the population share in the existing resources.

Crespo and Nudelman correctly insist upon the importance of pluralism and the institutional protection of dissidence to established authority, but they have very little to say about what is surely one of the key obstacles to any meaningful process of democratic change in the isthmus—the military's role as guardians of the status quo. Most Latin Americans would probably agree that the goal of political struggle in Central America should be to establish societies that are democratic, prosperous, reform-oriented, and peaceful. But the harsh realities of the region show us that Central American nations are actually wracked by conflict, politically polarized, repressive, and unstable. Whether these realities can be altered through gradual democratic reforms or through the traumatic spasms of violent revolution depends not primarily on those who want change to take place, but on those who want to prevent it. After all, most Central Americans who have tried to reform their societies in the past have attempted to do it mainly through peaceful means, only to find that it was impossible.

Crespo and Nudelman are convinced that the "narrow path" of democratic evolution is now a viable option, and argue that it would be the product of, among other things, a "negotiated solution of the Salvadoran conflict," the development of "a strong democratic option in Nicaragua," the "isolation and condemnation of right-wing terrorist groups," and, if necessary, the "use of military force" against those who would still oppose the new democratic order. They mention the Contadora Group's proposals and the Salvadoran elections as examples of the kind of initiatives that can make the "narrow path" that much less narrow. And yet I wonder if this is not too good to be true. What is the specific relevance of these recommendations about negotiations and peace to the concrete situation in Guatemala, El Salvador, and Honduras—where corrupt and repressive armed forces exercise firm control over steadily deteriorating political systems—or in Nicaragua—where a revolution is taking place that faces the unrelenting political hostility of the United States government and an increasingly powerful military offensive? How are these suggestions going to be implemented in an isthmus convulsed by a regional civil war? In short, is it realistic to expect change without revolution in Central America?

At one point in their paper, Crespo and Nudelman write that an analysis of the Alliance for Progress would be an excellent starting point for a thorough rethinking of United States policies toward the hemisphere. I agree, and I think that a study of the Alliance's failure convincingly demonstrates the incompatibility of a policy that strengthens the Latin American military with one that encourages reforms and democracy. In the case of Central America, the armed forces of Guatemala, El Salvador, and Honduras—with their profound ideological conservatism, their ingrained fear of retribution for past misdeeds, and their privileged economic[4] and political status in their societies—have never been, and cannot be, agents of democratic change—unless they are extensively purged and reformed, as in Costa Rica in 1948. Crespo and Nudelman refer to the Costa Rican experience as a good example of the potential of democratic politics in the isthmus, if there is "political will" to sustain it, but they fail to point out that this remarkable situation came about as a result of a revolution and of the dismantling of the military caste. They do not discuss the problem of the internal reform of the Central American military—who have traditionally been, and still are, the most important security threat to their own peoples—and this, in my view, reduces considerably the weight of their otherwise illuminating analysis. If a close connection is not established between ideals and realities, especially in such a complex and turbulent content as Central America, the discrepancy between what is hoped for and what can actually be achieved can only lead to increasing frustration or, worse still,—and this seems to be the Reagan administration's attitude—to an acceptance of the status quo, with a face of "reforms," as the "lesser of two evils." The contradiction between ideals and realities can, on the one hand, lead to disappointment for those who genuinely embrace the ideals, but, on the other hand, it can be used as a political weapon by those who are only interested in the preservation of the existing order. This is shown, just to give one example, in a reportedly widespread attitude among the Salvadoran armed forces which has been summed up as "Let the Yankees see what they want to see. Then do what you want to do."[5]

THE SIGNIFICANCE OF THE NICARAGUAN REVOLUTION

The authors do not explicitly discuss in their paper the Nicaraguan Revolution, but I think we can safely assume that their criticisms of those self-defined "progressive" regimes that boast about their "social conquests" without, however, raising the issue of democracy, are a thinly veiled reference to the Nicaraguan reality as they see it. Let me first of all declare my own position on this point by quoting Arturo Cruz's apt words to the effect that "the Nicaraguan Revolution, while in a state of sickness, is still worthy of an effort to heal it."[6] Mr. Cruz—whose intellectual honesty I greatly respect—has strongly argued that, first, despite all its failings and limitations, the Revolution is the most important event in the history of Nicaragua and a decisive landmark in the history of Central America; secondly, all efforts—short of invasion, blockade, or support for Somocista contras—should be made to ensure that the extremist zealots within the Sandinista movement do not irrevocably gain the upper hand in defining its course: and finally, that the United States should show by actions, not merely words, that it is prepared to coexist with a revolution in the isthmus as long as it does not transform itself into a Soviet satellite.[7] It is a pity that

Crespo and Nudelman did not address themselves to these matters, for what happens *in* Nicaragua and *with* Nicaragua will probably decide the future of the whole region for decades to come.

The United States government has repeatedly insisted that it would be ready to accept radical political and social changes in the hemisphere as long as Cuba and the USSR do not exert any major influence upon such developments; and in its report, the Kissinger Commission argued that "History holds examples of genuinely popular revolutions, springing wholly from native roots," giving Mexico as an example.[8] But this assertion totally overlooks the history of the relations between the United States and Mexico when the revolution was taking place, more than half a century ago. In his detailed study of the period, Peter Calvert has shown how the United States government "automatically and crudely" interpreted civil disturbances in Mexico as connected with the machinations of "outside powers," the internal disorders in Mexico were used as an opportunity for further United States expansion to the south, and United States leaders completely failed to realize that "the man on the losing side in the war of nationalisms in Mexico would always be the man with *gringo* support."[9] Many analogies could be drawn with the present situation in relation to Nicaragua. To be sure, contemporary Mexico is seen as relatively "safe" by United States leaders, but this is not how things were perceived when the revolution actually occurred.

I think that United States leaders have traditionally had a very poor understanding of, and an extremely low tolerance for, revolutionary change in Latin America, and this is being shown once again with respect to Nicaragua. It seems to me quite obvious, as well as legitimate, that after almost fifty years of United States support for Somocismo, a great number of Nicaraguans should feel strong antipathy and resentment against the government in Washington. It is also not surprising that, at least for a while, Nicaraguan *nationalism* will be defined in purely anti-American terms. When we in Venezuela fought for our independence against Spain in the early nineteenth century, we asked for the help of the other great empire at the time—Britain—and they gave it to us. The Sandinistas now ask the USSR and Cuba for help: this is, again, not surprising, though it may be considered regrettable. The Nicaraguan Revolution is a genuine revolution, not a pseudorevolution imposed by the Soviets or the Cubans. The United States government's undeclared war against it, and the support for the contras will not, I believe, destroy it, but these actions are certainly doing a great deal to help the extremist elements among the Sandinista Directorate push their case for more repressive political and military measures to defend the Revolution. If this process is not stopped, the Reagan administration may then succeed in calling into question the legitimacy of the revolutionary project in Nicaragua, to the detriment of that country and of Central America as a whole. As Arturo Cruz, Jr., has correctly argued, "While it is true that the Reagan administration was not directly responsible for the close ties between Managua and Moscow," it "did force a premature radicalization of the revolutionary process."[10]

Crespo and Nudelman write that there is among some Latin Americans a "strong resistance" to admitting the Soviet "presence" in the Central America conflict. Apart from those—not many—who are members of pro-Soviet Communist parties, or—perhaps a few more—who are uncritically committed to Castro's Cuba, I cannot think whom else they have in mind. Surely they cannot be thinking of the Contadora Group representatives, who have repeatedly emphasized in their public statements that they oppose the intervention of extrahemispheric nations in the crisis, and have condemned the militarization of the isthmus's conflicts by outside powers—including, of course, the United States, the USSR, and Cuba. To be sure, both the Soviet Union and Cuba are happy to see that United States tribulations in Central America are on the increase, but their role is not decisive, and political and military turbulence in the region would continue even if—to quote the words of United States Ambassador to Panama Ambler Moss—"Fidel Castro and the Soviet Union did not exist."[11] The plain fact is that the Central American crisis presents the Kremlin with a "no-lose" situation, and the Reagan administration's efforts to attribute to Cuba and the USSR the guilt for what is going on are no more convincing than the Soviets' clumsy attempts to explain away their troubles in Afghanistan and Poland as the product of a "Western conspiracy." While I certainly do not wish to deny the Soviet and Cuba involvement in fanning the flames of insurrection in Central America, neither do I want to exaggerate it, and I think it is important to preserve a healthy degree of skepticism toward the United States government's ill-fated efforts to make the Soviets and Cubans pay for Washington's own mistakes in the region. We only have to remember the fiasco of the famous 1981 "White Paper" on Soviet, Cuban, and Nicaraguan support to the Salvadoran guerrillas to realize how thin is the line separating fact from propaganda on this issue.[12]

There are aspects of Sandinista policies that leave much to be desired, but I am prepared to recognize at least that the government and the armed forces in Nicaragua do not behave toward the bulk of the population as if they were enemies, and that many of their actions are inspired by the "logic of the majority."[13] This is why—a fact corroborated by numerous independent observers—a great number of Nicaraguans are willing to defend their Revolution, and would impose punishing human and material costs on any invader. To be sure, other revolutions have begun with great accomplishments and have then degenerated into dictatorship. Nobody can be sure about what is going to happen in Nicaragua in the coming months or years, but there is one thing about which I feel certain: the United States government's attitude toward the Sandinistas is not only unhelpful but positively harmful. In any case, I do not see that we can realistically hope for anything much better in Nicaragua than an evolution along Mexican lines, but hopefully without the corruption and inefficiency that now characterize the PRI-dominated regime. For some this would represent a leap forward in the process of "democratization"; for others it would mean that the revolution has been "betrayed," and we can be sure that there are some who will not find a moment's rest until the remnants of the Somocista National Guard are reinstated in Managua.

One fact that clearly emerges from the Crespo-Nudelman account of the Central American turmoil is that for the countries of the Latin Western Hemisphere the hegemonic presence of the United States constitutes a key security problem. This is conclusively demonstrated by polls that show that for the peoples and elites of Latin America the terms "alliance" and "burden-sharing" on security issues with the United States not only have an almost purely metaphorical meaning, but also—more specifically—that for a substantial number of Latin American elites and mass populations the country that has to be "contained" is the United States.[14] For obvious reasons, this is something that has often been difficult for the European NATO members to appreciate, since their relationship with the United States is of a significantly different nature. Things, however, may now be changing, in no small measure as a result of the international impact of the crisis in Central America. The fact—however unpalatable—that a century of total military, political, and economic United States hegemony over one of the most backward regions of the Western Hemisphere has only managed to produce a massive revolutionary outbreak, is making many people in Europe realize that something terribly wrong has been happening for decades in this half-forgotten "backyard."

In their paper, Crespo and Nudelman refer to the "ambiguous" attitude of some European Social-Democratic leaders, as well as of certain "North American liberal sectors," with respect to the conflicts of Central America. They seem to imply that there is among these groups a lack of awareness about the "real" magnitude of the Soviet-Cuban influence in the region, and also a lack of understanding of the efforts that Central America democrats, not involved in the armed struggle, have been making to bring about social and political change in their nations. I do not think these criticisms are warranted. The European social democrats, and the Socialist International in general, have in fact been playing a highly positive role in moderating the bellicose instincts of the extremist zealots—this time of the conservative variety—within the present United States administration, but their attitudes toward the Nicaraguan Revolution have been far from condescending. As I said earlier, many Europeans also realize that, although the United States–Soviet confrontation is an inevitable dimension of the crisis, it is not its dominant feature *for the Central Americans themselves*. True, France, Norway, and other NATO members have given some help to the Nicaraguans, both moral and material, but these decisions have in most cases been the product of a careful study of the situation as it actually is—and not as sometimes described by Reagan administration spokesmen—and involving visits by parliamentary delegations to Nicaragua. The same has been the case with Venezuela, and, I believe, with Mexico. Aid has been forthcoming, but with intense pressure to save the Nicaraguan Revolution from the self-destructive tendencies that it apparently carries within itself. As far as the North American "liberals" are concerned, it seems to me that they are only trying to defend those principles that should presumably guide the foreign policy of a free and democratic nation: respect for self-determination and human rights, and solidarity with those who fight against intolerable conditions of life.

The Europeans—and Latin American Christian Democrats—have been deeply involved in the financing and running of J. N. Duarte's presidential campaign in El Salvador. They, as well as the United States government, have great hopes that this time the electoral experiment will lead to something more meaningful than merely providing a facade of democracy to a regime that remains essentially based on the autonomous use of power for popular repression by the military. I am afraid I cannot share their optimism, although of course events may prove me wrong. As we all know, Duarte has been head of government once before in El Salvador—during periods when repression actually increased. This was not for lack of good intentions on Duarte's part, but simply because he was the figurehead of an impotent civilian government, unable to curtail the military's power. Circumstances have changed, however, for there is now in El Salvador a strong revolutionary movement that can engage successfully the regular armed forces in battle. This is the crucial incentive for change in Central America: without the Nicaraguan Revolution and without the armed struggle of the Salvadoran insurgents, the tragedy of Central America would have continued almost unnoticed in United States decision-making circles. Now they, and the Salvadoran Christian Democrats, have once again the chance to experiment with gradual reform in a Central American country, with the tacit acquiescence of an unreformed military. We shall probably not have to wait long to see if it is possible.

In the meantime, the Latin American countries, under the leadership of the Contadora Group nations, can do little more than what they have been doing up to now, that is, trying through diplomacy and persuasion to defuse a crisis that has the potential for rapid and dangerous deterioration. Crespo and Nudelman call for a "new dialogue" between Latin America and the United States, based on a mutually held conviction about the importance of building healthy and strong democracies in the hemisphere. For a consensus about *objectives* to be reached, however, there has to be, as a first step, a coming together of views about *what* should be changed in Latin America. As long as Ambassador Kirkpatrick, and other influential United States leaders, continue to consider, for instance, that the Somoza regime in Nicaragua was only "moderately competent," "moderately oppressive," and "moderately corrupt,"[15] I very much doubt that a frank meeting of minds with Latin America democrats will effectively take place.

Notes

1. Samuel Huntington, *Political Order in Changing Societies*, (New Haven: Yale University Press, 1968), p. 1 (emphasis mine).

2. Jeane J. Kirkpatrick, "U.S. Security and Latin America," in H. J. Wiarda, ed., *Rift and Revolution: The Central American Imbroglio* (Washington: American Enterprise Institute for Public Policy Research, 1984), p. 355.

3. J. La Palombara, "Distribution: A Crisis of Resource Management" in L. Binder et al., *Crises and Sequences in Political Development* (Princeton: Princeton University Press, 1971), p. 275.

4. For a discussion of the Central American military's economic interests, see Thomas P. Anderson, "The Roots of Revolution in Central America," in Wiarda, ed., *Rift and Revolution*, pp. 110–111.

5. John Carlin, "Army's Soft Line Puzzles All Sides in El Salvador, *The Times*, London, 3 May 1984.

6. Arturo J. Cruz, "Nicaragua's Imperilled Revolution," *Foreign Affairs*, Summer 1983, p. 1046.

7. Ibid., pp. 1031-1047.

8. *Report of the National Bipartisan Commission on Central America* (Washington, D.C.: USGPO, January 1984), p. 84.

9. Peter Calvert, *The Mexican Revolution 1910–1914. The Diplomacy of Anglo-American Conflict* (Cambridge: Cambridge University Press, 1968), pp. 289–290.

10. A. Cruz, Jr., "The Origins of Sandinista Foreign Policy," in Robert S. Leiken, ed., *Central America: Anatomy of Conflict* (New York: Pergamon Press (in cooperation with the Carnegie Endowment for International Peace), 1984), p. 106.

11. Quoted in Walter La Feber, *Inevitable Revolutions: The United States in Central America* (New York: W. W. Norton, 1983), p. 107.

12. See Jonathan Kwitny, "Apparent Errors Cloud US White Paper on Reds in El Salvador," *Wall Street Journal*, June 1981.

13. For a detailed discussion of the basic features of an alternative economic model for the Central American region, based on the "logic of the majority," see *The Hague Declaration: An Alternative Policy for Central America and the Caribbean* (The Hague: Institute of Social Studies), June 1983. Mimeographed.

14. See Jorge I. Dominguez, "The United States and Its Regional Security Interests: The Caribbean, Central and South America," *Daedalus*, vol. 109, no. 4 (1980), pp. 127–131.

15. Jeane J. Kirkpatrick, "U.S. Security," p. 343.

Chapter 22

FAULTY MODELS

Arturo Cruz

AS A CENTRAL American, I find the piece by Horacio Crespo and Ricardo Nudelman to be a stimulus to the pursuit of social change and freedom. They reject the widespread erroneous notion that Central Americans lack aptitude for a real exercise of democracy. Moreover, they aptly remind us how both the authoritarian Right and the Marxist-Leninist Left give lip service to democracy and in fact abhor it. I share their view that a Central American nation like Costa Rica has proved beyond a shadow of a doubt that a democratic system is viable in our region. Mr. Crespo and Mr. Nudelman put the nature of the Central American crisis in its right perspective. There is a combination of mostly North-South conflicting relationships and, although lesser, yet real, East-West confrontation.

As a Nicaraguan, I think that Anibal Romero's commentary makes two important contributions. The first is the concept that civilian control of the military must be effectively exercised, which he says is one of the crucial aspects in the Latin American social democrats' definition of democracy. In my judgment, Mr. Romero is absolutely right in claiming that the Central American military have traditionally been, and still are, the most important security threat to their own peoples. This, of course, is true in traditional right-wing regimes as well as in the new left-wing regimes. Second, he has deemed it appropriate to expand the discussion of Nicaragua's Revolution. Our Revolution, or rather its leaders, have the historic responsibility of providing a revolutionary model— pragmatic and genuine for Central America. Their excesses and contradictions unwisely make the revolutionary process more difficult.

As Anibal Romero says, what happens *in* Nicaragua and *with* Nicaragua will probably decide the future of the whole region for decades to come. Of course, the United States must not only accept, but promote, revolution, that is to say, democratic revolution in Central America. Regarding the liberals of the Western world, although I agree with Mr. Romero that they have exerted, at times, a moderating influence on the Nicaraguan Revolution, I think it is still valid to tell them that if they really want to rescue the Revolution from external threats and its own self-destruction, they must stop any blank-check support to the Sandinistas. These democratic forces should give their backing to the third option, whether among dissidents or Sandinistas. Only confronted with the consensus of the nations friendly to the Revolution, Sandinista radicals may take heed of the advice of the moderates in their own ranks. Edén Pastora should not be abandoned. He is our best hope for the reconciliation of the revolutionary family in liberty and with national dignity, to satisfy the aspirations of our people, and to move toward achieving stability in Central America. Finally, I believe, as does Messrs. Crespo and Nudelman, that the narrow paths, as proposed by them, ought to be explored.

Chapter 23

RAPPORTEUR'S REPORT

Susan Alberts

SUSAN KAUFMAN PURCELL moderated a lively discussion focused on a presentation by *Horacio Crespo* and *Ricardo Nudelman*. They argued that it is a fallacy to believe that democracy in Central America can come only after economic stability is established. Rather, the United States must actively promote the development of democratic systems of government in the region. While the international dimensions of the current crisis are important, the situation has deep historical roots. Many Latin Americans, they said, view the crisis as a test of United States–Latin American relations.

The challenge to Central America, they believe, is to avoid falling into the political extremes of right-wing authoritarianism or left-wing totalitarianism. The Reagan administration blames the Soviet Union and Cuba for the upheavals in the region, looking at the situation in a completely East-West light. Unfortunately, this follows a pattern in which the United States has historically identified itself with the status quo and against change. Crespo and Nudelman stressed that as long as the United States continues to defend those who are unpopular with the majority of the people, the Soviet Union will have a good excuse for its involvement in the region.

The United States must face the complexities of the Central American problem. It is easy to belittle the Contadora Group, but they could exert real influence if the United States were behind them. The Reagan administration has given nothing but empty words of encouragement to this group—the only current alternative to solving the conflict with reason rather than bullets.

If security is the main concern of the United States, Crespo and Nudelman concluded, then we should realize that the best policy is one that consolidates democracy in the region. Revolts will recur until the reasons behind them are eliminated.

Anibal Romero argued that Crespo and Nudelman's scenario for democratic development glossed over the military—historically and presently the strongest political force in the region. Romero emphasized that the military cannot be agents for democratic change without first being fully reformed or purged.

Latin America as a whole has had a history of *caudillismo*—strongmen who took charge of the country, ruling with an iron hand in conjunction with the military. A lack of foreign wars and other traditional military matters with which to occupy themselves led the military to involvement in government and internal repression. Furthermore, the Latin American military, historically an anti-democratic institution, was and is involved in politics in order to maintain its privileges.

Practically speaking, democracy requires a situation in which civilians are actually, not superficially, in control of the military. Democracy must also include the idea of eliminating social and economic inequality. With the exception of Costa Rica, however, Romero asserted that the Central American countries are not at the point where they could meet these requirements.

Nicaragua holds out the possibility of progress toward democracy, but as yet it is more potential than fact. The Nicaraguan revolution was a significant break with the past, and possibilities for change still exist. The Sandinista's present actions should be considered in light of the fact that they are under attack and that anti-Americanism could well be part of their nationalistic symbolism. Furthermore, Nicaragua has a right to build up her armed forces until the United States halts covert operations.

Romero was pessimistic about the likelihood of a solution in El Salvador. Christian Democrats have never been truly reformist in Central America, and Duarte's faction made a mistake by not breaking clearly with the military in 1979.

The United States' continuing problem in relation to neighboring states is its inability to accept truly autonomous countries on its border, Romero concluded. This has more to do with national insecurity than with national security. The United States is reluctant to give up the habit of control over countries around her, or to tolerate their differences.

In the end, the internal dynamics of the Central American countries, not United States intervention, will be the determining factor in shaping their futures.

Arturo Cruz described the Central American conflict as a North-South crisis with East-West overtones. Exacerbating the situation is the lack of civilian control over the military, traditionally and currently the most important security threat to the people.

Cruz maintained that the Sandinistas have fallen into an excess of revolution, and must take moderates into their ranks. The narrow paths to democracy discussed by Crespo and Nudelman should be explored and, with reference to Nicaragua, this can best be done by convincing friendly countries to cease giving the Sandinistas a blank check of support unless it is truly deserved.

In the discussion that followed the panel presentation, *Ricardo Nudelman* suggested that Anibal Romero's analysis leads to the ultimate conclusion that a democratic government can exist only if the military is destroyed. The problem is more complex than that, however. Argentina, for example, overcame the military and installed a democratic government without waging a guerrilla war. In this case, democracy preceded military reform.

Susan Kaufman Purcell, broadening the discussion, contended that if she were part of the Reagan administration she would say they are succeeding in encouraging democracy in Central America. The elections in El Salvador are evidence of this. How can one argue that the Reagan administration is not following its stated intentions regarding democracy? What policies should Latin America and the United States pursue to bring democracy to the region?

According to *Horacio Crespo* the problem is not only how to form a democratic regime or what policies would lead to this end. The first step toward democracy is a government elected—perfectly or imperfectly—by the people. Second, the impact of conditions inside and outside the country that could affect the regime's survival must be taken into account. The best policies in the world will not ensure the survival of democracy, or even incipient democracy, in the face of overwhelming factors working against it. The external debt is an example of an element threatening the survival of certain regimes today.

Crespo also mentioned the long relationship between the militaries in Latin America and the United States, a linkage that stimulated and promoted antidemocratic intervention. In this context, any efforts to bring democracy to the countries of Central America must emphasize the regional consolidation of democratic regimes.

Anibal Romero added that United States policies stressing security (while giving due homage to the ideals of democracy) have given more and more resources to the military, building up that institution in different countries in spite of its antidemocratic history. Resulting military actions show the incompatibility of policies to strengthen the armed forces on the one hand while promoting democracy on the other.

The Reagan administration's policy in Central America repeats the mistakes of the past. Romero predicted that if the current United States policy continues, in a few years we will again see that strengthening the military in a country such as El Salvador is counterproductive to the goals of furthering democracy and United States influence.

The need for a "broker" between the United States and Central America was suggested by *Arturo Cruz*. The Contadora Group would be a logical choice, but it must have strong United States backing. Without a broker to act as intermediary and judge, any talk of changing United States policy in Central America is academic.

Viron Vaky, commenting on the gap between what is said and what is done in Washington for political reasons, added that the problems in Central America need time and will not be solved overnight. A broker is needed to mediate, he said, and further suggested a series of treaties between the countries, including Nicaragua, in which they would agree not to subvert each other's sovereignty and not to accept foreign bases. The problem that would occur is not so much verification as enforcement, as countries would have to submit to decisions they might not like. To implement the treaties a protocol could be set up that would include guarantees of compliance and a committee to hear complaints of violations.

Would countries participate in something like this so that the isthmus could get on with economic development and democracy?

Horacio Crespo felt that this was a reasonable option to break the impasse, and would probably meet with a favorable reception. *Anibal Romero* expressed his belief that Venezuela would participate in treaties such as these if Cuba were also included in the accord, but *Viron Vaky* responded that this was a long-term consideration needing hemispheric consensus.

Robert Leiken said there are many different ways of defining democracy in Central America. For the Reagan administration, democracy equals elections. Former Nicaraguan dictator Anastasio Somoza held elections when it was convenient, but they were empty gestures. Today Honduras is used as an example of democracy, yet in reality the military still dominates the civilian politicians. When people say the development of democracy is different in the Third World, they tend to link it to the need for prior economic stability. The question, then, is how can Central American countries develop and at the same time ensure political participation? Can democracy in Central America come from elections, or is prior negotiation between all parties involved, leading to a national consensus, necessary?

Horacio Crespo stressed that a national consensus is needed, but there are many ways of getting there. The basic question is whether the parties involved are really interested in consensus. Whatever the situation, however, they should keep struggling toward the goal.

Arturo Cruz added that elections are meaningless without prior consensus. The Nicaraguan elections will be held in order to solidify the institutionalization of the Sandinistas. The goal should instead be the institutionalization of the revolution, that is, an agreement on the future between the Sandinistas and all the vital forces of a pluralistic society.

Robert O'Neill asked whether United States policy in Central America should include a military element. He then asked what our economic relationship should be within the Sandinistas and what effect more United States support for the Contadora Group would have on the solution of any problems.

Arturo Cruz, Jr., responded first to the question concerning the economic relationship between Nicaragua and the United States. Even if all the necessary economic aid reached Nicaragua tomorrow, it would be meaningless because there is no social contract to assure that the aid is used to the benefit of the country's real problems. In the first year of the Nicaraguan revolution the aid received was dissipated. Nicaragua needs a political system than can allocate aid in an ecumenical manner.

Referring to the question of a United States military element in Central America, *Anibal Romero* argued that the military aspect should be almost entirely dismembered as soon as possible. The United States should develop economic and political means of approaching the situation. Specifically:

1. The United States should back the efforts of the Contadora Group by supporting negotiations in El Salvador between the government and the rebels, and by trying to agree on conditions under which the rebels could participate in political life in El Salvador;
2. Central America, including Honduras and Nicaragua, should be demilitarized. Stop supporting the contras in Nicaragua, and instead put diplomatic pressure on the Sandinistas to eliminate their totalitarian tendencies.

The Sandinistas realize they cannot create another Cuba in the region. Thus, it would be in the United States' best interest to give the Sandinistas new incentives in the form of economic assistance.

Expanding on the theme of the Contadora Group's efforts, *Ricardo Zuniga* expressed admiration for the Contadora Group's gestures but, because of their lack of strategic importance, he was doubtful that they could enforce any type of solution. He also pointed out that, while everyone talks about the Contadora Group, no one has asked the opinion of the Central American countries themselves.

Theodore Moran of Georgetown University asked how effective the Contadora nations could be in monitoring arms levels in Central America, and whether they could be of real use in preventing the United States from getting too involved in this question.

Arturo Cruz responded that the Contadora Group will continue to be only a fig leaf as long as the United States refuses to give it real support, as opposed to lip service, by allowing it to be a judge and submit to its decisions.

Regarding the patrol of the Costa Rican–Nicaraguan border, *Anibal Romero* suggested that several countries might commit troops for this purpose. According to *Horacio Crespo*, however, the border area is such thick jungle it would be extremely difficult to patrol it or operate militarily.

Wolf Grabendorff noted that whenever the United States perceives a security threat, "democracy" becomes a big word. After the 1979 Nicaraguan revolution, democracy in Central America became very important to the United States. Why wasn't it important when Somoza ruled or before the 1979 coup in El Salvador?

When the United States talks about bringing democracy to Central America, is that the real motive or is it a smoke screen to intervene because of strategic concerns? Grabendorff maintained that the United States is not all that interested in the concept of democracy. Rather, particularly to the Reagan administration, talk of democracy is a function of a certain security need.

Central America desperately needs consensus regarding the rules of the political game. Unfortunately, it is doubtful that this will happen in Nicaragua or El Salvador because of their particular histories. Elections can change parties but not systems. America wants elections in Nicaragua because it wants the system changed; however, the elections are clearly not going to accomplish this. Inversely, in El Salvador the FMLN does not want elections because they know only the political parties will change, not the system.

Alberto Arene, a representative of the FMLN, stressed the need for new ideas in shaping policy toward the region and an increased awareness of the influence of the region's history on the present turmoil. Central America's problems are a function of a history of poverty and repression combined with United States policies that make peaceful revolution impossible. The United States has always been involved in Latin American elections and Latin American militaries, and loves "democratic" countries that preserve the old order.

Unfortunately, the United States always comes too late with solutions that do not correspond to reality. El Salvador should be allowed to solve its own problems, preferably through dialog and a political solution. The FMLN has proposed a national accord, but there are forces in the country preventing consensus. United States policy must contain a more strategic vision that gives the countries in question room to breathe.

Ricardo Zuniga mentioned that the Honduran military is beginning to understand the relationship between the people, the army, and the United States. Honduras decided to change the structure of their military without the reactionary forces of the Reagan administration. His country is now in conflict with Nicaragua because the Sandinistas went straight to Marxism whereas Honduras chose capitalism. A definition of objectives, he argued, is needed to avoid a confrontation. If Nicaragua decides to legitimize her revolution without letting everyone in (that is, the rebels), they are asking for a confrontation and there will be war. If they open their election, however, and let everyone participate, there will be an internal solution.

Anibal Romero praised those sectors of the Honduran military who have broadened their perspective on Central America. But in spite of the fact that Honduras is capitalist and Nicaragua Marxist there is a difference between image and reality in Honduras. In that country, 1.1 percent of the population owns 40 percent of the agricultural land. One-fifth of the population has 70 percent of the income. In spite of its image, Honduras needs a revolution.

Concluding the session, *Arturo Cruz* noted that the term democratization is not necessarily the same as Americanization. Furthermore, Americanization should not be thought of as the unavoidable counterpart to Soviet control. Rather, both tendencies, Americanization as well as Soviet expansionism, must be checked so that Central Americans can develop indigenous solutions to the region's problems of economic development and social and political stability.

PARTICIPANTS AND PANELISTS

THE CENTRAL AMERICAN CRISIS AND THE WESTERN ALLIANCE

May 31–June 1, 1984
Washington, D.C.

Jonathan Alford
International Institute for Strategic
   Studies, London

Alberto Arene
FDR-FMLN of El Salvador

Cresencio Arcos
U.S. Embassy, Honduras

Bernie Aronson
Mondale campaign

Don Bandler
U.S. Department of State

Peter Bell
Carnegie Endowment for International
   Peace

Alan Berger
Boston Globe

Zbigniew Brzezinski
Columbia University and
Georgetown Center for Strategic and
   International Studies

Bruce Cameron
Foreign Policy Advocates and
Americans for Democratic Action

Rev. Phillip Cato
IISS and St. Francis Episcopal Church

Joseph Cirincione
Carnegie Endowment for International
   Peace

Peter Clement
Central Intelligence Agency, Office of
   Soviet Analysis

Horacio Crespo
Latin American Center for Strategic
   Studies, Mexico

Arturo Cruz, Jr.
Johns Hopkins School of Advanced
   International Studies

Arturo Cruz, Sr.
Inter-American Development Bank

Lt. Col. Alden M. Cunningham
Army War College

Piero Gleijeses
Johns Hopkins School of Advanced
    International Studies

Leonel Gomez
Former Associate Director of the Agrarian
    Reform Institute, El Salvador

Louis Goodman
Woodrow Wilson Center, Smithsonian
    Institution

Wolf Grabendorff
Stiftung Wissenschaft und Politik,
    Ebenhausen, Federal Republic of
    Germany

Roy Gutman
Newsday

Morton H. Halperin
Center for National Security Studies,
    Washington, D.C.

Michael Harrison
Johns Hopkins School of Advanced
    International Studies

Thomas Hughes
Carnegie Endowment for International
    Peace

Leslie Hunter
Department of the Navy

A. W. Jessup
U.S. Council on International Business

Josef Joffe
Carnegie Endowment for International
    Peace

Vic Johnson
House Western Hemisphere Affairs
    Subcommittee

Col. Robert Kennedy
Army War College

David Klein
American Council on Germany

Gert Krell
International Institute for Strategic
    Studies, London

Robert Leiken
Carnegie Endowment for International
    Peace

William LeoGrande
American University, Washington, D.C.

Gino LoFredo
El Dia, Mexico

Edward Luttwak
Center for Strategic and International
    Studies, Georgetown University

Christopher Makins
Roosevelt Center for American Policy
    Studies

William Maynes
Foreign Policy

Victor Meza
Centro de Documentacion de Honduras

James H. Michel
U.S. Department of State

Theodore Moran
Georgetown University School of Foreign
    Service

Ricardo Nudelman
Latin American Center for Strategic
    Studies, Mexico

Robert Nurick
International Institute for Strategic
    Studies, London

Lt. Col. Sigifrido Ochoa
Salvadoran Army

Robert O'Neill
International Institute for Strategic
    Studies, London

Sir Michael Palliser
International Institute for Strategic
    Studies, London

Robert Pastor
University of Maryland, College Park

Andrew J. Pierre
Council on Foreign Relations, New York

Susan Kaufman Purcell
Council on Foreign Relations, New York

The Hon. William D. Rogers
Arnold & Porter

Anibal Romero
Kings College, London

Stephen Rosenfeld
Washington Post

Nestor D. Sanchez
Deputy Assistant Secretary of Defense for
    Inter-American Affairs

Lt. Frederick F. Shaheen
U.S. Navy

Rodolfo Silva
Former Ambassador of Costa Rica

Wayne Smith
Carnegie Endowment for International
    Peace

Helmut Sonnenfeldt
Brookings Institution

John Steinbruner
Brookings Institution

John Stremlau
Rockefeller Foundation

Michel Tatu
Le Monde, Paris

The Hon. Viron P. Vaky
Georgetown University

Jiri Valenta
Naval Postgraduate School

Jenonne Walker
U.S. Department of State

Ben Welles
U.S. Department of Defense

Albert Wohlstetter
European-American Institute for Security
    Research

Roberta Wohlstetter
European-American Institute for Security
    Research

Major Ricardo Zuniga
Honduran Army

INDEX